The Cowman's Southwest

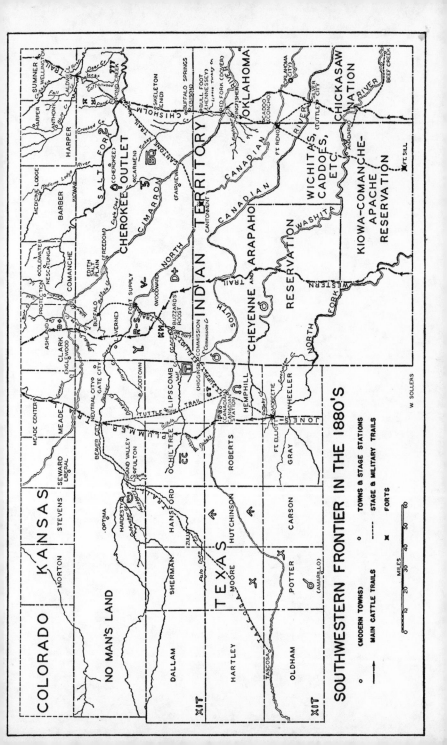

SOUTHWESTERN FRONTIER IN THE 1880'S

o (MODERN TOWNS)   TOWNS & STAGE STATIONS

                          STAGE & MILITARY TRAILS

o MAIN CATTLE TRAILS   FORTS

MILES
0   10   20   30   40   50   60

W. SOLLERS

The Cowman's Southwest

being the reminiscences of
Oliver Nelson

freighter, camp cook, cowboy, frontiersman
in Kansas, Indian Territory,
Texas and Oklahoma
1878-1893

edited by

ANGIE DEBO
Oklahoma A. & M. College

University of Nebraska Press
Lincoln and London

First Bison Book printing: 1986
Most recent printing indicated by the first digit below:
1   2   3   4   5   6   7   8   9   10

Library of Congress Cataloging-in-Publication Data
Nelson, Oliver, 1861–
   The cowman's Southwest.
   Reprint. Originally published: Glendale, Calif.:
H.A. Clark, 1953.
   Includes index.
   1. Nelson, Oliver, 1861–   . 2. Cowboys—South-
west, New—Biography. 3. Pioneers—Southwest, New—
Biography. 4. Ranch life—Southwest, New—History—19th
century. 5. Southwest, New—Social life and customs.
6. Frontier and pioneer life—Southwest, New.
I. Debo, Angie, 1890–   . II. Title.
F786.N44A3 1986   979'.03   86-11231
ISBN 0-8032-8356-3 (pbk.)

Reprinted by arrangement with the Arthur H. Clark Company

To the memory of my brother
CHARLES W. NELSON
Who worked with me on the range

Contents

Illustrations and Maps

Key to the Brand Marks mentioned in the text

♂	Frying Pan	M̄	Bar M
5	T 5	2S	2 S
X	L X	4D	4 D
2	Reverse S	⚱	Laurel S S
WP	W P	♤	Spade
Y	V Bar	D	J D
A	V Bar, variation used at Atterberry Camp	TAR	T A R
777	Three Sevens	◇	T Diamond
U	U	D+	D Cross
∩	Horseshoe	R-S	R Bar S
Y	Open Y	Y	Y L
H̲L	Bar H L	ᴗ	S Half Circle
B̄Q	Bar B Q	♂	Apple
XIT	X I T	PO	P O
KH	K H	Λ	Turkey Track
CT	C T	T	Box T
		C̄C	Bar C C

Foreword

In writing Prairie City *I learned to value the keen historical consciousness of the surviving American pioneers. Feeling that they have lived through an era that the world will never see again they will take infinite pains to assist anyone who aspires to write of their experience. They are entirely selfless; names and individual exploits do not matter, but the story matters more than anything else in their world. It must be told right. Their memory may trick them at times, but never will they deviate intentionally a hair's breadth from the straight path of truth.*

Knowing all this, I was not surprised when Mr. Oliver Nelson came modestly offering to help me with his reminiscences. He had jotted down a few sketches, he said; if they could be of any use to me, he would be glad. "I feel that much early experience that is lost should have been written and saved. Too many of the things that are written now are so far out of line; they don't reflect old times, just somebody's imagination." He placed in my hands a bulky ledger with penciled notes. I did not know until after he left that he had written a book.

I wrote at once and told him that as soon as other projects were out of the way I wanted to prepare his manuscript for publication over his name. He was pleased, but not elated. "I wrote that sketch so if any- one cared to they could read it and pass it on. You were kind enough to take it up, and I will be glad to handle it as you desire."

We labored together for a year in that spirit. I made many changes in arrangement; for even as he "worked" cattle I have learned to work thoughts, corralling, cutting, branding, putting each in its right "bunch." I added some explanatory material to assist the reader who is not familiar with the setting. In this, however, I was careful to distinguish my work from his. Throughout the text of the volume, italic type is used for editorial notes. Mr. Nelson's narrative is set in the usual roman type. Sometimes I had to call on Mr. Nelson for clarification; as he says, "I often find when I use the range jargon I have to explain to others words that are clear to me." But I was very careful to preserve his style. I enjoy the flavor it imparts to his story.

The manuscript passed back and forth between us several times in this year of co-operative work. In the whole process of editing he showed a humility, a personal detachment, an intellectual integrity rare among those who lay claim to scholarship. It was always, "At any time you desire a little more light on my script, drop me a line."

It is a story of rude, even lawless days, told without moralizing or defense. But it is also a story of light-hearted courage, of toil and hardship, and most of all of ready helpfulness. The invitation to every stranger to dismount and eat—" 'light and fill up"—was the spirit of the range. And if the writer shows some impatience with the groveling ways of the nester, some sarcasm over the plowing up of grassland that was "good only for the natural covering," that too reflects the prejudices of the cow country.

I am proud of the privilege of being the first reader. I hope that succeeding readers will enjoy the book as much as I did.

ANGIE DEBO

Stillwater, Oklahoma
May 1, 1952

My Folks Move West

*For seventy-four years old Oliver Nelson has been
an observer of the western scene. He has brought a
square of virgin prairie under the plow with his own
hands; he has watched a city's towers rise above the
place where the cowboys "bedded down" their longhorns; he sees a ribbon of concrete winding across
valley and upland following the trail cut by the
freighters' wagons. Thus the story he has written of his
life is also the story of the southwestern frontier. And
his quick, terse characterizations, his salty humor (with
his own discreet elisions) even his grammar, are a part
of the story.*

*He was born in Tippecanoe county, Indiana, Oc-
tober 6, 1861 – the year the Civil War started. "There
were seven of us children at home. We moved around
some, but wound up on a farm near Otterbein." Thus
he sets the key of restlessness and discontent that was
soon to launch the family on the historic westward
movement.*

*Life was still crude in back country Indiana. Was
not* The Hoosier School-Master *written in 1871?
Of his own schooling Mr. Nelson says,*

I went to school in a small log cabin with one log
out in the west end to let the light creep in. It was said
they had set up panes of glass in this opening, but the
glass was gone before my time. On cloudy days school
would dismiss. The teacher used a four-foot hickory

gad about like a broomstick at one end, and some less as it sloped down. He'd hammer us little fellows like hell a-beatin' tan bark.

We lived on an eighty-acre farm, well improved; flat, black, sticky land, poor crops. It was fenced with rails, worm fashion, cross staked and ridered. We had no barbed wire then, but a fellow was advertising a number 8 wire to be stretched and then clinch three-point barbs on. It was no good; the barbs would get loose and slip.

Young Nelson could not have known at the time that these fencing experiments were to be a major influence in his life. It was Joseph F. Glidden of De Kalb, Illinois who was selling smooth wire along with pincers and loose barbs to be clinched on by the fence builder; but when the barbs showed a tendency to slip and form clusters with smooth spaces between, he learned to fix them firmly on two twisted strands. This twisted wire was patented November 24, 1874; Glidden and his partner, Isaac L. Ellwood, opened a factory and took H. B. Sanborn into the firm to sell their product. In 1881 partly for demonstration purposes Glidden and Sanborn started the Frying Pan ranch where Amarillo, Texas now stands, enclosing it with the new fencing. It was an immediate success, the first practicable fencing for the treeless plains. The open range gave place rapidly to large enclosures, and the prairie homesteader also was enabled to control his holdings. All this was ahead of the Indiana boy, but his frequent mention of fences and fencing shows how acute was the problem throughout the west.

Times were hard in Indiana during the depression '70's, and the Nelson family sought the old American remedy: move somewhere else.

When I was fourteen, my father mortgaged the farm to buy more land; so he just blowed up. He decided to go west; sent my oldest buddy, Harry, four years older than me, down to Austin, Texas to look up a good location. And he sent me to act as flunky for a doctor half-brother who owned a drug store in Bement, Illinois.

It was September, 1876 when I started. Business in the store wasn't awful rushing, so I read a good bit; I think I did better than kids of like age did at school.

Thus young Oliver developed the intellectual discernment that was to set him apart from his fellows as an interpreter of the passing scene. He marked the struggles of the hard-pressed farmers. Many of them were sharecroppers in a condition approaching peonage. Everybody who could break away was fleeing to the west.

The winter of 1876-77 was very wet. Bement is between the Sangamon river and the Lake Fork of the Kaskaskia, and the land is black and flat. Standing corn fell down and rotted. Farmers would hitch four horses to the hind axle of a wagon to come in for grub and medicine. They used *a little* more flour than quinine. Many people went broke; abandoned their rented farms and drove west with team and camp outfit. Some lost their teams, the land owner overtaking them before they got out of the county and holding the team for the unfinished lease contract.

Meanwhile my own folks moved west. Harry hadn't liked Texas, so they tried Osborne county in western Kansas; then started for Arkansas and were stopped by high water near Eldorado, Kansas. The two oldest boys, Harry and the next one, Delos, went to work in the harvest field; so the family settled down there at

Murdock post office. The next spring, 1878, I went to join them.

The trip on the train was quite an experience. On the way to St. Louis the land was level, and about one-third covered with water. Geese and ducks by thousands, and blackbirds all around. Grass and more grass; very little fencing. Buildings scarce, and set on mounds that looked about ten feet high and three to ten acres in extent. So it went until night closed the scene, and we pulled into St. Louis after dark.

The next day we came to Kansas City. It was said to be quite a burg, but from the depot only a few houses showed up. I was told the town was on top of the hill northeast.

We went up the Kaw river; brush on each side, quite a sameness to the scenery. Then we got out on the open: nice rolling land, some places quite level; good grass, low timber along the streams, no fencing. The longer the train run, the further apart the buildings were. Most houses were half-dugouts. I learned all about them later: four feet dug in the ground, sod walls laid up two more feet, shingled with poles and earth, dirt floor. We soon got out where there were no depots, only side tracks. Teams on a dead run would come out to meet the train. Some one on the train would wave, and the ones in the wagons would wave back. Then all on that side of the train would wave and holler.

I reached Eldorado about midnight. Brother Harry came into the car and waked me up. He said we had twelve miles to go, and his team was a lame pony and a jinny. I piled my junk into the open wagon. Brother Charley, twelve years old, lay down on it and slept, while I talked turn about with Harry. We drove west; reached our destination at peep of day.

THEIR HORNS LOOKED AS LONG AS A BROOM HANDLE

Father came out to meet me; asked how I liked the looks of things. I could easily see over the eighty-acre place. I said, "It looks nice; good grass, soil laying nice and full of moisture." Father had built a limestone house twelve feet by twenty-four: two rooms separated by a cloth partition, attic sleeper reached by a ladder. He had a dugout stable. I said, "If we had used the economy in Indiana you are using here, we would have done well there."

We had forty acres of corn four miles northeast on land rented from another settler. Charles and I tended it. We slept in a covered wagon, cooked by a fire on the ground (bacon, eggs, and coffee) and mother baked biscuits and sent along enough to last a week at a time.

One night a bobcat passed close to our wagon making a terrible yowl. My spine just about froze. I tried to wake brother Charles, but I couldn't rouse him. I closed both ends of the wagon sheet and got the double-barreled shotgun. The night was warm, and I just sat there with the cover closed and sweat till morning. It was said that cats got a good many of the farmers' chickens, but they were not apt to attack anyone if left alone.

One cloudy morning a two-year-old doe passed our camp. And I shot my first jack rabbit. It looked as big as a small dog. In July we killed prairie chickens. The wheat stubble was full of them. I was told that many had been shipped east the winter before; during a heavy snow several men would follow the main flock shooting all the time, while three men came along with a wagon to pick them up.

Anything to make a little money, for the settlers were all hard run. Eggs were two cents a dozen, no sale in August; hogs were $1.50 a hundred. Flour cost sixty cents for forty-eight pounds. There was no work.

In the fall some farmers' boys began to come in from the range country: good horses and big saddles; could catch and throw with the rope; good clothes and free with money; and the way they would take with the young feminine population was just terrible. Some home boys toted a toad-stabber and wore a red sash – what we called a desperado flag – but they had no money.

In September J. M. Doubleday, an uncle, came from Harrison, Arkansas. He owned about two hundred head of cattle, and was looking for land. Father went along with him, and he bought twelve miles west of Caldwell on the Kansas border. Father decided to move there too, and buy stock and eat grass with it. Besides the eighty we had a cow and calf, three horses and a donkey, and a corn crop worth ten cents a bushel. Father butchered the cow, sold the eighty, and gave a neighbor the calf to haul a load of shelled corn to Caldwell – where the price was about the same. I suppose it was about October when we moved down – October of '78.

On this journey young Nelson got a glimpse of the most famous traffic in all western history – the great cattle drives from Texas across the Indian Territory to the Kansas railheads. The first herds that scarred the prairie along the Chisholm trail had reached the cars at Abilene, near the end of the Kansas Pacific, in 1867. That place enjoyed a brief prosperity and a lurid celebrity as a cow town. Then as railroads were built to the south, the drives shifted to other termini. Wichita was the "cow capital" for a few years following 1872. Caldwell was to ship its first cattle when the railroad reached it in 1880. Farther west on the railroad Dodge City, at first a hide market for buffalo hunters had, by

1875, become a cow town fed by its own set of trails, as the ranching industry had moved west after the destruction of the buffalo. Here is the way it appeared to the wide-eyed Indiana youth in the fall of '78:

The first day out we drove west. About fifteen or eighteen miles from Murdock we crossed an old trail seventy-five or a hundred yards wide, with ruts a foot deep, like lister furrows. Close by the trail was a two-story log house with an outside stairway. It was vacant, and the windows and doors were gone. We met a man riding a little pony almost covered by a big stock saddle; he had on a big hat, big spurs, and a belt of cartridges, and he looked like he hadn't shaved since he'd come west. We asked him how far it was to Wichita.

"You done passed *old* Wichita," he told us. "When the railroad come through, they moved the town away. That one building you see is the only one left; used to be a saloon and dance hall below, a gambling house upstairs. And this trail was the old Chisholm cow trail to Abilene. But they don't use this part of it any more; they just drive to Wichita and load on the cars there."

The Nelsons went on "about two or three miles to the new Wichita." Here was dramatic evidence of what the railroad meant to the frontier. They saw "a string of wheat wagons a quarter of a mile long waiting to unload; some had come as far as forty miles," hauling with underfed, skinny horses across trackless prairies and unbridged streams. The Nelsons drove west on Douglas avenue, following the Chisholm trail through the heart of the present city, and got their first view of the social life of a cow town.

The town was all strung out along this street; low buildings, about every third one a saloon. I noticed a

boy coming out of a saloon in a hurry, with a man
following. He turned and looked back, and the man
struck him in the face with a billiard cue. The boy
leaned against a hitch post and a woman came out and
went up to him; then he fell in the gutter. That was the
last I saw.

*At the west end of the street was the Arkansas river.
Here was the cattle crossing. (The modern Wichita
still treasures a faded photograph of the wide stream
and the swimming longhorns). But a wagon bridge
had been built there in 1872 – the year the railroad
came. Mr. Nelson remembers crossing the "low bridge
with a wooden banister about two feet high." On the
west end where the present McLean street intersects
Douglas avenue a monument now stands to show
where the trail turned south. And as they moved slowly
down toward Caldwell our emigrants got their first
view of the frontier traffic that flowed along that
famous thoroughfare.*

We drove on south. Soon we met a freight outfit.
There were four covered wagons double-trailed.
(Double-trailed means three wagons fastened together;
so there were twelve wagons in all). Each was pulled
by eight yoke of oxen – sixty-four oxen in the outfit.
The two front wagons in each unit were loaded clear
to the top of the bows with buffalo bones. There was a
Winchester carbine in a scabbard on the left side of
each front wagon.

We kept on going south. When we got to the
Chikaskia we saw a bunch of Texas cattle. It looked
like they covered four acres. They were on the trail to
the railroad to be shipped, but the boys had stopped at
the river to drink them. I know now they were four-
year-olds; their horns looked as long as a broom handle.

The cowboys all had pistols, though it was customary to leave off their pistols as soon as they passed Caldwell. All this was new to me.

We got to Caldwell, then turned west. About two or three miles from town we stopped for the night with a settler who had come out from Kentucky with his family, and was just building his house. He told us he'd been in Caldwell two days before, when some cowboys on a lark were shooting up the town, and two of them had needed burying after it was over. He was just about in the notion of leaving his land and going back home where the people were civilized.

We stopped on an eighty, eight miles west of Caldwell: black, sticky land; buffalo bones scattered all over. After night we could see half a dozen lights. There were three frame houses west of us, two east — four of them two-room. To the north all lived in dugouts or sod houses. There was a schoolhouse up a canyon a mile north; a dugout with dirt roof, weeds higher than the sod flue.

We drove twenty miles for firewood, to Pond creek down in the Indian Territory. In late November we hauled lumber for building from Wellington, about thirty miles northeast, which was the end of the railroad. (This road was building down fast; it had only got to Wichita when we were there).

Harry had a 56:56 Spencer. Some time that fall he took on a chum with a Sharps, and they went on a buffalo hunt in south Barber county. They got down there where everything looked rough and gloomy, and his buddy somehow got blood on one hind leg, and they retreated in a hurry. Mebby so Indians, next canyon.

If this hunter was shot by an Indian, it was almost

certainly an incident of Dull Knife's epic flight, famous in western legend. Two years before, this chief and his Northern Cheyenne had joined Sitting Bull and the Sioux in exterminating Custer's command at the battle of the Little Big Horn. Then they had been rounded up by the military and brought to the reservation of the Southern Cheyenne and Arapaho in the Indian Territory. Here many died of malaria, short rations, and plain heartbreak. Finally in the fall of '78 they suddenly broke away in the night – 92 men, 120 women, 141 children – and headed for their Montana homeland. They battled their way across several states, raiding as they went, eluding the soldiers that were sent to trap them. A few were killed, but the survivors went on to their own country, where they stayed, victorious over the policy-makers at Washington and the might of the United States army. Thus Harry Nelson and his pal, adventuring in buffalo hunting, brushed the stuff of history. Meanwhile in Caldwell other events were stirring that were to loom large in western legend.

Although the railroad had not reached Caldwell yet, it was already a cow town. It was about two miles from the Indian Territory line. Across the border lay the Cherokee Outlet or "Strip," a tract two hundred miles long and sixty miles wide, owned but not settled by the Cherokees. South of this were the reservations of the Cheyenne and Arapaho and other tribes. All this Indian land, with or without the consent of the owners, was occupied by cattlemen. Then there were the great herds coming up the Chisholm trail from Texas, besides the freighters' wagons and stage coaches which plied that frontier highway. To all the socially starved young men who drove the trails and worked the ranges, Caldwell

offered the first bright lights. Mr. Nelson says, "When
we came, the town boasted eighteen saloons."

One day two peelers (boys from the range) rolled
in. Their conduct somehow displeased George Flat,
the marshal. He treed them at the Moreland restaurant
and, without any preliminary, bored a .45 hole in each
one's back. The citizens planted them up in Boot Hill,
said a few nice things about the Last Roundup and the
Sweet Bye-and-bye, exonerated the marshal, but took
away his commission. Asked to give up his star and
guns he answered, "Come and take 'em." A few nights
later on his beat as he passed an opening between two
buildings a flash from behind opened the Pearly Gates
for him. Several shots scattered close around covered
all evidence, but it was said a well-known deputy was
near by.

A man named Danford owned a bank in Caldwell.
One day a card was hung up on the door, "Closed; No
Money." One of the depositors was a butcher. He
slipped in the back way, took Dan by the collar, drew
a steak knife, and said, "Out with my money, or out
comes what you been eatin' lately." The money came.
Other depositors got to milling around the bank door
some considerable, but the door was locked and
Danford managed to get to the Leland hotel.

Next morning early, the southbound stage with a
spiked team (that is, two teams, one ahead of the other)
drove up behind the Leland, took on the bank president, and pulled out. Some inquisitive chump watched;
then he moseyed up town and reported, "Stage goin'
south; spiked team in a high lope; Danford only
passenger." The depositors held a consult, then offered
"Twenty-five plunks to the man that brings 'im back."
A peeler named Jim Talbot, who had rolled in a short

time before and was engaged in exchanging kale for a
good time, happened along. He said he could use the
dough; he'd just take the job. He called to the stable
man a block away, "Hey, Jack! Saddle Slim and bring
him out; don't waste no time."

The trail south of town was upgrade two miles to the
Indian Territory line; then a level downslope about
twenty-five miles to Pond Creek, and change teams.
Talbot took an easy gait out of town and up the grade.
Then he said to his mount, "Go to it, Slim; we got to
gain five miles in twenty-five." So Slim lay low and
stretched out. Danford kept looking back. Finally the
driver said, "There's a fog o' dust comin' up just top
o' the rise." Dan said, "I'll pay for all the buckskin you
use; give 'em plenty." The stage horses were doing
their best; but after passing Polecat creek, a fifteen
mile run, they began to slow up. Talbot soon came up
'longside. He said, "Turn back, Mr. Dan; the town
wants to pin a ribbon on you and say good-bye when you
pass out." The stage Jack said, "You got no rights
here, so just come along." Jim drew a bead on the lead
horse with his gat. Then Jack said, "Don't shoot; I'll
turn back."

When the stage rolled in, the whole town was at the
reception. They had a lot of rope and some guns. They
unloaded Danford at the Leland, and a fresh single
team replaced the tired horses and took the stage back
south. Talbot was given the job of entertaining His
Eminence at five plunks a day. One mourner said he'd
give twenty-five dollars to anyone that would shoot
him. Talbot pointed his .45 full cocked, and said, "Out
with your money," but the fellow backed down. Then
Jim said, "I'll send him out for twenty dollars," but no
one would hand over that much. O'Brian, a heavy
depositor, said, "If we kill him, we get nothing."

Danford would get shaky during these discussions. But he finally got to Colorado. The depositors eventually received about twelve per cent of their money.

Talbot just blowed the town for ten days. Then somehow the city dads took the notion that his exercises wasn't exactly what fitted in with the town law. One Mike Meagher and company (Mike having a western rep) advised Jim and his pals to hightail it for the flat south. Jim's bunch – four of them – went to the north edge of town to start and had their mounts in high at the town center when the city bunch opened up. In the serenade Mike got a hole in his head, and rode up Boot Hill for keeps. The honor was attached to Talbot. One fellow not fixed for the show – he was a gambler, aimed to join the Talbot bunch – went to saddle a pony down near the red light run by Maggie Woods. A deputy marshal took a peek at him along the sights of a Winchester, pressed the trigger while he was smoothing the blanket, and he went into eternity bareback.

When the hurrah got close to a peak, the Talbot quartet moved south. When they got to the flat, opposition ahead turned them off the trail. They struck east for a cow camp on Deer creek, but were soon headed off, and on foot took to the breaks. To locate them, some Caldwell men put their hats on sticks and held them up. John Hall, a young fellow from west of town, got a hole punched in his hat, so they concluded their quarry wasn't far off. But after dark Talbot and company slipped out and took the trail. Next day they met some farmer freighters, took four horses, and aimed to leave Caldwell for good.

About 1900 a man came to the court at Wellington and said he understood there was a complaint against Jim Talbot; that was his name and he wanted it cleared. So a trial was held. But no Caldwell man

would swear that the well-dressed gentleman was the
boy in the rough cowboy garb that mixed up in the
fracas twenty years before. The case was dismissed,
and then he greeted all the witnesses by name. He was
never heard of again, but it was believed he belonged
to a very prominent family in the east.

I suppose there was some good people and some
good deeds done in Caldwell in those early days, but
I never heard any braggin' about 'em.

In the spring of 1880 Delos and I put forty acres in
corn on the W. S. (Buffalo) King place, four miles
east of where we lived. King had hunted buffalo, was
the way he got his name. He was about six feet tall,
weighed 305 pounds, and his yell would nearly knock
your hat off. He was in the freighting business, hauling
to the Indian agencies and military posts down in the
Indian Territory. Sometimes high prices were paid for
hauling: $1.50 a hundred pounds to Fort Reno, $2.25
to Fort Sill. The low price was sixty-five cents a
hundred to Reno, a dollar to Sill.

After we put the corn in, Delos and I went to freighting, using our own teams, but going along with King's
outfit. The railroad had just got to Caldwell, so we
loaded there. We were to haul to Anadarko, the government agency for the Kiowas, Comanches, Wichitas, and
other southwestern tribes. The goods was barreled
apples, canned tomatoes, and barreled whisky and wine,
and the price of hauling was $1.75 a hundred. There
were six covered wagons, each carrying three thousand
pounds and pulled by a two-horse team. Besides the six
drivers, two extra boys went along as passengers, paying
a dollar each to ride to Fort Reno, grub free. John
Stevens – a minister's son living west of Caldwell –
was boss of the outfit. Bright and early one morning we
started down the Chisholm trail.

Freighting on the Chisholm Trail

The trail led down the route now followed by the Rock Island railroad and U.S. highway 81. The Indian Territory of Mr. Nelson's day has become the state of Oklahoma, and the stage stations have grown into thriving towns and cities. The prairie is planted to wheat now, and grain elevators rise dramatically above the low horizon. In that spring of 1880 the land was carpeted with young grass, and there must have been white drifts of wild plum blossom and the soft glory of the redbud. Oliver Nelson marked none of these things; his mind was on other business.

It was a fifteen day trip to Anadarko, driving about twenty-five miles a day. As far as Fort Reno we followed the Chisholm trail. The old cow path was fifty yards wide, rutted and gullied out six inches deep on the level; much deeper in places. The weather was warm, the soil dry. We fed our teams corn. We also carried hay, but at night we usually stopped away from camp grounds and turned the stock loose to graze. We slept on blankets under our wagons, taking the covers off the wagons to spread over our beds.

South of Caldwell we crossed Fall creek; pulled up a grade over a mile long; came to high land with a gentle slope south, tough red soil. Prairie dogs were all over this heavy land. The dog hole was about four inches across with a ring of earth around it about six inches high; it usually went straight down several feet.

The dogs would stand across the hole showing their heads and backs. If you would shoot them with a shotgun they would fall back in, but a big bullet would knock them from the hole. They are about nine inches long with a five-inch tail; chuffy – weigh about two pounds – tawny yellow; have a sort of squirrel bark; eat grass, roots, hoppers, bugs, etc. If rattlesnakes get in the holes the dogs will leave. Owls, called prairie dog owls, live in deserted holes.

We crossed Polecat creek, Cottonwood creek, Osage creek, Pond creek. Pond Creek stage station was on Pond creek, a mile north of the Salt Fork. It was run by a man named John Hines. There were two marble tombstones leaning against the log cabin. They were still there when I saw the place four years later; must 'a' got the stones before they got the men.

These stones were probably intended to mark the graves of Tom Best, slain in 1872 by an Osage funeral party carrying out the tribal custom of taking a scalp to bury with the body of a warrior, and one Chambers, another Osage victim, killed in 1874. It is said that the graves were finally marked in 1889. They are on a knoll not far from the present town of Pond Creek.

We crossed the Salt Fork – low, sandy bed 150 yards wide, very little water. We passed a pile of buffalo bones eight feet deep that would cover a fourth of a city block. Later I learned they belonged to the freighter, George Laflin; he had nine piles near trails, waiting for railroads to come through.

That night we camped on Wild Horse creek. The next day we passed the Skeleton station about where North Enid is now, and camped four miles south on Boggy creek where there were a few big cottonwoods and a nice pool with a little spring at the north end.

Here we fixed a fire of cow chips and weeds, and cooked our supper on the present site of Enid.

Two miles north of the present town of Bison we came to a grave with a row of rocks around it. The trail forked, passing on both sides of the plot. I was told that two freighters killed by Indians had been buried here six years before. We passed west of Bison. The place was called Buffalo Springs: just a draw running east and west; a little spring west of the trail; and a foundation, showing a building had been burned, north of the draw. At the present site of Hennessey we passed a small plot with up-edged rock around the grave of Pat Hennessey, another victim of the same Indian attack. Just south was some ashes where another building had been burned. This, I learned, was what was left of Bull Foot station.

Thus again we touch the stuff of western legend. The story of the raid on the freighters' wagons and the burning of the two stations has passed into Oklahoma tradition. Every year the town of Hennessey reenacts the story in pageant; passing tourists visit the park on the city's edge at the approximate location of the Irishman's last stand where a stone memorial tower rises above a replica of his rude grave; and old-timers still tell their separate versions of the tragedy.

We went through blackjacks on our way toward Red Fork station, at the present Dover. Here, where highway 81 now turns west on the north edge of town, we passed through sand where the trail had been blowed out thirty yards wide and, in places, twelve feet deep. We followed it straight south, passing some distance east of the station, which was close to the present highway. About half way between here and the Cimarron was a crossed stake on top of a sand hill. I never did learn who it stood for.

We crossed the Cimarron – larger than the Salt Fork, same kind of bed, higher bank. South of the river we passed an Indian. He had a butcher knife, which he offered to sell for "two bits." Stevens took the knife, threw it on the load, and gave him a quarter. But it seems he thought two bits was fifty cents. He sulked and said, "No big." Then he went away and soon returned with a half dollar, wanting two bits like that. Stevens just drove on. The Indian followed us several miles, but finally turned off.

The next station was Kingfisher, run by a Frenchman named Filblock – a squaw man. It was about one mile west of the center of the present town, on the west side of the creek where it turns south.

This former stage station and present county seat of Kingfisher county got its name from King Fisher, fabulous outlaw-cattleman of the Eagle Pass country in Texas. He was killed in 1884 at a San Antonio theater, in a shooting affray still remembered as a lurid event in Southwestern annals. According to local tradition he once operated a ranch in the vicinity of the Kingfisher stage stand. The log house, stable, and corrals at the headquarters, about a mile north of the town, were still standing when the country was opened to homesteaders in 1889.

Next we camped at Caddo – now Concho – close to a Cheyenne Indian school. It was located on a spring branch, nearly on a divide. An Indian graveyard by the trail had broken wagons, carriages, baby buggies, toys, and horse bones all around. The dolls were interesting – buckskin filled with sand and dressed in Indian clothes.

Even yet Concho is a strange and remote place. Hidden in a fold of the prairie is a whole little town of government buildings – hospital, agency, school plant, employees' houses – and here the Cheyennes and Arapahos gather from all west-central Oklahoma to eat buffalo meat, transact tribal business, dance their ancient rituals, and relax in general fellowship. The Rock Island streamliner glides through unheeding, and on a ribbon of concrete across the wheat land the traffic flashes by on highway 81, unaware of this secluded ravine.

But all travelers stopped at Concho in 1880. An incident marked by young Nelson shows the demoralizing influence of the half-savage white men who passed that way; but it also shows how the native military society of the dog soldiers maintained discipline and order in the camp.

Stevens told a young Indian about eighteen he would give him four bits to throw a passing Indian girl in the creek. The young buck started to do it, but while he and the girl were scuffling an old Indian came along. He jumped up in the air, striking the boy in the side with his foot and knocking him down. Then when the youngster got up and ran, he followed, striking him several times. I was told he was a dog soldier, a fearless guard.

The school was a large two-story building with a court open on the east. The scholars were twelve to eighteen years old, all stout and well-built. At night we attended an exhibition of their work; their writing and drawing would beat the Kansas schools, but in spelling and arithmetic they were lost.

This school had been opened the preceding fall. Probably some of the pupils had had some irregular school experience before. A far from successful attempt had been made to establish a day school for them in

1871, and a small boarding school had been opened a little later. The good writing and drawing young Oliver saw was a characteristic development of their native artistry – the same traits that make Archie Blackowl, a modern member of the tribe, one of Oklahoma's greatest painters. But no wonder the white man's spelling and arithmetic were difficult for the Cheyennes in 1880. They were just emerging from a hunting economy. Though they had begun to settle tentatively on their reservation in 1869, they spent much of their time on the buffalo plains and were actively hostile to the whites, who were settling their hunting grounds and killing their buffalo. The disorders culminated in a series of raids in the summer of 1874, during which Pat Hennessey and his companions were killed. That same year Fort Reno was built to hold the Indians in check, and their resistance was crushed in an intensive winter campaign in 1874-75. In the following spring Fort Elliott was established near the eastern border of the Texas Panhandle to turn them back from their old haunts. There were no more open outbreaks; but for several years it was hard for the Cheyennes and their Arapaho brethren to be good reservation Indians, and there were times when their agents and teachers at Concho found comfort in the nearness of Fort Reno.

We went on to Fort Reno. We crossed the North Canadian – fifty yards wide with a sandy bed. We drove up to the fort, which was built on high ground; level alluvial soil covered with good grass. Here we left some stuff, and got an order to bring some sacked shelled corn to the post from Sam Garvin's place, near Beef Creek on the Washita. I don't know the haul price. We took on a new man to pilot us there, a quiet fellow about forty-five, who knew the trail. But first we went on to Anadarko.

South of Fort Reno the land was high and rolling, with no timber on the high land except blackjacks on sand ridges. We crossed the South Canadian, a bad sandy stream four hundred yards wide; shallow water. On the south side was George Washington's place. We saw three log cabins and some corrals, but did not stop. George was a Caddo; was said to be quite a leader in the tribe.

George Washington was indeed influential among the Caddoes. This once prosperous agricultural people from west of the lower Mississippi had been buffeted about for many years before they found a place to put down roots in the Indian Territory. And here George Washington set them an example of enterprise and thrift. When he died at the age of seventy-three, three years after Oliver Nelson's journey, a contemporary newspaper stated that he had a fine peach orchard and a farm of about two hundred acres under fence, and owned about seventy horses, seventy-five cattle, and one hundred hogs. He was buried in Caddo style: a jug of water was placed with the body, a large log crib was built over the grave, food was set near, and a fire was kept burning for several days.

We drove on from Washington's place, following Stinking creek for a time, then pulling up a sandy slope through blackjacks. We came to a beef carcass hanging in a tree. Stevens was going to cut off a chunk, but our pilot said, "Don't go near it. The Indian will soon be back, and if you disturb it we'll have trouble." We drove about half a mile, and met two Indians on ponies. They asked us to wait, while they rode back toward the beef. When they saw it was all right, they signaled us to go.

We reached the Washita, and camped near a long

pool of clear water about a mile from Anadarko. There were a good many fish floating on the surface; some were bass eighteen inches long. I was told the Indians had poisoned the water to stupefy them; likely they had taken the best, and these were left.

*This was the usual Indian way of taking fish. The drug was probably the bruised roots of the devil's shoe-string (*Tephrosia virginiana Pers*) which still grows abundantly in unplowed areas of the Oklahoma prairies. In this camp by the lagoon the leader of the freighters again showed his capacity for irresponsible mischief.*

In the night a young Indian singing a sort of "Ki-yi" passed about twenty feet from our camp. Stevens shot behind him. He kept up the song till he had gone about fifty yards; then he stopped singing and hit high. We could hear his bare feet patting the trail for quite a spell. Our pilot told Stevens, "You keep this up, and you'll find trouble. This is Indian country."

Next day we crossed the Washita[1], and drove into the stockade to unload at the sutler's store. They examined the wine and whisky close, but paid little attention to the other stuff. The apples were two-thirds rotted. An old Indian came in the enclosure, took a half-rotted apple, and was scraping the rotten part out with his finger. The sutler picked up a plumb rotten one and threw it in his face, smearing it all over, saying, "Get out of here, you old dog." The Indian must have been over seventy-five years old.

That night we camped about a hundred yards from some Indian tepees. I watched the women setting them up. A squaw would chop a circle of holes in the ground

---

[1] The agency had been located on the north side of the river; but apparently it had been removed to the south side – the present site of the agency and the county seat town that has grown up around it – shortly before Mr. Nelson's visit.

with a hatchet, pour a pint of water in each, and ream them out twelve to sixteen inches deep with the flattened end of a tepee pole. Then she set in the poles, and wrapped the cover around them, tying the edge to a loose pole that could be moved around as a ventilator.

After dark a dance started up. Of course we went. They used a piece of hollowed tree with dried raw skin stretched over it for a drum. They would strike light, then strong, keeping time to it with a sort of Ki-yi song. A row of young Indian men sat on the ground, feet out. A squaw would go up to one, draw his head down with her left hand, and pat him on the back several times with the other, then lead him to the center of the tepee. There all formed a line with locked arms, and danced to the sound of the drum: at the heavy stroke they would jump up clear; at the light stroke only the heel would leave the ground.

We all stood on the side except a boy named Turner – a boy about twenty-one with white hair and red eyes, said to have been in a side show as an albino. He sat down with the bucks, feet out in front. Two young squaws came up to him. He tried to get away, but they pushed his head forward, patted him on the back, and pulled him out to the line of dancers. He tried to shuffle while they jumped up and down to their Ki-yi music. After the performance they yelled for about five minutes – about as long as it took for one dance.

The next day the freighters pulled down the Washita and entered the country owned and governed by the civilized Chickasaws. The land was sparsely settled by this small tribe, but it was largely occupied by white farmers – five thousand Indians to nearly fifty thousand whites when the first census was made in 1890. Samuel J. Garvin lived about twelve miles northwest of the present Pauls Valley, where an Oklahoma county now carries his name. This section is one of the richest agricultural areas of Oklahoma. It was almost unbelievably fertile then.

The river bottom was very good all the way down – a red soil easily handled, not sticky. Some of the land was fenced with one barbed wire. (Wire was just coming on the market at Caldwell, selling at fourteen cents a pound). By Chickasaw law each Indian had a right to enclose what land he liked for farming; then he was allowed a quarter-mile strip all around it for grassland, which he could fence or leave open. We run onto some mule foot hogs – just like other swine except the solid hoof. We passed down a lane four miles long, twenty feet wide, mud a foot deep, and got to Garvin's place.

Garvin was a white man, born in Kentucky, who had worked in the Indian Territory during the Civil War as a freighter for the Quartermaster's department. Then he had settled in the Chickasaw Nation, married an Indian girl – thus becoming a tribal citizen – and acquired vast lands and herds. In 1890 he was said to hold two thousand acres of Chickasaw land under cultivation, which was farmed – in defiance of Chickasaw anti-leasing laws – by forty-five white tenants. Later when the Indian reservations were broken up in preparation for Oklahoma statehood, he removed to the new town of Pauls Valley and engaged in extensive banking and other business interests. Mr. Nelson remembers him as "a heavy-set man." He was thirty-six years old when the freighters visited him in 1880.

Garvin had a log house sixteen by thirty feet, with clapboard roof and stick chimney, several log outbuildings, and a long string of pole cribs filled with corn. We loaded shelled corn in sacks, and got some ear corn to feed on the way back, counting seventy ears to the bushel, and then they said it would overrun in weight. One of our fellows said, "You don't shuck the nubbins, do you?" Garvin said, "We don't raise 'em." Asked about the yield, he said, "I paid for shucking 110 bushels an acre on 160 acres. There is the corn," pointing to the pole cribs; "you can measure it and see if I paid too much." The ears were nine to ten inches long; and it wasn't hard to find one with thirty-six rows on. The grains were extra long. The finest corn I ever seen. The price was thirty cents a bushel.

When we started back we pulled across the Washita. One wagon lost some ear corn; it all sank like lead. Late in the evening we camped in a grove, fed our teams and fixed a fire. Later an ox train pulled into camp across the trail east of us: three teams, thirty-six head of oxen. One fellow came over to our camp – short, heavy set, auburn hair, easy talking, about fifty-five. He told us his name was George Laflin. Said he was just driving around to keep in the game; he had lost his string of teams three times to Indians, had U.S. claims pending, and ought to get the pay 'fore long, which would set him on his feet again.

"Where did you all come from?" he asked.

"Caldwell," we told him.

"Then you come down the Chisholm trail; you can't come no other way." And he told us the story –

"You all passed where Pat Hennessey was killed. It was July in '74. Pat was driving cattle for me. We had seven six-yoke teams hauling from the railroad. We loaded four teams, taking all the freight, and left the other three – that was Pat's outfit – to load as soon as the next shipment came in. We pulled into Caldwell. The Indians were ugly, and the government was furnishing a military escort to freighters going into the Territory. We took all the soldiers they had there and started south, leaving orders for the teams following not to leave Caldwell without an escort. But when Hennessey got there with his loads, it seemed safe; so they drove on.

"At Buffalo Springs the night herder stopped to talk with the station keeper, while the teams pulled on ahead. That saved his life; he was over a mile behind when the attack was made. When he saw what was happening, he turned back to Buffalo and helped the station keeper drive the stage horses up the trail north out of danger.

"The Indians made the attack from the head of a broad, deep gulch that comes close to the trail on the west. (You remember the broken red shale on the west; level prairie north, east, and south). It was so sudden the drivers couldn't make a corral of the wagons with the oxen inside.

"The men that found the bodies had to figure out what happened. The next day or so some people came up in a buckboard from Reno. They found Hennessey's wagon burned; and his body all burned up but a few pieces of bones. His gun was there with the ejector broke and a cartridge jammed, and exploded shells lay all around. It seemed that his team had turned square around right on the trail. The other teams had run northeast, one farther than the other. Each driver was laying near his wagon; neither man had been scalped. The Bull Foot station close by had been burned.

"They dug a hole in the trail, raked in the pieces of Pat's bones, ashes, and some busted shells, and covered them up. Later the other two bodies were taken to Buffalo and buried in the forks of the road. You all seen that. And they found the Indians had burned that station, too." Those were the graves I had seen and the burned foundation.

Here Mr. Nelson pauses to give another version of the tragedy, which he heard two years later from the cowboys on the T 5. This involves the notorious frontier character, Dutch Henry. This man is said to have been the head of three hundred horse thieves who operated between Vinita, Indian Territory and Pueblo, Colorado. They had a rendezvous in the present Oklahoma Panhandle, where horses stolen from the two ends of the line were exchanged, so that Indian Territory horses were sold in Colorado and Colorado horses were disposed of in the Indian Territory far from probable identification. About 1877 soldiers from Fort Elliott rounded up nine of the gang on nearby Sweetwater creek, and hanged them all. Shortly after this, Dutch Henry was captured and sent to the penitentiary for stealing government mules. These reverses broke up the gang. Many years later Dutch Henry was released from prison and settled down as a respectable citizen of Colorado.

According to the T 5 story, Dutch Henry and three of his gang were driving out a herd of stolen Indian ponies and the Cheyennes were hot on their trail.

The rustlers were camped on Little Turkey creek north of where Dover is now. They had a small team of mules and a buckboard to haul their supplies. They saw the Indians coming. Two slipped west on horses, and were not followed. The other two jumped into the buckboard and rolled up the creek north; one sat behind, smoking the pursuers with a Sharps .45, while the other whipped the mules. The Indians split: one bunch took to the trail to head the rustlers off, while the rest followed the buckboard to push them into the trap. But when the trail bunch saw the freight outfit coming, they flagged the others; so all left the thieves and lay for the ox train. They hid in the gulch, and when Hennessey and his wagons came by it was soon over.

The morning after they camped with Laflin our freighters saw what was apparently an instance of white outlawry, probably bootlegging, and almost witnessed a sample of the law enforcement in the Chickasaw country.

It was a calm morning, April, 1880. About two inches of snow had fallen in the night. We pulled northwest, following an old trail, and drove about four hours, when we met a pony coming on a dead run. It had a pack saddle, and a small keg on each side. Close behind came two horsemen, each armed with two .45 pistols. Both had their ropes down and were larrupin' the pony, which was doing its best to stay out of reach. We were crossing rolling country. Nearing the next rise we met six or eight Indians strung out about two hundred yards, and moving right along. Each had a pistol and a carbine. Our pilot said, "Indian police. We'll wait here a while, and we'll hear something." But nothing happened. He said, "I guess they didn't catch up."

We drove on out of the snow. We passed Silver City or Silverton, said to be an old trading post. It had four log cabins with clapboard roofs.

By this time the freighters had struck the Chisholm trail. Silver City was one of the important stations on that route. It was near the south bank of the South Canadian, about two miles north of the present Tuttle.

We came to the South Canadian. Some driftwood lay on a sand bar. Stevens was needing wood, but our guide said, "Don't go near it." When we got to the north bank, there stood an Indian. He asked us to wait. He went back and walked around the drift, then signaled for us to go, and we went on. This Indian came from a camp north of the river, and it seems they claimed the wood. It was a good thing we hadn't touched it.

We soon got to Reno and unloaded the sacked corn. I think our pilot was relieved; all the time he'd had to hold us back to keep us from having trouble with the Indians.

Our business done, we started up the trail home. When we were passing Kingfisher, our butcher knife Indian came to us and wanted some corn. Stevens gave him twelve ears. He said, "Me was mad at you; me no mad now."

This time we turned off the trail to the Red Fork station. It was run by a man named Chapin. There was a log house, twelve by fourteen feet, with dirt roof and dirt floor, a door in the west, and a one-sash window in the north and south; a pole corral; and a grass-covered shed stable.

Near Skeleton station we overtook an ox train; three teams. Jim Kerwood, quite a western character, was driving the lead. There was a pony's head sticking out of his wagon. One of our bunch asked, "How come, Jim?" He said,

"I God, I come 'bout Kingfisher rise, two Injuns overtook us leadin' this cayuse, wanted five dollars for it. I give it 'em, dropped the trail, took the hind wheels off a the lead, blindfolded the hoss, led it in, put on the wheels, tied down the sheet, put back on the trail, and drove on. Purty soon a bunch of Injuns come up. An old buck tried to talk chicken to me. Seems the first two had stole their pony, and they trailed it to where I loaded; then the trail quit. I didn't want to take any chances of 'em seein' it in the wagon. I shot the old buck's cayuse on the stern with my bull whip, and he nearly fell off behind. Bill there got a pull at the back of a young buck, and it looked like he'd leave his mount. They'd turn back, then pick up the trail and come again. But we gave them ponies the buckskin till they wouldn't come a-nigh our outfit. I'll get forty dollars for that hoss at Caldwell."

There were a good many ox trains on the trail. A three-wagon train would have six yoke to a wagon, thirty-six head in all. The lead wagon had four and one-fourth-inch spindle, broad tread (four-inch tire), bed four and one-half feet deep (bows and sheet making seven feet), carried four thousand to five thousand pound load. The second wagon had three and one-half- or four-inch spindle, carried four thousand pound load. The third wagon was the "trap" wagon: it carried blankets for bed, also ax, shovel, water keg, bucket, Dutch oven, fry pan, coffee-pot, knives, forks, spoons, tin cups, bacon, flour, coffee, sugar, baking powder, salt, and tobacco. The whips had a three-foot stock, a lash fourteen to sixteen feet long, and on the end a snap of buckskin nine inches long and one and one-half inches wide. The driver carried a ball of bees' wax to grease the lash. He always carried the whip with the lash looped up in his hand; to let it drag would have worn it off and ruined the popper.

These drivers were usually quiet, easy-going, hard to change. On the road they took things as they came; in camp they sang songs, told stories – sometimes plain lying. Some carried pistols; others had an easy way of getting them when they felt the need. They were nice fellows when things run smooth, but when out of sorts nice to let alone; and you could rely on them.

When we got home, Delos went to plowing. I, with several others, loaded up and went south again, this time to Fort Sill.

Fort Sill, the most important military post in the Territory, had been established in 1869 by General Philip H. Sheridan of Civil War fame. Troops stationed there had been active in subduing the Kiowas and Comanches of the Texas plains and forcing them to settle on their reservation in the vicinity of the post. Unlike Fort Reno, Fort Supply, Fort Elliott, and other military establishments of the Indian wars, Fort Sill has continued in use. In 1930 the Field Artillery school of the United States army was permanently located there.

Two wagons were loaded with mule shoes boxed in hundred-pound boxes; then we had canned stuff, bottled wine in boxes, barreled whisky, and flour. It was a hard trip, no pleasure, just rain, water, and mud all the way. The streams were all up. We had to double teams at the creeks. The rivers were worse. We would take all the horses and lead or drive them back and forth till we made a kind of solid trail across the quicksand, then hook all six teams to one wagon and pull it over, making six trips crossing. We didn't happen to get any wagon mired down.

We crossed the Salt Fork that way without much trouble. When we got to the Cimarron we had to wait a day for the water to go down. At the South Canadian we waited several days, and the water was still too high to pull across. Then a mule outfit came up. They said, "Just watch us." They unloaded, spread their oiled wagon sheets on the ground, placed a wagon box on each sheet and loaded them with freight, tied up the sides and ends of the sheets to make boats, and pushed them across; unloaded, returned, loaded again, until they ferried all the stuff over. Then they strung out the running gears of the wagons, hooked on all the teams, and pulled them across. We did the same – water over four feet deep – loaded again, and went happy on our way, finally getting to Sill.

On our return when we came again to the Canadian it was a half mile wide. Turner just sat down and bawled; he said if he ever got across that river he'd never come back. The trip took over twenty days. We met very few on the road. This ended my freighting for a spell.

The Call of the Cow Country

In July I worked a while for my Uncle Doubleday. He set out forty thousand apple grafts, and two hundred apple trees. He had eight mules and a cow all strung out on picket ropes. We didn't have one good rain all summer, so we irrigated the whole outfit from a forty-foot well: the stock at the trough with a tow line, the trees and grafts with barrels and buckets.

A dance was announced at Sherm Richmond's, four miles east. I didn't take too strong, but Uncle said for me to go, so I went. There were four of us. John Hall piloted us over. Down the line a piece Old Sam Garlet had changed the road unbeknown to John: so we followed the old trail, broke down a paling fence, and cut through Sam's garden. Now Old Sam had drove all his kids nutty with his fog horn, so we aimed to drown him out 'fore he got a good start. As soon as he came out, wearin' a kind of white robe, our crowd set in to sing,

> Way down on the Pecos stream
> Where the wild wolf howls
> And the terrifying owls
> Wake us up from our midnight dreams.

We got to the shindig after the small containers had been laid aside. They passed a gallon bottle to John. He being unsteady, hung the bottle on the floor, scatterin' refreshments around in bad shape. Several of us had our smokers on, so very little was said, but the dance began to stop right now. We went back across Uncle Sam's garden, but knew the road this time and got across 'fore he got well keyed up.

Here in this pioneer settlement young Nelson again saw concrete evidence of the desperate need for railroads. This was the period when Kansas counties and communities were bonding themselves ruinously to lure construction their way. In some cases the whole promotion scheme was a fraud capitalizing on the settlers' urgency.

In September Delos and I hauled wheat to the mill at Anthony for one Willis Graham. Near the mill we saw some grading and tie marks that looked like a railroad had been there and left. On inquiry was told the town and township had voted bonds to pay a bonus for the road. The road was built in, and the bonds turned over to the construction company. Then on a Sunday morning the company run in a bunch of workmen, who took the track up as far as the county line that day, and let'er go. If a bunch of cowboys had been there, they would have spoiled that little game.

The mill used hay for fuel. They didn't have anything else. Brother Delos asked the darky fireman how he told when the water got low. He said, "I'll jes' show you how I tell." He looked at the gauge, said, "I's out of water now. You all git out of here quick." He shut off the engine, raked out the fire, and sat down and sweated; he said, "I's glad you is 'quisitive like you is."

One evening a Texas man came to Uncle's place to look at his mules. He said his cow camp was on Deer creek, east of southeast, about twenty miles; he would make it all right – he would watch the stars. I couldn't see how anyone could go twenty miles after dark and strike camp. But later I learned the star map and the penknife-thumbnail compass. And a camp fire will show a long way.

I took a notion to cook at some camp. A fellow told me that a Bates and Beals outfit on Pond creek wanted a cook. So I borrowed a horse and rode south across the prairie.

This outfit belonged to the great LX *ranch of the Texas Panhandle, founded in 1877 by the Bostonians, W. H. "Deacon" Bates and David T. Beals. At one time the company owned 210,597 acres and used an equal amount of public land, with headquarters north of the present Amarillo. About 1880 an additional range was acquired in the Indian Territory, on Turkey creek; this was used as a maturing ground, where cattle were brought to fatten before being driven to market. But young Oliver Nelson missed being an* LX *employee.*

When I got to the place, I found the outfit had left. But at noon I run onto a through herd. (A through herd was a herd just brought in from Texas, whether held in the Territory or on its way to market). I told my errand to the boss. He said Overall, across the Salt Fork, needed help; "but have a bite to eat." There was a grub box built into the back of the wagon, three feet deep, three shelves, lid dropped down and resting on a stake for a table. They had strong coffee, bread solid as cheese, and jerked beef. This beef tasted like chips of wood. To cure it they cut it in strips, salted it, and hung it on ropes to dry. The cook said it would never spoil. In a spell of rainy weather it would get damp and they would fry it in hot tallow. This had had three fryings. It was brittle as crackers, but strong. The cook said, "The taller was ransom."

After the meal I pulled south. Trying to cross Salt Fork, I mired my plug in the quicksand, but finally got him out. I took up the south bank of the river looking for Overall's outfit, and run onto an abandoned camp site. Nothing doing there, so I crossed the river again and rode back north. After it got dark, I could see a camp fire several miles further on, and rode to it. Here I found a man named Linch, his wife, and three hands, with a small tent and a buckboard, on the bank of Crooked creek. I got a biscuit, a piece of bacon, sorghum, and coffee, and filled up; tied out my horse, bedded down with head on saddle and carcass on ground covered with wet saddle blanket, and went to sleep wondering if I'd ever learn to like such a life. This was September, I think, 1880.

The land I'd been over had good bunch grass in the sand hills along the river, and some plum brush five feet high; on the hard land was buffalo grass and prairie dogs. Along the creeks were a few cottonwood trees; and there were blackjacks in the sandy land north of Salt Fork and west of Crooked creek. Buffalo bones were scattered around everywhere away from the trail.

We had breakfast at daybreak: coffee, sow bosom, sour dough bread minus soda, flour gravy, and sorghum. Sour dough is made by mixing flour and water, and letting it stand till it ferments; or one can start with yeast—it's not needed, but it starts quicker. Use half the batter to make your biscuits; then refill the container with water and flour, add sugar if you like, mix well, and let stand for next time. On the roundup a kerosene can is used to hold this yeast batter; at camp, use a jar.

The biscuits are made by adding soda, salt, and lard, and stirring in flour with a spoon to a fairly stiff dough. Use plenty of lard. They are left to stand overnight, then baked in the Dutch oven. During nice weather

THERE WAS A GRUB BOX BUILT INTO THE END OF THE WAGON

N U N Outfit, Texas Panhandle, 1896

they are real light; but during a cold, rainy spell they get downright tough and are called sinkers. Biscuits made without soda are flat if baked at once; if left to rise overnight, they are light and rather tart. I finally got to liking them, but at the time they just beat going without.

Mr. and Mrs. Linch were both a little dusty, some greasy (no chance to wash up) but nice folks. He owned several thousand head of cattle. He told me he had an outfit up above, camped on a side branch, branding; and could use me. I pulled up the creek, missed the side branch outfit, but rounded up at a wagon camp of Henry Stunkel. Rube Pennington, the boss – a tall fellow, badly tanned – said he'd take me on till Stunkel came down from Peck, Kansas. (The old man owned a farm up there). So that was the beginning of my work on the range.

Cooking for the Reverse s

There were six boys in the bunch: Rube, Judge Butts, Billy Stunkel (Old Henry's nephew), Charley Laughorn, Henry Lewis, and a carpenter. The camp was in a draw near Crooked creek: a nice grassy plot, some elm and cottonwood in sight south, blackjacks six miles west, no fencing. They burned surface coal (cow chips). There was the general run of cow camp furniture: a cook stove setting out on the ground and a covered wagon filled with grub and plunder. We had two large ticks made of feather ticking, which I filled with buffalo grass; we put them on the ground, and all crawled up on them that could. Some bedded down on the grass and covered with saddle blankets that smelled too much like a tired horse.

Life slid along amazin'. The weather was dry, but turning cool. The grass was fine, cattle doing good. There were bunches – five hundred to two thousand head – scattered along the creeks three or four miles apart. About half were native, not so wild as Texas cattle. The boys would herd them during day time, bed them on high ground, spend the night in camp, and look them up early in the morning. The carpenter was building a winter camp in a gulch a quarter of a mile south: on the north side, a barn open on the south; then on the opposite side, there was to be our dugout, open on the north so we could look across and watch the horses, Dutch fashion.

I went to a plum patch a quarter of a mile away and

got firewood. I didn't use the stove; found I did best with an open campfire on the ground. I had a Dutch oven, fry pan, and coffee-pot, and nearly enough knives and forks to arm the crowd. I tried yeast bread without much luck. Baking powder was too expensive; seems it would break the old man up. So I turned to sour dough, but nobody seemed able to put me on the right line. I finally tried the sour dough with soda, and learned to do fairly well.

I would have breakfast 'fore day so the boys could get to the cattle bed early to strike a damp trail if any led off. The carpenter would lay till late, then want me to warm up his chuck. One morning when the moon was getting ready to set I put his boots twixt him and the moon saying, "I'll bring you out"; took a bucket and began pouring water down beside his boots. He said, "You little son-etc., etc.," and cocked his gat. (He was the only one that carried his hog-leg all the time). I slid under the creek bank; then I told him, "I didn't pour water in your boots, you crazy fool." But I stayed under cover till he ate his bite and left for the building site. When Rube came in I told him of the happening. He said, "I'll leave my pistol in the grub box, and when he comes in you shoot him in the back." I said I didn't want to do that. So he paid the carpenter off, and the building rested a spell.

The rain soon set in; a good rain about twice a week. We had two large comforts filled with wool. We would pile up on the ticks and cover up, but the beds would bog down in the middle, and soon the cool water would being to creep in at the edges and run down towards this sink. The middle man would crawl out, put on his slicker, and set on his saddle or roost on the wagon tongue. In about ten minutes of heavy rain all would be strung out on the tongue 'cep'in' the boss, Rube, who would say, "If you would lay still, it wouldn't run in." No one else ever tried it. But he'd sticker out, and at daybreak he'd be half under water.

One night Rube said, "Cook, day's a-peepin'." We had no watch or lantern. It was dark as tar. I said, "Rube, I've just got good to sleep." Rube said, "You're half asleep all the time. I'm hungry." I said, "I aim to cook when you're hungry, so here goes two suppers together." I soon had a skillet of bread baked and another started. I called the boys; they didn't seem interested, but I said, "You fellows roll out. There's a heavy storm coming. Pull on your tarps, swallow your bite, and do your stretchin' later." We each got a sinker and a cup of coffee. Then a dash of rain put the fire out, just flooded things. It came from the northwest where all the storms had come from. As soon as it passed Rube said, "It will be day 'fore you get to the cattle." So the boys left. Rube sat on the wagon tongue, covered his face with his hat. I sat down by the front wheel. We both went to sleep. At good day I woke, cooked a bite, and went up on the bank. I saw the boys laying off about four hundred yards. I went to Rube, raised up his hat, and said, "Go tell the boys to not lay on the wet ground." He called them in, and they had another breakfast. I think the first meal was at about twelve.

Old Henry Stunkel came down and looked things over. He said it was handy to have a cook; so I got to stay, at twenty dollars a month. He said he'd send a team down to haul some wood, and better finish up the winter camp. Pennington said, "Send down a sack of fish bone." The boys were all singers and they roosted on the wagon tongue about every third night; I had raised it to a level by putting a tomato box under the

end. But I guess they didn't look like canaries to Old
Henry, for he didn't get the joke. He nearly got sick
laughing; said, "Vy, Rube, vat you do mit a sack of
fish pones?"

When he got back he sent down a man named Foegal
with a large team of mules. Foegal hauled poles and
brush to the place where they had started the camp.
We all worked on it except a couple of boys that held
the cattle. We used pick, shovel, ax, and pitchfork. We
made rafters of poles and shingled the barn with brush
and bluestem grass. Then we dug a square in the south
bank for our quarters; we shingled it with dirt – less
liable to burn than grass – and floored it the same way.
Then Foegal hauled down some corn and we put it in
our dugout and laid our beds on it. He hauled up a big
pile of green water elm for firewood, but it was no good
so I kept on using the plum brush. On one of his trips
down he brought turnips and potatoes from Old
Henry's farm; queer stuff to eat in a cow camp.

An outfit moved in above us: four hundred cows
with calves branded w p (Warren and Prigmore).
They had been driven from Van Buren, Arkansas to
Las Vegas, New Mexico; then back to Crooked creek.
They were engineered by an Arkansaw Democrat from
Van Buren named John Mathews, and two Mex kids –
Lebrow, twelve, and Frisco, fourteen. The kids were
ornery little devils, especially Frisco. He had two
pellets stuck in one hind leg just under the skin, brought
about by a strong talk with a Gringo about the same
age. The impression was left they'd had to sew up the
other fellow a little.

*Apparently life in a cow camp was hardly a refining
influence for young Frisco. Mr. Nelson tells of an
altercation he had with Henry Lewis.*

Lewis was a transient handy man, who would grub one place, then move on. He got Frisco to drink some kerosene; then told him it would kill him, that was what he'd intended. Frisco took it serious, wished for a little revenge; he asked Rube if he thought it safe to go behind Henry and hit him on the head with a branding iron. Rube said, "If you take both hands and give him a good one, he won't hurt you." But Frisco couldn't rouse up the nerve. The branding iron was a two-pound iron on a three-foot rod. Our brand was a reverse S.

Even the owner was not exempt from the robust humor of these cowboys. Mr. Stunkel drove down one day with his mule team to get some big steers to take back to his farm for feeding.

The cattle were off half a mile, and there was no horse at camp, so he walked out. He was about sixty, weighed 170 pounds, and was somewhat clumsy. A boy rode up and let him have his mount and spurs. Charley Laughorn had cut out a cow that outran his pony and got away. Henry said, "Let me show you somedings, Sharley," and gigged his horse in the flank, aiming to head off the cow. But the horse tipped up behind, and the old man went over forward and sat on the ground. The boys hollered and laughed. Henry said, "You iss all tamn fools; dere iss notting to laff at." He walked back to camp, said they tricked him – gave him a bad horse –"Dey iss all tamn fools." I said, "Rube never tricked you." Rube was quiet, lots of times easy, too. I told him how the old man felt. He spilled a little sympathy and Henry seemed relieved.

Stunkel cut out his cattle, drove them twenty miles to Wolf creek, missed three big steers, and rode right back. He reached camp about midnight; found his team of mules tied to the wagon, and no hay. He just went wild. I fixed him a bite, the mules got fed, and he got a nap; and the next day he drove his cattle north.

That night it snowed about three inches. This was November 13, 1880. Mathews had no shelter. He turned his cattle loose, got rid of his lice, and turned in with us. And it just kept snowing. We soon had ten inches.

I could not find plum brush. The elm limbs would not burn. I wanted Foegal to get blackjack wood – it was not as far off as the elm – but he said there was no road to the jacks. By this time he had brought several loads of corn, and Stunkel had sent down twelve very large hams that were spoiled. I would put a little corn in the stove, sandwiched with ham properly sliced, and when the fire was going good add a stick of elm. Sometimes when getting chuck ready, I would half fill the stove with corn and finish with wood. The boys would eat and the fire would begin to cool as it hit the elm. If they tried to tinker with it, it would go out. They soon learned that if they wanted a warm fire they better go off for a spell and let me work on it alone. They would go to the shed stable, and on their return they would find the stove hot again.

Rube had tried to warm up the fire several times, but couldn't maker go. One morning he came in before I'd had time to monkey with the stove. He said, "Now I want to see how you fix that fire." I said, "I've been usin' boxes to start it." He said, "We've got no boxes." I said, "Sometimes I put in a little corn." He said, "Well, get your corn." I said, "And I put in a little ham." "Well, get your ham." I put in the duke's mixture, the ham began to broil, and the fire started up pretty good. He said, "So that's the way you do it." I said, "Sometimes." He said, "You know damned well that's the way you been doing it ever since the snow fell." When the fire got to going good, I went to put in a couple of sticks of elm, but he said, "Keep that damned stuff out of there."

After that, when it was about time for the boys to come in, Rube would fill the stove with corn, put in about two pounds of ham, set in front of it with a foot on each lid, and say, "Let it alone; it'll burn." The boys would say, "I don't like to see a feller burn corn." But Rube would say, "I don't like to see a feller freeze."

The weather soon bore down to zero, with snow over a foot deep. Our camp was half a mile south of the Timberlake crossing on Crooked creek, where peelers passed by on the way to Caldwell, thirty miles northeast. On the way there they would stop in for news, or coming back with news stop overnight. We would never turn a man down: when they came, it was, " 'Light and fill up;" when they left, it was "So long, boys; stop again."

About the last of November a bunch of beeves dropped in above us: about twelve hundred belonging to Bates and Beals from the Texas Panhandle, to be shipped at Caldwell. It turned cold. The boys lived in a tent and were short on bedding; they came to us and we let them have all we could spare. Later their boss told us they just rode and slept in the same blankets – wrapped the blankets around them in the daytime, and slept in them at night. The snows came only one or two days apart. The herd passed our dugout several times during the storms. We could hear the guards singing.

One bad morning we looked north, and the tent was gone. Later we were told that their boss was at Caldwell the day before, looking for cars to load. He found none there, decided to give up. He got back to camp at 11 p.m. A bad storm was on. He went to the herd; said, "Boys, turn 'em a-loose. We'll go to town in the morning." The boys said, "We'll unsaddle in Caldwell." The cook said, "Here fellows, you bring in my team." The snow was over a foot deep, but they got to town, thirty miles distant, at 8 a.m. Then they returned to the ranch, two hundred miles southwest, aiming to gather the cattle on the spring roundup.

The cattle held up fine on the range that winter. The grass was good because it got snowed under before it froze. Cattle will not paw the snow off like a horse, but they will root or move it with their nose so they can get to the grass.

We cut ice so they could get water. I helped at that – would rather ride out than stay in camp. Two of us with an ax and shovel would ride down the creek, two others would ride upstream; we cut the ice, cleaned out the holes, then drove the cattle down to drink – an all-day job on the start. Later as they got more used to the watering, they got so they would bawl for us and follow us up, gathering around so close we couldn't clear the ice away. So we would cut a short time, then when they crowded up we would mount, ride a mile in a high lope, and start another hole. They came to drink by the thousands; there was no fencing, and we were watering all the cattle in that part of the range. Their weight would press the ice down around the holes and push the water out on top; in the night it would freeze, and we would have to cut it again. This watering kept up till in March.

This was about all we did. In camp our library was principally Sam Bass, Dick Turpin, Claude Duval, the Forty Thieves, or anything else that was good.

Somehow we didn't take to cards. Finally Rube wrote a letter to a Miss Emily Cumpton he had met somewhere in Texas – I have forgotten the post office – telling her where he was, of his surroundings – snow, cold, and how lonesome he was. He mailed the missive and bided his time.

Soon his love bait got a nibble – a nice letter. The writer was surprised but not displeased, had wondered at the life and trials of a cowboy –"perhaps you are not in just the right company"–"you have my sympathy." Rube wrote an answer, showed it to Mathews, saying, "I'm going to send that." Mathews read it, said, "No, you won't. I wouldn't send that to my mother-in-law. Let me show you." He wrote a letter and handed it to Rube; Rube looked it over and sent it. After that Mathews did most of Rube's writing. One of his sentences I remember was, "Your letters are as an oasis in the desert of my dreary existence." (Yes, it had a happy ending; Rube and the lady finally united for life).

News came up that the Indians were killing cattle below the Cimarron, and the stockmen called a meeting at Red Fork (Dover) about sixty miles south, to decide on a course of action. Rube went from our camp. On his return he reported that one of the United States Indian agents had turned two thousand grown steers over to a well-known cowman to winter for his Indians. They were branded I.D. (Indian Department) but the cowman had slapped on his own brand burned deep to cover it. And those were the cattle the Indians were killing. So the meeting decided they had no call to jump on the Indians; let the agent and his friend do their own stealing. In the spring the cowman drove the stolen cattle west – it was said to Billy the Kid. (But he eventually died broke).

In the cow camps where the favorite reading was of Sam Bass or Dick Turpin, the exploits of the fabulous Kid (William H. Bonney) made good conversation. And it is possible that cattle stolen from the Indian Territory were finding their way to his New Mexican hide-out. Two years before he had spent some months around Tascosa in the Texas Panhandle, selling stolen New Mexican horses and studying the lay of the land; then he returned to his old haunts, where he gathered up cattle that drifted – or were driven – from Panhandle ranges. The Panhandle cowmen were hunting him down at the very time Oliver Nelson was cooking for the Reverse S; but his depredations continued until he was killed the following summer.

Meanwhile the Reverse S hands were having milder, but yet annoying, troubles with strayed cattle, for barbed wire had not yet come to enclose the herds of the ranchmen or protect the fields of the homesteaders. And young Oliver Nelson was learning the ways of the range.

We were ten miles from the Kansas line. The Kansas settlers lived in bunches – several close together, then several miles to the next bunch. The cattle would wander for feed and get up into the settlements. If the settlers had no place to shut them up, they would shoot them. (I always will think they killed cattle to live; they had nothing). But if they had corrals, they would pen them, ride down and tell us, and get ten dollars' damage and a fill-up on our fare – turnips, beans, and potatoes. Then two of us would go up and bring the cattle back. I rather liked to go out, but sometimes the coming in was bad. We would start back about sunset, get in about midnight. I had no overshoes, and I froze my feet pretty bad.

On one trip up the line I struck a bull trail. (Bulls will bunch up in winter). I followed it several miles northeast, and came in sight of my uncle's house where I had worked the summer before. I went there and took dinner. They had me stay till two o'clock. When I got ready to leave, my uncle said there was ten bulls back of his barn and he wished I would take them along. I took them and got started. They drove fairly well for a while, then strung out single file. I had a quirt, but no rope to lam them with. It was awful cold. The snow was twelve inches deep and crusty; I had to break a trail twenty miles to camp, and I was riding a horse that was never good at finding his way in.

I followed the bulls till sunset; got so I couldn't holler, then left them and started back alone. I aimed to go southwest. After quite a ride I came up to the twin mounds south of Anthony. Then I knew I was close to ten miles north of camp – I had gone more west than I intended. I turned south. It was a calm starlight night. The country was fairly level, sloping southeast. I rode quite a while, and a light appeared off to my left. I thought, "Now that's just too low down for a star; it must be someone's camp." I turned for it and ran off of a bank into a snow drift. I got off and tramped down the snow till I managed to get my horse out. I led him to level ground; then I started out again. The light would appear and disappear, but I kept my course. Finally I could see I was getting pretty close. I came to a level flat where the snow was light. I thought I would learn my pony how to travel; I got into a high lope – and the light flashed on a hillside to my left about half a mile behind me. I turned back, and there was *our* camp! And how did I feel? Rube said, "When you ride Old Paint, find camp 'fore night, for he just won't come in."

Toward March we ran out of corn. Foegal drove up to Peck for another load. Old Henry said, "Vy, vat you do mit dot corn?" Foegal said, "The cook, he burns it." "De cook, he purns corn! De cook, he purns corn! Vy, his beople iss poor folks. May be dey didn't purn corn, dey vouldn't be poor folks like dey iss. I'll learn dot cook somedinks." For several days after the wagon returned to camp, the boys talking among themselves would say, "Cook is goin' to get fired." When the wagon was fixed to go to Peck again, Rube said to Foegal, "You tell Stunkel it takes money to fire a man down here." So the next time the wagon came down, I was paid off and "resigned."

Rube Pennington quit soon after. He had come up the trail with Billy Stunkel at twenty-five dollars a month; now he went to work for the Lundy outfit that held cattle southwest of us, at three times what Stunkel paid, and Stunkel got another twenty-five dollar boss. Rube met Henry at Caldwell that spring, and told the old man *he* was the one that burned the corn, that the boys had been afraid to tell on him and so laid it on me.

A couple of rustlers made a figure 8 out of Henry's reverse S, and run him out of the Strip. But when he died it was said he was worth several hundred thousand dollars. He had come to Wichita with very little, and he could not read or sign his name.

Life on the V Bar

After I left Stunkel I went home for a spell. I took two trips freighting to Reno. Then I plowed out some sod on the place and planted a crop. In June I went to cook for Ben and Perry Garland at twenty dollars a month.

Ben was good-natured; Perry had to be soaked in coffee and tobacco juice, and even then he didn't feel just right. Our brand was the v Bar. There were two camps: Garland, where I worked, a through camp with near a thousand head of through cattle; and Atterberry, six miles north, with about the same number of wintered stock. Our mealtime bunch was from four to ten, just owing to convenience.

We had an ox team for pleasure drives, which I tried out a time or two when the fuel situation got low; but having a very poor ax I turned to surface coal, which I mined with a gunny sack. This ox team had a spread of horns of close to eight feet. We had three other steers with horns equally broad; a year later when they loaded them to ship, I was told they took an ax and cut one horn off of each to get them in the car.

Our camp was a wagon on a bend of Pond creek, about four feet north and ten feet east of a twenty-foot drop in the bank. The wagon jet with the sheet on was set on the ground north of the wagon, and here we kept our grub and plunder.

A covered wagon often had overjets or extensions built out at the top of the box, and to these the bows were fastened. This increased the width of the covered space, and the entire jet with bows and canvas sheet could be removed without dismantling.

There was a board platform under the wagon to hold our dry salt bacon, and a bacon box for cupboard and table. We had the usual supply of stuff at a through camp: coffee, flour, meal, bacon, salt, and soda. I suggested beans and dried apples, but was told there was plenty there if I'd find them. (More of that later). We had a coffee-pot, two ovens, a fry pan, a bucket, two knives, one fork, and one spoon. I suggested more knives and forks and a few more spoons, but was told it was no use. (More of that later, too).

The weather was warm, the ground dry. We would spread our blankets on grass close to camp. The cattle – a mixed bunch – bedded away about fifty yards. They were gentle, so unless a storm came we didn't stand night guard. They would leave the bed ground at good day. The boys would point them out towards fresh grass; at ten o'clock turn them to graze towards the creek; at twelve come in to dinner, leaving them till about two; then point them to other grass, aiming to have them drift to bed around dusk. The land sloped away from the creek, so they could see them for several miles. It was mostly red soil, with good buffalo grass and pea vine; no timber east, blackjacks five miles west.

We had a good rain every ten days. When a storm came at night we would roll up our beds and put on our slickers. Then I would put my bed roll on the protected side of the grub box and sit on it, leaning back against the box. Each of the boys would place his saddle on top of his roll and sit in the saddle to sleep, leaning against a wagon wheel. Thus we all slept dry, and breakfast always tasted good.

IT TOOK GOOD ROPERS TO HEAD AND HEEL AND GOOD HORSES TO STRETCH THEM OUT

Branding on the prairie, southwest Kansas, about 1896

Laying on our blankets at night, we sometimes discussed astronomy. Once a boy named Billy Edwards said if a certain star was to fall it would hit him on the breast. Another boy said it would hit the cook. Asked what I thought it would hit, I said if that star was to fall, the chance of it hitting the earth was about as good as his flipping a bean up and hitting the star. Billy wanted to know, "How big is that star?" I said, "Many times larger than this earth." Billy asked, "Do you believe that?" I said, "Yes." He said, "I'll bet you Old Fuzzle"– Fuzzle was his private mount –"that star ain't no bigger than my fist." I asked him, "How big is the sun, Billy?" He said, "About the size of the bacon box." I said, "Billy, there is holes in that sun the earth could drop in and have thousands of miles of space on each side." We just didn't each have the same notion about the planets.

Some of the cattle got to coming to the wagon at night and licking salt off the bacon, so I moved my bed up beside it. One night a warm air waked me up. I opened my eyes, and there was a coyote's nose not four inches from mine. I drew a long breath, and darn near passed out. The coyote growled, his bristles raised, eyes turned green; he started to run, but kept looking back, and fell over the bank into the water. I crawled into the wagon jet with the grub, and listened to that coyote yip and yell on a hill west till peep of day. I couldn't forget that inquisitive look. But I kept mum about it.

Young Nelson worked in the best cow camp tradition to make his meals appetizing. He developed considerable ingenuity – even if he did draw the line at "marrow guts."

I got hold of a .22 rifle; would kill soft-shell turtles fourteen to sixteen inches across. I would cut up the meat and soak it in salt water; then cook the white one meal, the dark the next, and have the boys guessing what it was. I got hold of some potatoes and vinegar; I would slice the potatoes, soak in salt water overnight, and put on vinegar, and the boys ate them raw for cucumbers. Once we run nearly out of flour. I mixed sour dough and meal and fried it in plenty of lard, and served it with turtle meat and molasses. I cut a small square out of the rock bank at a spring, and placed my yeast batter there to keep cool. Once Billy Edwards brought in some marrow guts (calf entrails); he said they were good to eat, that no food passed through them. I threw them in the creek.

The grass was growing fast, and some of the cattle died from bloat. A peeler passing said there was no need to lose any, just to stick a knife in and let the wind out and they would get over it. Billy came in one morning and asked for a butcher knife; had me sharpen it. I asked what he was going to do, and he said, "None of your business." He took the knife and rode out of sight around a bend in the creek. I dropped down the bank and ran to the top of a high bluff. Under the bluff close to the creek lay a yearling, swelled up till all four feet were off the ground. Billy walked up, knelt down between its feet, and said, "Here's where I save a steer." He drove in the knife, cutting a six-inch hole in its paunch. The whole side blew out; blowed his hat off, and he fell over backwards. The calf bawled, got up, walked off about fifty yards, and layed down for keeps. Billy went to the creek and washed his face, coat, and knife.

I slipped back to camp. When the boys came in, I took the position Billy had taken, said, "Here's where I save a steer," made a wild stab with the knife, and fell over backward. Ike Davis said, "Cutter wide open, did you, Billy?" The boys roasted Billy good.

A boy with a herd close to us was learning things, too, that summer. One time while he was on guard, a young cow lay off to itself and would fill up on wind and blow and grunt like full cattle will. The boy felt sorry, went up to the cow, said, "Poor bossy," and put his hand on her; and right now she got up and went through the herd like a bat out of hell. The boy headed the bunch off four miles away.

A few sheep men from New Mexico were bringing in their flocks to graze in the Strip, some with ten to twenty thousand head. Small bunches would stray away. Our upper camp caught about fifty head and corralled them in a bend of the creek, killing as they could eat them along. They wanted me to cook some. I said I didn't think much of a sheep thief. I came near having trouble about it.

Cow men didn't like sheep, for range cattle wouldn't feed where they grazed. Once several boys – not working for our outfit – run onto a big herd crossing Salt Fork. The sand bed was about two hundred yards wide, the channel six inches deep and twenty feet wide. Half the herd had passed the water, was on the sand bed. The boys began to shoot, and the lead turned back and piled up in the water. They piled up five feet high. The boys rode away, leaving the herder pulling out his sheep; likely several hundred head drowned. There was a lot of cussedness in some boys.

It seemed nearly everyone took cattle, too, when it looked safe. So there was always fighting over brands. One day Garland came in and told us, "Garfield is shot," (meaning, of course, President Garfield). Billy said, "Another poor devil killed over a cow." At another camp when the news came in, a boy asked, "What brand did he run?"

We wanted to put the Garland brand on our through cattle before we turned them loose on the range. Where there were no corrals or pens, cattle were often branded out on the open prairie, but it took good ropers to head and heel and good horses to stretch them out. We had neither, and anyhow it is slow work. So we drove the cattle to the stock pens at Caldwell. The pens were right on the state line two miles south of town. It was my job to fix a bite to eat, and heat the irons and hand them to the branders. Garland said it was easy work. They picked up a load of trashy wood – cottonwood and elm – and made the fire close to the branding chute on the north side of a seven-foot-high corral, where not a breath of air could strike it. It was about August 10, 1881.

My clothes were wet with sweat, but in the middle of the afternoon they turned dry and I could not see. I told Ben Garland, and he said, "Go lay in the shade." A man had been standing there watching me work. Now he came to where I lay under a wagon and said, "You stood that longer than I thought you would; they didn't fix that fire right." Ben asked what he would charge to fire and handle the irons. He said, "Ten dollars a day and blackjack wood." So Ben told him to go ahead. He took a blackjack pole twelve feet long and eight inches thick and laid it twenty feet from the fence; placed another above, with an eight-inch space between the two for the irons; then made a fire close up behind them, letting the irons rest on the bottom pole. That way, the two logs held off the heat so a man could work.

We kept the whole bunch of cattle in the pens. We

would take them out to water and graze a short time, then bring them back and burn again. They let one of the work steers into the branding chute by mistake. It took over an hour to work him back on account of his long horns.

Ben said we'd take our slumgullion at a grub shop close by on the bank of Fall creek so's to save time. Right then I thought of our horrible condition about cutlery at camp, and resolved to improve it if I could. So I put on a coat at dinner time. I noticed Billy Edwards and Ike Davis did the same. The mercury was close to 110°. When I sat down I got the knife, fork, and spoon on each side of me and stowed them in my inside pocket. Men sat down at those places and yelled, "No knife or fork here." The main stoker came out with another supply; he said he had a damned ninny helping that never did anything right. When I got done eating I took another side knife and fork and helped myself to a glassful of spoons he had on the table. Then I went back to the wagon to hide my haul. I saw Billy and Ike there, but I said nothing, and went out to the pens.

After about three meals of this, when I got set down at the table there was not enough chop sticks to go around. I wondered how my taking six or eight pieces could cause such a scarcity. The chuck boss acted like he had swallowed something hot: called his flunky an auger-eyed son of a coyote, throwing his cutlery in the creek; said he had a notion to heave him in the water and stand on him till he raked it all out. He sent a hurry-up man to town, two miles away for more implements.

At the last meal, someone took my knife and fork, but I had a-plenty. I yoked up the ox team and rolled into Caldwell, got a full line of grub, and trailed the herd back toward camp. I crossed Bluff creek and pulled up the grade. I believe it was the hottest day I ever met up with. The team took a desire to lay down. I had an equal desire to keep going, and a four-foot club to drive it in. I finally got to the top and came out on the flat land about noon; then I seen the herd all laying down two miles ahead. I unyoked, and the oxen layed down all hungry and thirsty. I started a fire (wasting nearly all my water to hold the blaze), fixed a bite, got on a lead pony, and took the lunch to the boys. All of them was under a tree. I asked why they didn't drive to water, and was asked why I didn't drive down to the tree. I said, "The oxen layed down;" they said, "That's why we stopped, too." This is the only time I ever knew of hungry cattle refusing to graze. We all ate lunch and lay there till nearly four. Then the cattle got up and started grazing. We got to camp late in the night.

Next day I went to the wagon to check up. I found about twenty each of knives, forks, and spoons slipped away under the stuff. I knew what I had done, but this was overdone. It seemed wrong somehow. But I put them in a small box. About noon Billy got in the wagon, scuffled from front to rear a couple of times, then said, "Oliver, diju get my cutlery?" Ike said, "You fellows been stealin', too? I got a-plenty to go 'round." Ben came down in a few days, and seen the plunder. He said, "You boys ought to be ashamed. Didn't you hear that fellow cuss his poor flunky?" But he let it pass. Anyhow I had enough kitchen machinery now to feed the bunch without using their hands.

One day we had a heavy rain that brought a stand of water down the creek. It made a wash in the bank, and

a little later the soil began to swell up there. Next day
or so, new beans began to peep through. When Ben
came in, I took him to see the wonder. He said, "That's
where the cook before you hid the prunes, rice, dried
apples, and beans – just too lazy to cook."

We now moved into a tent. Ab Hall and Charles
Larkin began fixing line camps for the winter. It was
all prairie country, no fence, so they just rode lines
around a claimed square, and let the cattle drift inside.

Old Perry had moved out. Ben said he would have
to pay us less. Prices at K.C. were three and one-half
cents for stockers and feeders – a big price for those
days – but he thought he wasn't making enough. I said,
"Get a cheaper man," and I gave him my resign to take
effect when help showed up. Billy and Ike traded their
mounts for two nice fat 'riginals ("originals" were
good-looking, high-life horses), and rode to Caldwell
with Gube, a brother to Ike. They came back all new
togs, guns, chaps, and spurs, and pulled south. I was
told that when they got to the Red river Billy was so
afraid of the broad stream he cried.

Soon a gentleman from Arkansas, a Mr. Harkleboad,
hove in to relieve me. A drizzle rain set in that evening
and kept up all next day. We were cooking out of doors.
Mr. Hark told me he'd rather I didn't help him, so the
next morning I layed still while he got up and stormed
the works. About fifteen minutes later I looked out, and
he was trying to set fire to a wet cow chip using one
match at a time. I seen the matches wouldn't hold out
if his patience did, so I saddled a pony and rode to the
upper camp for chow. Then I pulled out for home.

Trail and Range

When I got home, John Mullin – a cousin – and I went to hauling freight to military posts down in the Territory. We took several loads to Cantonment, one hundred and twenty miles southwest of Caldwell.

This post was located on the North Canadian, just above the present town of Canton. It had been established March 6, 1879 to restrain the Cheyennes. It was abandoned by the War department the summer following Mr. Nelson's freighting trips, but the stone buildings were used for many years as a school plant and a sub-agency.

On the "Cantone trail" the freighters saw evidence of the ruthless slaughter of game carried on by white men in the Indian country in violation of law and treaties.

It was late in the fall of '81. About Christmas time hunters from the north would drop in on the creeks running into the Cimarron and shoot turkeys on the roosts; they would shoot half the night, pick up the next day, and pull north to market. If the weather turned warm, the meat would spoil and they would begin to throw them out one at a time; in some places they would throw out the whole load. The trail was lined with coyotes waiting for turkeys. Sometimes we would pass twenty-five deer hanging in the jacks ready to be hauled to Wichita and sold.

On one trip we were loaded with boxes of bottled wine, barrels of whisky, and canned corn and tomatoes.

We camped on Sand creek that runs into Salt Fork. (There was a whole lot of creeks called Sand creek). One John Haines and pard camped close to us; some soldiers camped to the north. A cold rain set in. We bedded down under a wagon and covered up, heads and all. In the night we got quite warm, and when we moved, our cover would crack. We were wakened by the bugle call. Then Haines throwed a club and struck our bed; it sounded like breaking glass. Cousin laid the cover back, and snow fell all over our faces; the sheet was stiff with sleet and covered with snow three inches deep. We filled up with bread, bacon, and hot coffee, and pulled south feeling pretty good. The south wind soon took off most of the snow. It was all open country.

We made a trip to Anadarko. On the way we met two squaws with a donkey loaded with firewood. The trail was washed out, so the donkey couldn't get out; and the lead team knocked it down. We all passed, but no one would help to tail up the donk. The squaws shook their fists at us, and said "Damn you!" They had to unpack to get the donk up.

White men were more co-operative when they found each other in difficulty.

On our way back, we found the Cimarron up when we got there. On the south bank was an ox train, empty, going north – six wagons, seventy-two head of oxen. On the north side was a U.S. mule outfit, loaded, going south. Cattle pull with the top of their necks, holding their heads down, so they can't pull in water a foot deep. And the mules couldn't pull their loads up the sandy bank. So the mules would take the loaded wagons across the stream; then the ox drivers would hook on twelve yoke of cattle, holler, "Hold back your mules," and start in with their whips popping like pistols. They soon got up the bank; twelve yoke will pull the tongue out of any wagon that won't move. Then they hooked the mules to the empties, and pulled them across to the north side, and both outfits went merrily on their way.

Once a storm struck us at Reno, snow ten inches deep. On the way back north we stopped behind a small mound about one hundred yards southeast of the present Enid public square. We scooped away the snow, and slept very well. But at Pond Creek one boy froze his feet sleeping in the cold.

My last load was to Reno. There were several wagons in the outfit. I usually fixed the mess, some one caring for my team. I had two small mules and a pony I had bought on Little Turkey creek north of Dover. One night my cousin fed my team and turned them out, tying the hitch rope around the mules' necks instead of taking off the halters. One caught a hind shoe in the rope, and in the morning we found him choked to death. When I got home I wanted to get another mule, but Daddy said I was wasting my money, so I went to work to fix up our place.

Brother Charley and I hauled logs from Osage creek down in the Indian Territory to a sawmill Joe Richmond had on Bluff creek. We had some broad boards cut to make a shed stable; also fixed a good corral. Then I put in the crop. When this was all done, I hired out to J. C. (Charley) Plake at Caldwell. He was a tall slim fellow with a big hat and spurs.

Charles and his brother, Doss, had brought up a small through bunch of cows and calves from the Yaller House canyon – the Lum Slaughter range in west Texas. They branded three sevens (777) on each side. The bunch was on Deer creek, about twenty miles out from town: nice-laying red ground, mesquite grass, and a prairie dog hole every fifty feet. There was little rain and everything moved along nice. Cows and calves are not much bother, so it was little trouble to stand night guard. (Standing guard means to ride around the herd. The night was divided into three guards, each boy waking his relief as he came in).

A man named Terwilliger had a bunch of horses – 3500 head – just below us southeast. One of his men rode up to our camp one noon. I said, " 'Light and fill up." He tied his bronc to a hind wheel of the chuck wagon. I said, "Don't tie him there; he might get scared." But he said, "I'll watch him." He tied him with about fifteen feet of slack rope. We had a grub box built in behind, door dropped to rest on one leg for a table. The horse got his rope under a stirrup and made a jump, and the table went down with all the tin pans. The horse left with the wagon. Then the wheel broke, and he went off with the tire, which would bounce and land on him, and every time it hit him he put on some extra speed. The boy took out after him, but the bronc reached the herd first, and it began to bunch up. It took some time to get a tug on the scared bronc, but to corral the herd and ease the fright took all afternoon. The boy never came back to our camp. We propped the axle on a box; then Plake took the hub to Caldwell on his saddle, and later a buckboard brought the new wheel out.

When standing night guard we kept a slow cow chip fire so we could have a pot of hot coffee – couldn't well stay up without it. One night I came in for a drink. When getting off my horse, I stepped too far back and the wind blowed my slicker against his hind leg. He kicked me in the side and knocked me down. When he fell, I dropped his rope and he got away. He ran toward our bunch of saddle horses (called the "remuda") which were loose-hobbled; they started to run. One had a bell on.

I seen stars a-plenty, then remembered I was standing guard. Charley Plake's – my relief's – mount was tied to the wagon saddled. I took it, led it from the wagon, and rode slow, singing same as always, till I got past the herd. The bell was headed southeast. Soon as I got past the herd I turned my horse to a dead run – right across a bad dog town. I soon began to strike bunches of Terwilliger horses. Then I came to the main bunch, all running. Their hoofs sounded like a storm. I soon passed them, and heard our bell ahead. It was very dark. The horse that had got away from me was white, and trailing the remuda. I headed him, caught his rope, and drove our horses back; tied Charley's horse to the wagon, waked Charley, and layed down.

Day soon peeped. The saddle horses were brought in and unhobbled. Doss Plake hollered, "Oliver, did the horses run last night?" I said, "The Terwilliger horses were wild; I never noticed *our* bell." He said, "These horses' legs are skinned up to the knees. They must have been running with the hobbles." Then Charley Plake came in and took off his saddle; he said, "Look, fellers; this horse has been covered with foam." The Terwilliger horses ran all day. They broke up in small bunches; one horse would nicker, another bunch would answer, then they would come together and all would tear out. One of their boys told us they had to corral the whole herd and let them stand a day to stop the run. Nobody could understand how it all happened; nobody except me, and I kept my mouth shut.

A heavy rain came one night when I was standing guard. Water covered the ground two inches deep.

When it passed, the stars came out clear. Soon the full moon came out overhead, shining against a bank of clouds. The top rim of clouds was alive with electricity. I thought of a column of marble a mile high. The water on the ground looked like ice; the drops on the grass sparkled. Soon a rainbow formed in the east, the circle about half as broad as a rainbow in daytime, but dazzling as electric light, the colors as clear as any I ever seen. The cattle stood still. The boys were sleeping on a little rise, covered with a heavy duck sheet. I rode up and said, "Charley, look out." He asked, "What is it, Oliver?" I said, "Just look out." He laid back the sheet, said, "Boys, just look out." One little fellow asked, "Is this the end of the world?" I said, "No, Billy, that is just a midnight rainbow." I have never seen any other light so brilliant.

All this seemed remote and peaceful, but news of lurid happenings traveled fast over the cow country. Western books still tell of the death of Marshal G. S. Brown of Caldwell at the hands of two celebrating Texans. The boys out on Deer creek heard it first when the boss took a trip to town. Then Charles Nelson added some later details. Charles, now seventeen years old, was working for Major Andrew Drumm, prominent Strip cowman, who ran the famous U brand and controlled an immense range on the Salt Fork with headquarters near the present Cherokee.

Charley Plake came in one day from Caldwell, and told us about the Bean boys. They had come up the trail with a through herd for the Texas Land and Cattle company (brand T 5). While they were at the red light in Caldwell, George Brown, the marshal, tried to take a pistol from one; the other shot over his brother's shoulder, and hit the officer square in the forehead.

Then they went to the livery barn and got their horses; rode up in front of a hardware store and called for pistol cartridges; paid their bills and rode leisurely out of town. The deputy marshal, John Neal of Boston, took off his star, not wanting to clash with them.

The boys slept that night on the prairie. The next morning they rode up to a Major Drumm camp on Polecat creek, twenty miles out. My brother Charley was working for Drumm – he told me all about it later. He said one boy stood back, and the other did the talking. They ate breakfast the same way, one at a time, the other holding the mounts; then said they had a long ride to make, wanted fresh horses, would leave theirs. So they got fresh mounts and rode south. They stopped eight days with the outfit they came up with – the T 5 through camp on Sand creek, which runs into Eagle Chief. Then they pulled for the Pecos. Officers from Wellington passed them somewhere and with the help of the rangers trapped them near Wichita Falls, Texas; they killed one, and crippled the other so he couldn't navigate and died while they were bringing him back to Caldwell. I was told they were sons of Judge Roy Bean, "the Law west of the Pecos."

One feels that the picturesque judge should have been their father; but sober history does not credit that famous frontier character with any sons answering to this description.

Other cowboy frolics in town brought laughter rather than bloodshed. As Mr. Nelson says, "If it wasn't one kind of excitement it was another for the boys at Caldwell." And he describes one prank from which the good people of the place emerged looking less righteous than they had intended.

Along about this time the meetin' house ladies put on

a baby show, selling votes at a dollar each on the most popular kid, with a fine baby buggy to the winner. Several idle peelers decided it would be a good scheme to enter the name of a little darky from the low end of town. So just before the contest started, they sent a committee to tell the church bunch that a poor lady in the south part of the city had a very beautiful child, which they would very much like to enter in the contest. "Oh, of course," purred the church ladies, "bring the little one along; it's no disgrace to be poor." So they gave the kid's name, but plumb forgot to say it was black.

Meanwhile another delegation proceeded to tog up the coons: they had the piccaninny dressed in red and yellow, and the mammy in blue and yellow with some white and black trimmings. They layed low till after the performance started; then they led up their hope. The reception committee, not knowing what else to do, put the new entry on a bench at the far end of the hall. Finally several of the boys came in – well teed, of course – and began to look at the babies. They never in their lives seen such beautiful children – and how was the contest going? Well, it seemed the vote was pretty heavy on two; the lead stood at forty bucks, the next at thirty, and coming strong. Finally they got down to Snowball, dressed fit to kill, face black as tar; and they started the little coon's tally about where the two leaders would stand added together.

The church people had to do something. So when the boys went out for a chaser, the white tickets were all slipped to one kid, to put it ahead of the black diamond. The contest was to close at ten. And right at ten the boys came back, and planked down fifty dollars' worth of votes for Snowball. One cowman just up with a bunch

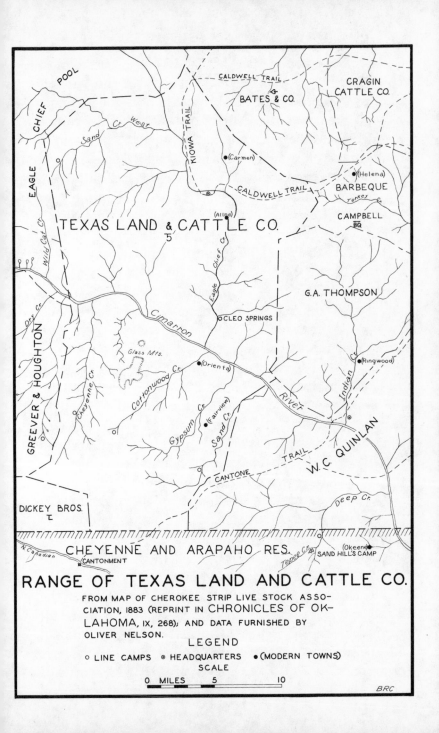

RANGE OF TEXAS LAND AND CATTLE CO.

FROM MAP OF CHEROKEE STRIP LIVE STOCK ASSO-
CIATION, 1883 (REPRINT IN CHRONICLES OF OK-
LAHOMA, IX, 268); AND DATA FURNISHED BY
OLIVER NELSON.

LEGEND

○ LINE CAMPS ◉ HEADQUARTERS ● (MODERN TOWNS)

SCALE

0 MILES 5 10

BRC

of beeves said, "That coon is goin' to push that tram car if it takes my last steer to do it." Well the church people plumb lost heart, and Black Beauty won. Then the punchers paid the mammy coon to coast the piccaninny around town for a week.

The baby coon – I forget the name – finally came to Oklahoma after the country was settled, and lived west of Hennessey. But I'm gettin' plumb off my range.

The Plakes soon sold their cattle, so my job was over. I went to Caldwell; met a tall, starchy-lookin' fellow – all dressed up like a preacher, only he had a big hat on and high-heeled boots. I asked if he was running an outfit. He said, "Yes." He was J. Will Carter, manager of the T 5. I asked him if he needed a cook. He said, "I pay twenty-five dollars, and you furnish your own bed. If that suits you, meet me at Witzleben's supply store Thursday noon." It seemed a T 5 bunch had come up to Caldwell to ship a beef herd, and would be ready to start back Thursday. And so that was the way I joined up with the T 5. It was my first experience with a big outfit.

Starting in with the T 5

Thursday noon I called at the supply store; was told the wagon had already loaded and gone out. So I went down to the stockyards, and got there just as they were driving the last bunch into the pens. They had the restaurant man lead a tame cow into the car to start the others; paid him a dollar for it. The man in charge of the loading was rather small, neatly dressed, about thirty years old. His name was Real Hamlet. Afterwards I got to know him well. He was always pleasant, but would expect most of the willing man. Some way we got to disliking him.

I told Hamlet my business. He said, "You take that horse and ride out four miles; you'll see a wagon about two miles east of the trail. Tell the fellow there you've come to take his place."

I rode down the Chisholm trail south, turned off to the wagon. A bald-headed fellow about my age with dirty drab overalls on and low shoes – kind of a hard looker – was washing a black kettle with a rag almost as black as the kettle. I told him, "I've hired to the Carter outfit to cook." The boy – Ed Mathews – throwed the kettle one way, the rag the other, wiped his hands on his breeches, put on a good Stetson hat, took the reins out of my hands, and swung into the saddle. I asked, "What am I to do?" He said, "You're the cook," and rode off toward town in a lope.

I picked up the kettle, het up some water, and washed all the tin dishes again. I took an inventory of the load:

forty pounds Climax Plug, twenty pounds Bull Durham, and several caddies and packs of smoking tobacco; a dozen .45 Colt single-action pistols and twenty boxes of cartridges; a roll of half-inch rope; ten gallons of kerosene and a caddy of matches; one hundred pounds of sugar, one 160-pound sack of green coffee, five hundred pounds salt pork, twenty sacks flour, two hundred pounds beans, fifty pounds country dried apples, a box of soda, and a sack of salt. There were bows on the wagon, a grub box on the rear end, a kerosene can cut in half for sour dough, two sixteen-inch ovens five inches deep, a coffee-grinder nailed on the side of the grub box, six bull's-eye lanterns for night herd. Blankets were spread all over the ground to dry.

A darky rode up – Henry Jones, called "Mistuh Jones" or "Nigger Henry." I said, "You belong to this outfit?" "Uh huh." Then I asked, "What am I to do?" "Is you de cook?" "Yes." "Den do as you please. Dat's de way we all do." "How many shall I fix supper for?" He said, "Cain't speak fo' nobody cepin' myself. I won't be heah." He left a pair of spurs and rode off for town.

I fixed supper for ten – bread, bacon, flour gravy, coffee, and a cup of sugar. I stacked the blankets half width, full length; there was a pile about two feet high, and some duck sheets. At dusk I ate all I could, drank two cups of coffee with plenty of sugar, sat there a while, took another cup of coffee, lay down on the pile of blankets and counted the stars. The coyotes turned loose all around. After a spell I forgot and went to sleep.

At peep of day I fired the cow chips again. The coyotes were getting ready to quit. Pretty soon the bunch began to string in. No one was hungry. They had spent the night in Caldwell, and ate breakfast there. Hamlet said, "Throw out the grub. Help him load and hitch up, boys. What's your name?" "Oliver Nelson." "Well Oliver, just follow us."

They had about fifty horses in the remuda. There were ten men: Real Hamlet, Ed Mathews, Nigger Henry, Jim Hudson, George Hudson, Oscar Mayes, Ed Rucker, Jim Erwin, Russell Hannah, and Ed Reid. Another boy, Mike O'Shea, had come up with the beef herd, but he had started to ride up town from the stock pens with a railroad track man on his tricycle. The tricycle had jumped the switch below the station, and they took both men to the Leland hotel for repairs. Mike got to camp about two weeks later.

They went off on a trot to the Chisholm trail, then turned south. I had on a load of about 2300 pounds. I let the little mules trot downgrade, had to hold them back upgrade. One boy stopped till I drove up; he said, "You're a new man?" I said, "Yes." He said, "That team has followed the remuda till they'll hurt themselves to keep up. Just hold 'em back and take it slow. Follow the trail; don't follow us. We aim to go ahead and graze the horses. We'll find you at noon." I asked him, "How far is it to camp?" He said, "It's eighty miles from Caldwell."

We stopped two hours at noon. I've forgotten just where we camped at night. It was a nice night, warm, somewhere about the middle of July, 1882. We spread our blankets on the grass and rolled in. The boys were full of steam, kept me awake till late.

Part of their talk was of the meteoric career and dramatic death of the flashiest juggler of cows and dollars in all southwestern annals.

I learned that the general manager, A. H. (Gus)

Johnson, out with a herd of cattle from the Texas Panhandle, had been killed by lightning near Dodge City, Kansas. This Johnson had come up the trail in '74 and '75 for wages. He kept watching; and as soon as he learned the trick, bought stock but invested the most money in men. They drove all they could gather across the Red river in '76 and started the T 5 with nine thousand head, selling forty-nine per cent to a Scotch company. In '78 he drove a bunch to the Texas Panhandle and formed the Horseshoe; again he sold the Scotch company forty-nine per cent. Just before he was killed, he bought the Kenedy interest in the King ranch (*El Rancho de los Laureles,* Ranch of the Laurels) near Corpus Christi, Texas. At that time he was general manager of thirteen different ranches owned by the Texas Land and Cattle company. But July 3, 1882 he died near Dodge.

The second day out we crossed the Salt Fork, and took the Cantone trail. It was cloudy, but not windy; rain set in near noon. The boys were waiting for the wagon. Hamlet said, "Oliver, can you fix us a bite?" I asked for a slicker, stretched it on the side of the wagon for a shelter, and soon had them filled up.

The second night I roosted off by myself to keep away from the talk. The third day, as usual, I drove slow. The boys said, "Take the first trail west to camp," and struck off across the prairie. It seemed everyone was expected to know his part. I turned off on a dim trail, a wagon track. I passed a spring branch and there was a line camp: a wagon sheet marked T 5 stretched over a pole, several ovens, a coffee-pot, a bucket, and a pile of sticks. Six miles farther on I came to Eagle Chief creek. The bank was steep, but the little mules made it. A quarter of a mile up the creek we came to the home (headquarters) camp.

We got in hungry at 2 p.m. Marion Hildreth was chief cook. He was about six feet tall, with bacon rind complexion, long underjaw, keen gray eyes, and long nose with a big hump in the center. Also I found he was somewhat slovenly, but nobody ever pointed that out. He seemed to have no trouble with the boys. Our first meal was dry salt bacon, strong coffee, biscuits about the size of a silver dollar, five inches high, real light, crusted over with sugar. One of the boys said, "Marion is the terrapin's hide on bread."

The camp was on the south bank of Eagle Chief creek, two miles west and one mile south of the present town of Carmen. The memory of the place still lives in local tradition. When the Cherokee Strip was opened to settlers in 1893, Barney (William Barnett) McAdoo, an old T 5 *cowboy, established his homestead there. He died a few years ago, but his daughter, Mrs. Belle O'Shea, still lives in the big white old-fashioned farmhouse he built on the exact site of the ranch cabin. With her own childhood memories lengthened by the tales her father told her, one can fit Mr. Nelson's description of that long-vanished cow camp into this modern scene.*

The Eagle Chief is marked by a heavy growth of timber — mostly cottonwood and elm — as it winds through the farm, but Mrs. O'Shea's father told her it was almost bare around the camp in T 5 *days. Conspicuous to the south about two hundred yards, as Mr. Nelson remembers them, were "three sand hills about twenty-five feet high, covering three acres." These have been worked down by the plow, but the wheat field still has a tendency to blow into low drifts in dry seasons. Here was the setting for the headquarters buildings — all made of materials at hand, for the* T 5 *like all Cherokee Strip ranches held only the most precarious title to the range it used.*

The cabin, thirty feet by sixteen, lay east and west; it had doors in the north and south, fastened by old-fashioned string latches; a sash window east of each door, and one in the west end. The walls were of cedar poles ten inches thick. The roof was of split cedar covered with four inches of mud and about twelve inches of earth; it rested on two parallel ridge poles about five feet apart, which were supported in the center by two upright posts set in the dirt floor.

In the northwest corner was a double bunk, pullman style, with poles for springs and hay for feathers; it was apt to have seam squirrels (lice), but no bedbugs. In the northeast corner was a cupboard with four shelves; here were tin plates and cups and iron handled knives and forks, four sixteen-inch ovens, and a fry pan. Between the two doors was a twelve-foot table, with boxes around it for chairs. There was a fireplace with a stick chimney, and an iron hook hanging in the center to hang a four-gallon coffee-pot on; a coffee-grinder was nailed to the side of the fireplace, and below the grinder was a shelf for a three-gallon sour dough jar. Under the window in the west was a box desk to hold extra pistols, tobacco, or anything the boys didn't want to drag around. Then we had a gun rack in the south-west corner, and half a dozen guns.

On a spike driven in one of the two roof props a gentleman had hung his head; a half-inch hole in the back indicated he had went out in a hurry. I was told a hunter had camped on Sand creek west, and that the man who was then the T 5 range boss had brought in a bay team and a gun; that later a prairie fire burned the wagon, and still later a T 5 boy brought in the skull. It was hinted this ex-boss could wise me up, but somehow I didn't care to dig up ancient history. When I got to running the camp I took down the skull, cleaned out some improvements made in it by mud dauber wasps, and polished it a little. In '83 a secretary sent out from Clarke, Underwood and company of Kansas City, which did the bookkeeping for the Texas Land and Cattle company, took it back with him.

The camp buildings were strung out quite a distance along the creek. About eighty steps west of the cabin across a washout was Carter's house. It was a picket house – that is, cedar posts set in the ground close together to form the walls – of two rooms, with board floor and dirt roof. East of our cabin about twelve feet was the old cabin, a smaller one, about twelve by fourteen feet, built in '76. Now it was used as a storeroom, and the space between the two, roofed over, was used as a buckboard shed. Just east of this storeroom was a dugout chicken house built in the creek bank, where Marion had raised a hundred chickens – also a few white turkeys – to supply the camp with eggs and meat.

The stable and corrals, as Mrs. O'Shea locates them, were a few rods farther east across the present section line road. Mr. Nelson describes them also.

Beyond the chicken house was a shed stable about sixty feet long, built in the bank. (Later – after a new one was built – the boys used it mostly for a shooting gallery, setting up a target at one end). Beyond the stable was a bunch of old wagons where I was told several boys slept perpetual, but little noticed. (They still sleep there). A pole corral with several pens and a branding chute covered about two acres on the flat above the creek bank.

The range was thirty miles north and south, and twenty-five miles east and west. It all lay in the Cherokee Strip; the south line was the division between the Strip and the Cheyenne and Arapaho reservation. The Cimarron crossed it about the middle, running a little south of east.

It comprised the level wheat lands north of Carmen, which now grade gradually into the belt of sand hills bordering the Cimarron; the ragged breaks along the river's innumerable tributaries; the great spring near the mouth of the Eagle Chief, which gives its name to the present town of Cleo Springs; the rich valley south of the Cimarron, now surrounding the county seat town of Fairview; and the sparkling, gypsum-covered buttes and scarps known as the Glass mountains rising above the river on the southwest.

Most of it had good buffalo grass, with mixed grass in the breaks on the south side of the Cimarron, and bunch grass and bluestem in the sand hills north of the river. There was a strip of blackjacks east of Cleo Springs.

There were about forty men on the ranch. We had five permanent line camps: on Sand creek west, which flows into Eagle Chief; on Cheyenne creek (now Skull creek), Cottonwood creek, and another Sand creek, south of the Cimarron; and at Cleo Springs, on Eagle below headquarters. There was another camp about six miles west of headquarters on Sand creek west, where twenty thousand head of through cattle were close herded. This was the Bean boys' camp, but they were gone before I got there. Then there was a tent camp six miles west of Cleo to hold the wintered stock south of the Cimarron.

Each line camp had a cook and two riders. The riders rode the boundaries of the range; at daybreak they would leave camp, and go in opposite directions until each met a rider from the next camp. All the stock they saw they turned back toward the center of the range, and if they found any trails leading out, they followed and brought back all that had crossed the lines. When I came, there was no fencing on the T 5.

A man named Henry Williams had been range boss; Hamlet, boss of the beef herd. Billy Smith had been horse wrangler, but took over the through herd after the Bean boys left. Jim Mathews was put to holding the horses, but couldn't keep track of them somehow, so Williams quit to look up several private horses that had strayed away, and Hamlet bossed the ranch. George Martin was the freighter, hauling whatever we needed from Caldwell.

It was my job to help Marion Hildreth, chief cook, who was all around with "Hey! Don't do that." Besides cooking he milked ten cows, using a throw rope and a club. (Later when several of them died of murrain, I noticed they all had broken ribs). In the evening he would put several large sticks of blackjack in the fireplace and cover with ashes; at peep of day he would uncover the bed of coals, put on the ovens, and bake the bread. Likewise in the evening I would grind the coffee and slice the bacon and put it in water to soak out the salt. In the morning I would wake the boys, put on the coffee, fry the bacon, and compound the sop (flour gravy), and we had 'er ready for the first man in. After breakfast I would clean up the dishes and skillets, replenish the sour dough, and get bacon and coffee ready for the next meal, while Marion beat out about four gallons of milk (half churned).

There was a nice plot of buffalo grass south of the cabin where we all slept during good weather. After the dew was gone, I would spread out the blankets to dry, and then roll them up. Most all the boys had a duck sheet for cover. During bad weather we piled in under shelter as best we could – mostly on the floor of the cabin. Marion and I got to bed about ten, but we generally found time for a nap in the afternoon between two and five.

A couple of days after I came, they killed a beef. Hamlet hollered, "Cook, come jerk the beef." I was busy at something, but Marion said, "You go out and help; I ain't goin' to." I went out and cut the meat in strips three inches wide and one inch thick. Then I stretched ropes from posts, hung the strips on to dry, and built a smudge to keep the flies off. We fried this jerked beef in tallow and ate it dry; but some cooks boiled it, thickened it with flour, and seasoned it with salt and plenty of pepper to make a dish called jowler, which was said to be awful fine.

Carter told me to look up the branding irons. I found ten: three-eighth-inch rods four feet long with a five-inch T 5 on the end. Then he had Martin bring twenty-four more from Caldwell. About August 1 we began putting the brand on the twenty thousand through cattle: one-, two-, and three-year-old steers. They had been branded with the road brand, open Y on each side. I believe the bunch had been bought for the company; naturally they had different brands and the road brand was used to mark them before they came up the trail. I never could see much use in a separate road brand; it looked like they just wanted to torture stock.

Carter had all the men come in that could be spared from the lines. Some days we would have forty men working at headquarters camp. They started at sunrise, rested an hour at noon, and stopped an hour before sunset. They would drive twenty-five steers into the chute; one would hold the head with a rope, another grab the tail, and a man on each side would slap on the iron. One day a heavy rain fell, and at about 2 p.m. it turned very hot. They filled the chute, and the cattle began to fall from the heat. When they got them out, nine were dead. Then they set poles in the large corral, roped the steers, snubbed them to the posts, and threw and branded them there.

They would bring in about two hundred at one time – enough to brand in about half a day. They put most of them in smaller pens (ketch pens), leaving only about thirty in the large pen at one time. Several boys would hold the branded cattle till they finished with that bunch; then drive them into a ketch pen and bring out thirty more. When they were all branded, they would drive them to the main herd on Sand creek west. The branded and unbranded were kept in separate herds, guarded night and day.

Sometimes Marion and I would go to the corral at nine and work till eleven. One day about 10:30 a.m. a new man asked who did the cooking. One boy said, "Them fellers over yonder." Then he wanted to know, "Well, when do we eat?" They told him, "That tall feller just hollers, 'Dinner!' and by the time we get washed up, it's ready." After working a little longer we got on the corral fence, and Marion said, "Well fellows, you just as well get ready to take it." Our meals were pretty slim; we could have had beans and apples, but we didn't.

One day in the pen I tossed my rope over a yearling's horns and threw a hitch on a post as it passed. The calf changed ends and fell. Mistuh Jones caught the upper hind foot with his hand, sat down, pushed the low hind leg forward with his foot, and held it there. I took hold of the horn and jaw and pulled its head back. Ed Mathews slapped on the brand, we turned it over, and he put a brand on the other side in half the time it takes to write it down. Mistuh Jones said, "We ain't no slouch, is we?" In branding larger steers one boy would rope the head and snub it to the post, another would catch one hind foot with his rope, and a third would tail down (seize the tail and throw).

It was a run all day to dodge the wild mad and catch the unbranded. Several boys got hurt, but none bad, for there was always help close. One time Ed Mathews was holding a steer's head. Another steer on the prod came up. ("On the prod" means he got mad). He got Ed on his horns, and threw him clear over the steer he was holding. Ed kept on working, but he was pretty sore.

One day Mistuh Jones was off his feed. We had a medicine kit that had been sent down from Kansas City, and all the boys wanted to help save the coon. One gave him six Compound Cathartic tablets, another two large spoonfuls of Commonsense liniment; Billy Smith said a half cup of kerosene would help, so he took a drink of that; Real wanted to give him a half box of axle grease, but then some of us stopped it, so the darky went away without that dose. I told him I would fix anything he wanted to eat and lock him in the storeroom where he wouldn't be bothered; but he could not eat for two days, though he kept on working. Real said they might as well kill the no-account nigger.

One night Marion was ailing. The next morning the boys were tired, and a little late in getting to the pens. While I was cleaning up in the cabin, Carter went out where Marion was milking and rounded him up; said he must have breakfast earlier. Marion said he was sick, but that the men could have been out earlier if they hadn't loafed. That didn't satisfy Carter, who was pretty high-strung, and he howled a little louder about having breakfast on time. Marion, some high-strung too, said, "You tell me what I must do. Now let me tell you what you must do. You get me my check and you do it damn quick"– and he called him some nice names. Carter jawed back a little and paid him off.

Just then Williams came in with the stray horses he'd rounded up – Marion's among them. The cook got his bronc and started off. It pitched so that later I picked up two large plugs of Climax tobac on the trail, that had been jolted out of his pockets.

But for the present I didn't know Marion had quit. He had been gone two hours; the cows were still in the pen and about a gallon of milk in the bucket. I asked what he was doing, and was told what had happened. I told Carter I couldn't run it alone. He said, "Try it out." Milk ten wild cows, cook for thirty men, dry out and roll up all the blankets, cut wood for Carter's house and the camp, look after the storeroom, take care of a hundred chickens and a few turkeys, and tend a garden Marion had – and loaf the rest of the time. I found out Mrs. Carter was packing down butter, so I had a confidential drive off all but four of the best cows so's I couldn't find them. And I let Marion's garden grow to weeds. It was a good garden, and he had threatened to shoot anyone going into it; but after he quit, the boys went in and I let it go rather than have trouble. Yes, and the coyotes soon got most of the turkeys. But I cooked as best I could. The day after Marion left I boiled a pot of beans with bacon and fixed some dried apples – black from the pot.

Martin was getting ready to go to Caldwell. (He

went about every thirty days). I gave him a list of stuff I needed including a sack of green coffee. When the wagon came back I said, "George, I told you to get coffee." He said, "Yes, but Carter cut it out." I went to Carter and told him, "The coffee won't last two weeks." He said, "You use too damn much coffee." The men half lived on coffee, and we had two outfits on guard with the through herd – the branded and the unbranded – with coffee all the time.

When we ran short, Carter sent to the line camps, but got little. Then Mrs. Carter sent over to replenish her batch. I parched a flour sack full and sent back word I had none to spare. In a few days I told Carter I was out. He said, "Ain't you got tea? Use that." I put a tomato can of tea in the four-gallon coffee-pot. It was green tea, which made the brew look light. When I poured it one boy asked, "Did you save any for dish-water?" I said, "Now if that ain't the right color, you just set back while I add life to it." I added another can to the mixture, boiled it a spell, and there was no more complaint. A twenty-five-pound box of tea lasted about four days. Then Carter sent to Kiowa, on the Kansas line forty-five miles north, for fifty pounds of green coffee. From August, 1882 to August, 1883 I used up thirteen 160-pound sacks of coffee.

I still didn't know everything about cow camp cook-ing. There was about eight hundred bulls with the through herd, one, two, and three years old. One day Nigger Henry brought in half a peck of the clippings from the bull pen, and poured them in my dishpan. I bawled him out, and dumped them in the creek. When the boys sat down to supper they said, "Henry, where's the 'oysters'?" "Mistah Olivah done trowed dem in de creek." I came near getting into trouble. I said,

WE BRANDED THE CALF IN HALF THE TIME IT TAKES TO WRITE IT DOWN

On J J Ranch, Texas Panhandle

"Fellers, I never heard of eating such. I thought Henry was putting up a job on me. I'll cook anything you'll bring in to eat, only let me in on it." There was some sour talk, but we eat our bacon for supper. The next day we had a big "oyster" fry, which kept up for four weeks.

About this time young Nelson met a boy whose lonely life and tragic fate was to impress him more than anything else in all his range experience. But of this he had no premonition that summer day in '82.

One day a boy rode up with four extra horses – one with a pack on – all strung out, each tied to the tail of the one ahead. It was about 2 p.m. I went out, seen the T 5 on the horses, and said, "There's no use invitin' *you* to turn in. Had hash?" He said, "No." I said, "Your chuck'll be ready soon as you're ready for it." That was my introduction to John Potts. He had been out on the roundup. Some hands would follow the rounding up of the different ranges all early summer. In later years I worked the roundup myself, and learned all about it.

Everything on the big ranch fell into a practiced routine, all geared to the habits and needs of "cows." At one time –

The mosquitoes got bad, and the cattle milled all night. The boys hauled up chips from an old bed ground and kept smudge fires. This through bunch was long-horned, wild south Texas stock, but they just lay quiet in the smoke while the boys kept up the fires, walking by the herd.

Then there was the mysterious Texas fever, cause of more bitterness between north and south in the cow country than any other War between the States. Southern cattle had built up an immunity to the disease, but they carried infected ticks, and these dropped from their bodies and spread the sickness to any northern cattle that grazed over the area. But these facts were not scientifically established until the experiments of Theobald Smith and F. L. Kilborne, carried on in 1889 and '90 and published in '93. Meanwhile south Texans knew that their cattle were healthy; how then could they spread contagion? Northern owners saw the native stock sicken and die when the long-horned foreigners came in. How could either side account for known facts except by asserting that the other lied? The T 5, truly cosmopolitan in its investments, accepted both and, as Mr. Nelson indicates, some of the cowmen had worked out a theory very near the truth.

Even after they were branded, the through cattle were close herded west of the home camp till after heavy frost; this was to keep them from the wintered stock on account of Texas fever. I think we knew at that time that ticks caused the fever, and that southern cattle that appeared well would infect the native cattle.

As soon as they finished branding the through herd the boys rounded up three thousand head of cows, to brand their calves. They had to night herd this bunch, too. They would cut out fifty cows with their calves, pen the cows and calves separate, and take the calves to the branding pen to rope, brand, and mark ears. After all were branded they turned the calves back with their mothers. After each cow had found her calf, they drove them off a couple of miles toward the river and turned them loose; then brought in another bunch. This work kept the boys on the run. Sometimes when being penned, a calf would get away from its mother and break back to the range. We had only a few good ropers to bring them in. Once I saw a boy bring in several. He passed behind the calf, threw the rope over its neck, and spurred his horse; when the calf got to the end of the rope it turned ends, landed on its back, and went into the pen sled fashion; and the boy reached down and took off the rope. Good work!

Some brands were burned too deep; sometimes the irons were red hot, and pressing hard burned through the hide, making a running sore. The green flies got after these and made screw worms, which ate a sort of pocket under the skin. The boys cut out seven hundred head, and held them in a bunch to themselves. The green flies followed. The smell was awful. They used up several cases of cresylic ointment to treat them; they would drive a bunch in the corral and push the ointment under the skin with a long stick paddle, digging the worms out by the pint. They didn't have to throw any; the steers did not seem to mind. They kept this up till December, but they lost about four hundred head.

I Learn About Horses

Oliver Nelson was to be told later that Billy Smith, the boss of the through herd, had "worked" with Billy the Kid. Probably this cannot be established. Western historians know him mainly for an especially lurid exit from the outlaw scene, and that was still in the future. In his comparatively innocent T5 days he stands out only as a good hand who knew horses and was willing to help a youngster learn. His deductions seemed like magic to Oliver. "He could tell more about a horse by looking at the trail than the average person could by examining the horse." But he studied his problem carefully.

After the branding was finished, Hamlet, Potts, and Smith went to look up several horses that had left the range. They rode off south. Smith came in next day. I asked if he had found the strays. He said, "Jesus Christ, man, I just went to look at the bunch that's here. When you go to find anything, you want to know what it is you're a-huntin'. I found out we're three horses short; Old Marshal and two others. I'm ready now to go after 'em soon's I get a fresh mount." And he started out again.

Hamlet was out about three days. We found out later he and Potts crossed the Cimarron, and he suggested they ride together to the Indian camps. But Potts said, "It don't take two men to find a horse. I'm goin' alone. If you don't want to do that, just go over to the Bar HL (Bickford) camp and stay a couple of days; then drift in." So that was all the horse hunting he done. The Bickford camp where he laid up was southwest of Cantonment.

Smith came in about the fifth day. Carter came over to the cabin and asked if he'd found the horses.

"No," said Smith, "but I struck the trail. Marshal and another horse is goin' back to Texas. Then they's a poor horse with a sore back, that took down the Cimarron."

"What made him quit the others?" asked Carter.

"Wy, 'is back is so sore it was hard for 'im to make it down and up the dry runs. When he come to the river, that was too steep and he wouldn't try it."

"How do you know he has a sore back?"

"Wy, Jesus Christ, man, he'd go down the dry runs sideways."

"And how do you know he's poor?"

"Wy, Jesus Christ, man, he's got an awful sore back and he's bound to be poor; and then I can tell by the way he takes it uphill. And Marshal's goin' home."

"How do you know it's Marshal?"

"Wy, Jesus Christ, I know the horse. I ain't herded horses all my life for nothin'. And the other horse is trailin' 'im."

"How do you know someone isn't riding Marshal and leading the hind horse?"

The answer sawed Carter off. Smith said, "Why, man, you'd have to have a trot line to lead it, they're so far apart. Marshal would leave the trail at the old trail camps, feed and water, and take the trail again. The other horse would leave the trail farther up, then strike it farther down. That showed how far he was behind." Another reason Smith knew both horses were loose – a loose horse always stops to perform nature's requirements.

Smith said he had written a letter to a fellow coming up with a herd. "If he gets the letter 'fore Marshal passes, he'll bring 'im back; if the two horses stay together, he'll bring 'em both back; but the hind one's showin' signs he won't keep up. If Marshal passes 'fore the fellow gets the letter, he'll go home to Texas."

We got Marshal by the letter route. We never heard of the one with him. But Potts soon brought in a poor horse with a very sore back. Smith knew horses.

Potts also had a story. His search took him into the Cheyenne and Arapaho reservation; and here one sees how hard these Indians – distinguished among the tribes for their legal development – were trying to maintain order and protect their people from the irrepressible actions of the cowboys.

He went down the river and located the poor horse. Then he rode among the Indian horses to look for the others. He could talk Mex pretty good, and some Cheyenne. The second day out he run onto a squaw on a sand hill, who seemed to be mourning for someone. She would cut herself with a butcher knife, rub sand in, and howl, but would not talk to him. Two young Indians rode up, took his horse's bridle, and led him away. He soon run onto another squaw; he would tap her with his quirt and talk Mex and Cheyenne, but he couldn't make her say a word. Again some Indians led him away. Then he run onto a third squaw – same result. After that, two Indians led his horse from one horse bunch to another. At dusk they came to an Indian camp. He took off his saddle, and they turned his horse in with their bunch; he ate their chuck and slept in their tent, but would not give them his pistol; the next morning they brought in his mount. He turned east and rode almost to Reno. Then as he came back, he picked up the poor horse.

After the horse hunt they cut out twelve hundred native steers to take to Caldwell to ship. I fixed up a chuck wagon for them to take along. Carter went with this beef herd; and I think Mrs. Carter was away somewhere, too. I was supposed to keep the camp and care for any transients that might drop in.

Jim Mathews, the horse wrangler, took sick. His brother Harry came down from Kiowa to see him. When he left Jim said, "Don't worry, the kid'll take care of me." But that meant I had to look after 150 head of horses. I went it green; didn't know the range or the habits of range horses. I had nothing to ride but three no-account pelters. I rode most of the time, and got nowhere. Then Mathews went to Caldwell, and I was alone.

Smith still rodded the through cattle. (That is, he was boss. We called the boss the "ramrod"). He came down to camp one noon; asked how I was making it. I told him I had too many horses, and didn't have my bunch either. After dinner he said for me to bring some in so we could have fresh mounts; he'd take a nap, then go out and look them over. I went to the first bend in Eagle, where some half dead pelters hung up, cut out several, and put them in the corral.

When Billy saw them he told me, "Turn them plugs out; we'll get *horses*." We started out south, me on my pelter. Billy said, "You ain't got no mount at all; you're afoot." We soon came to a bunch. He roped one. I said, "That's Castleberry's mount." Billy said, "Where's Castleberry?" I told him, "Caldwell." Then Billy said, "Put your hull"– saddle –"on it. I won't tell him." He roped another. I said, "That's Hamlet's." He said, "Cinch up and shut your mouth, and come on." We mounted, me on Castleberry's, he on Hamlet's – he wanted to keep from tiring his own mount – turned the loose horses north, and rode about five miles in a high lope to another bunch. Here we changed mounts again, turned the bunch, and took another good run, turning all horses in toward one point. We sat on a rise and watched them about two hours; then rode around the herd on the south side, turning them back gentle; and rode to camp near sunset on the mounts we started out on. Smith said, "You're out five, got thirty head that don't belong here – several they been hunting all season." He described the ones I was out, and told where I would find them. "In the morning you bring in a bunch from north the creek. I'll be down at seven. We'll round them all in, and show you how; and you won't have no more trouble."

Next day I brought in the bunch from north the creek. Bill came down, we took good mounts, and turned the rest back. Then we took off in the sand hills southwest in a high lope, driving small bunches ahead, then throwing to one side to pick up on our return. We worked the sand hills, passed north of Eagle, then turned east, turning north of camp by noon; we cut the bunch and drove the extras that didn't belong to us down toward the Cimarron; then we rode to camp. We had changed mounts four times.

I got dinner while Billy went to sleep. At near two he got up smiling. We had bread, bacon, flour gravy, and coffee; saddled up and rode out; counted the herd, turned the leaders back, and sat on a rise, letting our mounts graze, and watched the bunch. They were scattered over about two sections.

Mr. Nelson is referring to a surveyor's section – one square mile. The herd was spread out over about two square miles.

The day was pretty warm. I suggested going to camp. Billy said, "I'm waitin' to learn you sumpin. Soon some of 'em 'll lead out. They know which direction they want to go; they're tryin' to locate for winter. You must notice which course they take. But stay with 'em late, and just before you leave, turn 'em back in towards the herd; then they won't go far, for horses ain't apt to cross water after night. Then in the morning get out early and ride after 'em; you can follow their trail pretty good when it's still damp. But you got to ride. You can't go on your old plugs. Pick out a good horse. (But don't let anybody catch you on their mounts; leave yours out, so if you see anybody coming in you can change). Don't ride 'em too far. Change often, then ride; that's all. And see every stock sign."

Next morning I rounded them up early. At noon I roped a long, slim buckskin belonging to George Hudson. I got up in the crow's nest, and it started pitching. It felt like I was hitting my spurs together above the saddle. I had to reach down, but I held the strings. I didn't dare to quit my horse; once I got afoot I couldn't catch another, and there was nobody nearer than ten miles. We rounded the corral and got to the creek bank, fifteen feet straight down. Old Buckskin wouldn't do it. The show was over. But after that I would saddle my horse in the evening and let it stand overnight with the saddle on; then it wasn't so apt to pitch. I took a chance the boys wouldn't come back and find one of their horses saddled.

One day off from camp I roped a good-looking horse, turned my mount loose, saddled, and got on. Then I found the horse couldn't lope; it had got its back strained roping a steer. Luckily the one I'd turned loose was grazing, and I managed to catch it without any trouble. But I found out I'd have to be careful. I could learn a little any time.

Several rains fell. The creek was up ten feet. One night after dark about ten men came in – Billy Smith, a boy they called Tall Horse, John O'Shea (Mike's brother), and some others. It was raining hard. Smith said he was going to wash his feet. I said I was short on water –"If you use that up, you'll have to get some first thing in the morning." The well was about ten feet down in a dry wash forty steps west of the cabin.

The next morning I got up 'fore day. It was still raining. I took the five-gallon water keg and started for the well; went west about ten feet – *and ran into the creek.* The water had backed up in the wash nearly level with the creek bank. It was warm, but plenty wet. I went in past the belt line. I made up my mind to get Billy in; thought I'd make him half mad so he'd start off without looking. So I went back in the cabin and turned on him. "You was so damn nice last night you *would* wash your mud hooks or sour; now I'm out of water and late with chuck. Roll out and make good." He got up growling, took the keg, and made a run west into the creek. He went in about two-thirds up; said "Jesus Christ!" and backed out. I followed him out of the cabin, and said, "Keep still; let's get Tall Horse in." Now this Tall Horse would do anything the boss told him to.

Billy went back and pulled his boots off. Then I razzed him for water, and he pretended he couldn't get his boots on; so Tall Horse grabbed the keg, and was out in no time, and into the creek to where it nearly would float his hat off. When he got out, I said, "Let's get O'Shea in." Now this O'Shea was a little red-headed son of Erin, somewhat slow, and not strong on a joke. He took the keg and went out; but he stuck one foot into the creek, said, "Oh, Hell!" and backed off. By this time it was getting light, and the fun was over.

All streams were high that October, '82. The beef drive to Caldwell usually took ten days for the round trip, but this time the outfit was gone twice as long, having been held up at the Salt Fork. One day I came in at about 11 a.m. from rounding up the horses. Soon the outfit began to string in – eleven men. After dinner they all lay down. I said, "Boys, the horses are hard to hold; you fellows better round 'em up and lay out on the ground a while to watch 'em." One boy said, "We've herded horses." At about three I reminded them again; was told, "You're the cook. We'll tend the horses." When they finally went out they couldn't find more than half of them. They had to let them go that night; you look for stock only when it's light so you can see a long distance. The next morning the whole bunch strung out hunting horses, but it was several days before they got them all rounded up again. We aimed to keep them all in the sand hills north of the Cimarron.

Late in October while the outfit was gone on another beef drive, two boys – Hank Siders and Hoos Hopkins – came up from the Horseshoe to pilot a bunch of cows and calves that Carter wanted to send down to that range. They waited with me about ten days. I would have breakfast 'fore day, round up the horses, go five miles east to the jacks and get a small load of wood, come back at two, fix things at camp, and round up the horses; had little else to do. Hop went with me, said he'd rather go than lay in camp.

Hop was a good talker; so was I; and Siders ditto. One day Siders asked me, "Young man, what wages do you get?" I said, "Thirty dollars a month." "Do you know what you're worth?" I said, "They must think I'm worth it, or they wouldn't pay it." He said, "You're worth seventy-five dollars a month. We have a woman with us gettin' fifty who don't do what you do in the house, and a man at $125 who don't do what you do outside." Hop added, "And when the Carter family is here he keeps them in firewood too, and milks the cows." Siders said, "Young fellow, you could run our ranch. And what do you get to eat?" "Bread, bacon, coffee, and sometimes beans." "If you come to our ranch, I'll give you oysters for dinner; and I'll guarantee you forty-five dollars through the winter and seventy-five on the roundup next spring."

When Carter came, he said he aimed to market the rest of the beeves before he drove away the cows and calves, and so the boys went back to the Horseshoe. But the oyster story seemed like such a good joke I told him about it. We had a big laugh. He said he always took Siders for an honest boy, "but oysters in a cow camp! That's a damn lie. That boy came to me afoot two years ago on Mulberry creek south of Dodge. I gave him twenty dollars a month, and I'll bet he ain't gettin' more than you are right now."

Later I learned that Siders was getting $125; Hoos Hopkins and the other cowhands, fifty dollars; and the foreman of the Horseshoe, Bee Hopkins, a brother of Hoos, $150. And this from the same company that owned the T 5. Carter was getting two hundred dollars, his bosses thirty-five dollars, and the hands twenty-five dollars. Later our bosses got fifty dollars, I got thirty-five dollars, and the hands got twenty-five dollars and thirty dollars. As for the oysters, I little thought at the time I would ever have a chance to check that part. While tending horses I was expected to look over every herd of cattle passing through our range, cut out our brand, and turn back all strays or unbranded stock and all fresh brands without a bill of sale; let nothing pass but the road brand. One outfit came through with three wagons and thirty-nine men. It took over an hour for the herd to pass. I asked one fellow, "How many you got in this little bunch?" He said, "Twenty-four thousand." In grazing they would cover more than a section. The herders just kept them headed north and took their time. At night they stopped on high ground with the wagons perhaps two miles apart forming a triangle around the bed ground; had a fire and hot coffee at each camp. All through the night three men would be on circle, each riding from his wagon to the next around the herd. In bad weather all hands were out. Where the range was rough, they would cut in three herds.

Finally the beef drives were over, and we all settled down for winter. It was my first winter on the T 5.

Winter in Camp

Curtis and Kerchner came down from Kiowa in the fall to put up hay for the horses. They stacked about twenty tons southeast of camp. Then two brothers named Deatley brought lumber from Caldwell, and a Mr. Spiker came down to build a barn – about eighty steps south of the cabin; would hold about twenty head of horses. He also put weather boards and a shingled roof on Mr. Carter's house and painted it white.

Late in November a man named Wilson, secretary to Clarke, Underwood, and company, came down from K.C. and cut out the cows and calves to drive to the Horseshoe. This range was in the Texas Panhandle, below the Springer ranch on the South Canadian. Billy Smith went as boss; a Mexican named Manuel Odcan was cocinero (cook); and there were Billy Ward, Billy White, Russell Hannah, Jim Hudson, Jim Erwin, Dave Duniphant, D. H. McPherson, and some others – thirteen in all. Expecting warm weather, they took no tent and no winter clothing.

Wilson talked with several boys, trying to find out things. I was just too dumb to give him any information. But it seems Hamlet had told one of the boys that Carter would be put in charge of all the company ranches, and he himself would get Carter's place. Wilson got hold of it, and told Carter; and Carter got mad and fired Hamlet.

I began hauling wood for winter. I went to the jacks about six miles east and picked up several loads of posts Barbecue Campbell had cut.

B. H. Campbell held the range at the head of Turkey creek, joining the T 5 on the east. He was one of the most prominent cattlemen of the Indian Territory. In 1885 he became the first general manager of the great X I T ranch, which owned three million acres of land along the western side of the Texas Panhandle. His nickname of "Barbecue" came from his well known Bar B Q brand.

Campbell was just too slow in hauling his posts, and I got there first. But that was too far to drive and cut a load, so when the posts were gone I cut on the creek. There in the heavy timber I found a half fallen tree leaning south, with poles laid against it and then brushed over. I was told this rude hut had been used by Dutch Henry, the rustler, in 1875. I never took the poles away from it – just sentiment, I guess.

The weather was nice, some ice but no rain or snow. But pretty soon the bunch rolled in from the Horseshoe, and they told a different story. They said a storm struck them the fifth day out: a ten-inch snow, the weather awful cold. They kept on the high land away from the timber, and only hauled wood for cooking. At night they would scrape away the snow, spread down the wagon sheet and cover with what blankets they had, put their feet toward the wind, and the snow would bank up over them. The cattle bawled all the time. The boys got so they couldn't holler. Some days they drove only five miles. One boy went snow-blind, and had to ride behind the wagon for three days.

McPherson gave up his gloves, eartabs, overshoes, and overcoat to younger boys. He said he had been around Cape Horn three times as a rigger, and didn't mind the cold. One night he came in from standing guard, and called to his relief, Billy White, "Time to go on guard." Billy was twenty years old, but he cried; and Mack said, "Lay still, Billy; I'll stand your guard." This McPherson said his dad was Governor-general of Canada, and that his mother sent him a three hundred dollar draft every three months. I know that he did get the drafts, and the letters he got had on the royal crown.

One can only speculate as to the antecedents of this chivalrous wanderer. Canada never had a Governor-general by that name, but Sir David Lewis Macpherson served as a cabinet minister during the early 1880's. "Remittance men"— dissipated scions of proud English families, who were paid to stay away from home — were often encountered in the cow country. But the hard-working cow hand, McPherson, hardly fits that classification.

Part of the way to the Horseshoe the boys had no trail to follow. They cut across the Greever range, west of the T 5, *and then followed the divide to Fort Supply. This post, established in 1868 during the Indian wars, had become an important stopping place on the trail to Dodge City. By the time they got there, the* T 5 *boys were out of food, and they had no money to buy more. They found a friend in the famous scout, Amos Chapman, who became their surety. Their chuck wagon replenished, they turned their herd southwest on the trail that led to Fort Elliott. Following it, they went up Wolf creek to the* K H *(New York Cattle company) ranch, drove up Little Wolf, crossed into Texas, passed near the* C T *headquarters, and turned southeast to the Horseshoe.*

They drove the cattle across the Canadian on the ice, and the herd struck a trot over the snow-covered hills south. The boys reached the headquarters camp at 2 p.m. and set down to the best coffee, best bread, best beans and beef that ever was fixed up. They layed down in featherbeds a foot deep; was dead till they got hungry next day. Billy White took the stage line for the Pease river; decided he wanted to work in a warmer cow country. The rest came back. On the return they camped in timber every night and built fires – to make up what they lost on the trail out. They left most of their horses at the Horseshoe, and the ones they rode back was in bad shape.

Carter came over to our cabin and asked how they got through. Billy Smith said, "We had a hard time: snow, zero weather, and no feed. The third morning after the storm started we left three calves and two horses froze on the bed ground. The horses had been rode that afternoon. The boys done their part good, but we lost some cattle; turned over 3728 head and fifty horses." Carter went to his house and got his ledger; he came back and asked, "How many did you turn in?" "3728." Carter said, "That ain't bad; you left with 3725." (It's fairly easy to miscount a bunch of moving stock).

Thus these cowhands – whether outlaws, adventurers, or boys who cried from the cold – worked to the limit of human endurance to hold their tally true. Here was something beyond their duty to the great corporation that paid them twenty-five dollars a month, with bread, bacon, coffee, and perhaps beans. "Cows" was their way of life, and everything fused in loyalty to this. It was only when the work slacked that they were conscious of other interests. One of these was the abundance of game on the range.

Turkeys began coming down from the brushy streams where they'd hatched, to winter in the heavy creek timber and eat acorns in the blackjacks. The first we got was young ones, partly grown. Four of us run a small flock out of a plum thicket. They flew about two hundred yards, all in a bunch; then settled in high grass and tried to hide. (Turkeys can't fly far after the first flight). I had a hoe handle to strike them on the neck; the others used ropes. We got fifteen and was back to camp in thirty minutes. Once a bunch went to roost in a small tree near the cabin. I stood in the door and killed three at one shot.

About a mile above the cabin on the creek was a bunch of timber we called the Elm Mott. The turkeys would come there; then afraid to pass the new barn, they would leave the creek and run east nearly three-quarters of a mile across an open space to a bunch of timber on a branch. Three different days in October there were turkeys in sight all the time crossing that open space, sometimes in a line halfway across and thirty or forty feet wide. The boys would stand and watch, saying, "Now come and just look at the turkeys." There was a turkey roost down the creek about six miles southeast of camp in a heavy grove that we called the Big Timber. A path in the snow ten feet wide led from this roost to the blackjacks two miles east.

Gobblers will bunch up by themselves late in the fall. One day Byron Long came to the cabin on a run and said, "There's ten big gobblers south of them sand hills; get your gun and we'll get them all." I saddled up, and we started to drive them away from the creek, farther south into the sand. But they run up a mound and took to the air; first flying south, then doubling back over us (circling like buzzards), and sailing down the creek far as we could see.

We had turkeys hung up during most of November. About Christmas time hunters on Walnut creek, east of

Eagle Chief, would shoot all night, and pick up next day to haul to market. But Carter would not allow hunters on the T 5 – mostly for fear they would let fires get away and burn off the range. "This is a cow camp, not a game preserve," he told me.

In the spring at roundup time the turkeys crossed to the south side of the Cimarron opposite the mouth of Eagle. Some of the boys offered to bet every turkey on earth was in that bunch; one boy told me he believed it would cover forty acres. But that was our last turkey season. Cholera got among them in the summer of 1883, and the next fall I never seen a turkey, though there were a few south of the river.

Deer were plentiful also. In the spring they would bunch up in brushy places. But Carter told us not to hunt them; to kill grown cattle for our meat. "And see that the company brand is on all you kill. Don't kill strays; turn 'em back." I made several boys mad telling them to turn back cattle they aimed to kill, and we did without meat sometimes. In the south camps they were not so careful what brand they ate.

Fred Creigh came up from the line camp at Cleo Springs and told how one of the boys there tried to rope a wild cat. It run up a tree near the camp – a picket house on the present townsite of Cleo Springs. Fred went to help; he leant over and patted his leather chaps to scare it to the other side of the tree toward the boy with the rope. But the cat jumped on the rump of Fred's horse. Fred got off sudden, but the cat rode a piece. The other boy caught the horse a mile away, but lost the cat.

Cep Good, who rode the line between Cheyenne and Cottonwood creeks, came up to camp one day and told Carter two calves had got up on the lone butte south of the Cimarron and it would take help to get them down. Carter said, "Why don't you push 'em off?" Cep said, "Just as well let 'em die there as kill 'em gettin' 'em off." So the next day Carter took a boy that I'll name "Dan George" – I'm changing his name because of something he done later – and went down. They found a dim path up the south side. One steer was dead. The three men put ropes on the live steer, and one pulled down while the others held back. They got it down O.K. That butte was over a hundred feet high, a break from the flat land south. To the west there were several such buttes, which ran northwest to the bat caves on the Greever range and Sleeping Bear creek on the Bar M.

This butte, the most conspicuous of the so-called Glass mountains, is about twelve miles northwest of Fairview. Glistening white with gypsum crystals, it rises rather impressively from the flat valley floor, completely detached from the escarpment that forms the edge of the high plains to the south. It is visible for many miles across the level wheat fields of northwest Oklahoma.

The gypsum caves, known since early days by the cowboys, are still largely unexplored. But one on Cedar canyon near the present town of Freedom, in the neighborhood of "Sleeping Bear creek on the Bar M" – has been lighted for tourists. Here in these "alabaster caverns" is an underground world of gleaming crystal from which innumerable bats issue forth on summer evenings in a dense, funnel-shaped cloud.

Apparently scenery was not enough to hold Cep Good's interest in the lonely work of the line camp.

One evening he dropped in on us and said he was going to quit. Carter came over and asked, "You leave your line open?" "Yes, I've quit." Carter said, "You've quit? Now that's doing me dirt. That's got to be settled between two men. You go back, and when I want you to quit, I'll let you know." Cep went back and rode his line till Carter sent a man to take his place.

Too many men were laying around the home camp with nothing to do. Carter aimed to hold about ten of the best and let the rest go; but he gave them no satisfaction, did not pay them off, just kept them waiting. All was morose – just set around glum. I looked for trouble to break out any time. One evening about dusk a man named Churchill came in from the south on his way to Caldwell. It was drizzling rain. I told him to drop his wagon south of the barn, and I sent a boy out to help him put up his team. The boy soon came back. He told me, "When I got out there, that feller was across the creek and goin' in a trot." Later the man told my brother Delos at Caldwell that he met Oliver at the T 5 –"He wanted me to stop overnight. There was about forty men there; every one had a gun on and half of them had on a butcher knife. I'd just sold a team, and had five hundred dollars. I wouldn't stay; that's all."

There was a boy working at our camp when I came on who used to have me lock him up in the storeroom so he wouldn't be disturbed, and in a short time he would have several letters ready for Martin to mail. One day I asked him if he wasn't out of his latitude. He asked, "What makes you think so?" I said, "Sometimes you use good language; then again you act just *too* ignorant." So he showed me what he could do. He had me sign my name on alternate lines of note paper, marking each signature by a dot on the back; then he copied the name on the blank lines, and cut the signatures apart. I could not distinguish my own writing except by the dot, but he would pick it out quick. He told me the misuse of a pen got him in a cow camp – a poor place. He said he could make money that would pass among us, and he told me he could speak German, French, and Spanish. He soon left the T 5.

Carter finally paid off all the extra men, and moved with his family to Caldwell. I had only three boys and the transients to cook for, so life slid along plumb smooth. The coyotes got a lot of my chickens and finished the white turkeys.

Billy Smith came to my camp several times and took dinner with me, then rode back to the west camp. Once he asked me to get him six .45 pistol cartridges. I knew something was wrong, but I got them from the store-room. He loaded one of the guns in the desk under the west window, and told me to keep my mouth shut. One day while he was in, Mike O'Shea rode up. Billy went to the desk and began to stir the stuff there. Mike came in and the two started to growl. I didn't want to be in anyone's range, so I stepped out of the door. Soon Mike came out, mounted, and rode off. I went in and told Billy, "I've got a notion to boot you, starting a ruckus around camp." Billy said, "I was ready for him, but when he turned and left, I didn't want to shoot him in the back." Mike soon took to other pastures as marshal of Kiowa, but his brother, John, still worked for the T 5.

One day a young fellow from Kansas City – so he said – came down with a note from Carter to Billy Smith. He was bleached out, fat, well dressed, wore a little black hat and shiny shoes. The boys took him for a bar keep. Billy said, "Chuck's ready; come and gitter." The man came in, took a box, sat up to the table like he was at home. All evening the converse was of K.C., whisky, terbaccer, and the nice girls, but he only answered questions "Yes" or "No." Asked if he would not like to ride over the range next day, yes he *would* like to look around. In the morning they caught up a good-looking, high-life horse. Smith put the saddle on and told him how to get up on the left side and hold the reins. Then they all stood back.

But the fellow kicked the horse in the left flank as he mounted; he took his seat, held a loose rein, and as the horse started off pitching he looked back and called out, "Come on, fellows; let's all get together." When they caught up, Smith said, "Where you from?" He said, "Dogtown." They had a good laugh. Dogtown was a noted hangout sixty miles south of San Antonio. I'll call the fellow "Ben Adams" because his real name's not important and I never happened to know a peeler named Ben Adams. He soon went over to Quinlan's (brand 2 S) southeast of us. Jones, the boss, was aiming to quit soon, and Quinlan asked Ben to hang around till he left, then take his place.

THE BOYS AT THE LINE CAMPS HAD CONSIDERABLE TROUBLE WITH THE INDIANS

Cheyenne camp, with Glass mountains in background

Cheyenne Neighbors

The Quinlan home camp, where Ben Adams went to work, was on Indian creek near the Cheyenne line. Part of the range was on the reservation, so they aimed to keep on good terms with the Indians. But Jones couldn't handle the Johns; they nearly took the place at dinner, crowding the boys back from the table. One day Ben got up to get a cup of coffee, and a young buck dropped down in his place and started in. Ben came back with his coffee; then took the Indian by an arm and a leg, slung him in a corner, sat down and finished his meal. No one ever tried Ben out again.

Jones soon went back to Indiana, married, and dropped out of sight; and Ben took over. Ben never gave the Indians any ground. One day near noon six bucks came in and waited for chuckaway. Ben said, "Cook, when you get things ready, let me know. And you fellows set up quick." The cook soon said, "She's ready." Ben said, "Fall in, boys;" and they all moved up to the table. Ben placed a plate, knife, and spoon before each one; then gave each a cup of coffee, dished out beans with a cup, gave each a biscuit, and set in; he with the others. The table was full. The Johns growled; but Ben said, "Cowboy heap hungry. Ride long ways. Mebbe so, pretty soon Indians heap chuck- away." The Johns didn't like it, but they stuck it out. After the boys had finished, Ben said, "Cook, got any pepper?" Cook said, "A pound of cayenne." Ben said, "Trot it out." He put about half of it in the coffee boiler, and seasoned the beans with what was left. Then he told the Indians to set up. He put a biscuit and a cup of beans on each plate, gave each a cup of hot coffee, and they fell to.

They ate beans till their blood began to boil, then took a drag on the coffee to put out the fire. Then they said, "Woo-oo-oo!" and made a break for the creek. Indian creek ran west and south of the cabin; in the bend was a garden fenced with willow pickets. The path went around the garden, but the Indians broke down the fence, tore straight through, and jumped down a steep bank into water four feet deep. They soaked up all they could manage handy. Then they went into the shallow water, got down on all fours, and drank like stock. When the flurry sort of subsided, they strung out across the sand hills and never came back at feedin' time.

Quinlan was supposed to give the Indians beef for the use of their grass. Ben would kill for them at regular times. Once he sent word to three camps – Sand Hill's, Buffalo's, and Big Horse's – that he would kill wohaw tomorrow. Sand Hill and Buffalo were on hand with their people, but when Big Horse came up, the guts were gone. (Ben would not divide the beef, so first come, first choice – which was the entrails). Big Horse said, "White man no treat Indian right." Ben told him to "Take wohaw and go." Finally Big Horse said, "Indian no want to live." Ben said, "Here's my gun; take it and kill yourself." Big Horse went to his tepee, took his own Winchester, and shot himself; one squaw took the same gun and wound up her little ball of yarn; another swung herself out on a rawhide rope. (At least that's the way Ben told it. Ben set in as boss for us in the spring of '83).

The cowboys probably did not realize that the Cheyennes were hungry; that their buffalo herds had been destroyed and they had not yet learned agriculture. Ben Adams of course did not understand the Indian code that would compel a chief to take his own life to prove his cause. The boys moreover had all of the frontier callousness in their feeling toward the race with whom their people had fought for every step of the westward trek. This was accentuated by the tendency of these recently tamed hostiles to drive off cattle from the southern boundary of the range. But even with these allowances, in the intercourse between the races the cowboys appear the more savage of the two.

The boys at the line camps had considerable trouble with the Indians, who aimed to scare them off and then kill the cattle. Jim Oberly rode the line from the home camp to the east side of the range, then south to the picket house at Cleo. One day in February of '83 he got a .45 hole in the crown of his Stetson; just clipped his hair. He said he heard no report nor saw any smoke; he speeded up a little, and after that he stayed farther off from the jacks.

The boys used to get careless and waste all their cartridges, then leave their pistols at home. One day Jim Hudson and pard, unarmed, run onto an Indian skinning a steer. The Indian raised his gun, and Jim started toward him. The other boy said, "Take your gun down, John; and Jim, you stop where you are." The John lowered his gun, Jim stopped, and the John rode off. The boys took what beef they wanted and went to camp. Another time two boys rode out from the Sand creek camp with one pistol and one cartridge, and run onto several Indians. The Indians were going to take the unarmed boy, but the other would point his pistol and persuade them to back away. They fooled around an hour before the Indians left. Carter used to say he wished they would kill every man that went without a loaded gun.

Some time early in '83 they scared a boy off from his line, and he came in to the home camp, his horse winded. Carter happened to be down from Caldwell. He came over with a Sharps carbine and a box of cartridges and said to Potts, "You go down and try to ride that line; if you can't, I'll go." Potts said, "You try it first; and if you can't, I will." Carter said, "You go ride that line." Potts said, "That's the way to talk. They ain't nothing I can't do."

One day soon after he started riding, a bunch of about ten Indians rode toward him in a high run, aiming to chase him off. He tied his horse out of sight and went to the top of the ridge. The Indians had stopped in a bunch of brush on a hillside off about four hundred yards. Potts went to slinging lead. They left the brush; had to run a quarter of a mile 'fore they got under cover. One horse fell down and lay still; the John took it afoot, nearly kept up with his crowd. Potts thought he touched some other horses, too. After a few such brushes, the Johns quit Potts's line.

The boys at our camp on Cheyenne creek claimed a Texas boy worked at Dickey's, southwest of our range, who said his folks had been killed by Indians and he aimed to kill all he could. He was always on the watch for them, but one dark night he slept off from camp, and was frozen in a storm. I was told that Henry Brown, marshal at Caldwell, once worked for Dickey. The Indians bothered some asking for meals, so he salted their hash with wolf bait. It got so no Indian or squaw would eat at the Dickey camp. Then he poisoned dead cattle. The Indians, half-starved, would eat the carcasses and pass out. All I know about this is that a lot of them did die from some cause.

An old fellow named Kirk at the Greever camp said he had been a Texas ranger, and had served with Mackenzie.

Here Mr. Nelson probably refers to Colonel Ranald S. Mackenzie, who broke the power of the hostile Kiowas, Comanches, and Cheyennes in the Texas Panhandle in the winter campaign of 1874-75. He afterwards served as commandant at Fort Sill.

When the boys got to talking about Indians, wishing them all kinds of torture, Kirk would say, "Boys, if you knew what I know, you'd keep still. I'm pretty hard, but I've seen rangers do things to them Indians down in Texas that made me shudder." I've heard stories myself too hideous to tell.

Sometimes, however, the boys met the Indians in a friendlier mood. They especially enjoyed the society of the Indian girls. The courtship was formal, for Cheyenne women were noted throughout the western tribes for their chastity. It had its elements of pathos: to the Indian girls, it meant the prospect of marriage; to the girl-starved cowboys, it meant only a brief experience of the feminine companionship they craved.

One old Indian came to the Sand creek camp, who likely had been to Washington. He had a big time telling his experience: how he got in a long house, how things run along by, and the black house 'way up would go "Wo-oo-oo-oo-oo-oo-oo!" He said he met some white squaws; he talk big, white squaw all go 'way quick.

He told the boys he had two papoose. The boys said, "Bring 'em over." He came over with two girls, about sixteen and eighteen. The boys would fix beef, bread, and coffee, and have a feast. Sometimes instead of Old John, an old squaw came along that for hard looks couldn't be beat. She sat in a corner of the dugout, but kept her eyes on the papooses. The boys and girls would eat first, then turn the old woman loose on the chuck. She would work like a starved hound. The boys promised, "Go agency get married, when leaves come," but they soon left the range. Two new hands took their place. The girls came over several times with the old man, and these boys tried to make up to them. But it would not work – they would go away crying. They soon quit coming.

Jo Kerr rode the line west from our Cheyenne creek camp. Two of us rode out with him one day when the weather was nice, and on our return we stopped at an Indian camp where old Buffalo was chief. Jo got off and shook hands with the Indians, and started making up to a girl they called Paddy. She was eatin' on a piece of a calf that had been taken from a dead cow. As we rode off, he said, "The poor thing don't know any better." After that he would put a chunk of beef and some sinkers in his saddle bag, stop at a big tree to meet Paddy and her sister and father, and make sign talk while they ate. Then he would ride in to camp, his face shinin' like a smoked ham.

Then came several days when Paddy failed to show up at the tree. Finally Jo rode down to the Indian camp. Some squaws were weaving a long willow box, and a lot of howling was in progress at one of the tepees. A young fellow came out of this tepee and told Jo, "Paddy heap sick, mebbe so Paddy die." That night at the card game, the boys heard the tom-tom starting up. They asked Jo, "What's transpirin' at your wickiup?" He said, "Paddy is dead!" And the card game stopped right now. The next day when Jo was passing the tree, some squaws with a trappers' ax and a piece of elk horn were digging a grave. One said, "Paddy want to sleep under big tree she love."

The next day four of us was at the big tree. Two young Indian men came leading a pinto pony pulling a travois. This travois was made of two poles like buggy shafts, the small ends tied to the pony's neck, the heavy ends dragging, with sticks tied between to hold them apart. There was a buffalo skin tied from pole to pole, and resting on this was the willow frame with Paddy sleeping inside. Following this was a long line of silent Indians. Four squaws took this coffin and laid it in the grave. Then they covered it all up with earth except a woven trap door over the face, which they left so they could open it to put in food. Old Buffalo said, "Papoose go tepee, Paddy no there, papoose cry, Indian heap heartsick. Paddy go where great sun all time shine. Paddy see buffalo." They laid some meat and bread by the dead face; then leaving a little pony by the grave, they silently turned toward the home tepee.

Jo soon left the Cheyenne creek camp. The rider that took his place would lift the lid and shoot holes in the dead face, and put cigarettes in the holes. The Indians finally put up a sign:

WHITE MAN PLES LET DED INDIAN LONE

But the boys kept right on.

Cheyenne girls knew how to repel unwanted advances. Mr. Nelson relates an instance when the Quinlan outfit was branding at the camp on Indian creek in the spring of '83.

A boy named Bert Espey got to annoying two Indian

girls. Bert was about fifteen, the girls a little older. They took him to the creek and doused him in. He came back at them a couple of times, and the girls put him under again. Then some of the older boys run in and got him out; but they told him, "We helped you this time; you go it alone now." The girls said, "You no quit, you die." He quit.

Bert's brother, Ernest, was also working for Quinlan. He came first to my camp late in the fall of '82, and stopped several days – a neatly dressed, nice looking young fellow. When he went to Quinlan's he was set to ride on Tepee creek; his line passed within a couple of miles of Sand Hill's camp. He would go to the camp and play monte with the Indians. He picked up a few Cheyenne words and signs, and got to slinging them at a young Indian girl named Woki (Antelope). Soon he was passing more time with Woki than at the card game.

He had a pearl-handled bowie knife. One day he took off his belt, with the knife, and buckled it around Woki's waist. A short time later she was wandering along Tepee, when she saw a doe and two fawns coming toward her on their way to the creek. She squatted down behind some bushes. The doe and one fawn passed and went to the water. The other stopped with its head hidden by a large oak tree. Woki made a short run and threw the knife, sticking it in the fawn's side and killing it. She put it on her shoulders and carried it to their wickiup. An old fellow seeing her coming gave a couple of wolf yelps –"Woki killum deer!" Then Woki's stock run high. All the young bucks wanted to take her in.

In a few days Ernest came again to the camp. Woki mounted up behind his saddle and rode to where she

A GIRL ABOUT SEVENTEEN, IN BUCKSKIN AND BEADS

Fanny Whirlwind, Cheyenne girl, with elk tooth costume, 1890

had killed the fawn. She got off, showed where she was when she had first seen the deer, where she dropped down, where the fawn stopped with its head behind the tree, how she ran and threw the knife, how the fawn struggled, and how she carried it in. Ernest put his arm around her waist, said, "When flowers come, we go agency get married," then kissed her. (The agency was at Cantonment, just west of the Quinlan range).

Late in April two of our boys fixing to go to Quinlan's to see about separating the two ranges before the spring roundup, said to me, "Cook, come along." I said, "I'd like to, but I can't leave camp." Another boy said, "Go on. You ain't got nothin' to do. I'll keep camp." A saddled horse was soon brought up and we three started south. We crossed Eagle five miles southeast of camp, took dinner at the Quinlan camp on Indian creek, and stayed overnight at the line camp on Tepee. When we were ready to leave, Ernest said, "I'll ride up to your camp with you. I'm goin' to Wyoming, and I want to see all the boys 'fore I leave." Another Quinlan boy, Cal Smith, said, "Wait till I saddle; I'll ride along."

The five of us started back west, but soon Ernest headed a little south. One of our boys said, "Now tell me how you're goin' to get to the T 5 headin' south." Smith told us, "He's froze on a young squaw up the creek, and it don't make no difference where he aims to go, he always heads up Tepee." Then Ernest said, "Fellows, there's an Indian girl up there nearest like a white person of any Indian I ever seen. Sometimes I'm almost sorry for her. I want to tell her good-bye." Then we all rode toward the Indian camp.

We came up to about ten tepees – round tents with a pole tied to the top and a loose flap to move around to

draw the smoke out. There was a circular fence about
five feet high of bluestem grass tied together, around
each tepee; and a higher fence of willow shoots and
grass bound tight, to form a windbreak on the north,
south, and west of the camp. And a lot of dogs – some
looked like coyotes. Several squaws were tanning hides,
pulling and stretching with hands, feet, and teeth.

Ernest dismounted and led his horse up to one of the
tepees. A girl about seventeen came out, all dressed in
buckskin and beads, quick and bright, real nice looking.
Ernest said, "I'm going to the northern tribes. When
the leaves fall, I'll come again. I've come to say good-
bye." The girl's eyes got dead black; she turned, walked
slowly to the bunch of squaws, lay down on a skin and
began to cry. The squaws chided her.

Ernest went to another tent. An old fellow came out
with several young bucks. Ernest spoke the same piece
to them. The old fellow said, "Ernest heap talk straight.
Ernest heap good." He said something to one of the
young bucks, and the boy went away. Then he took
Ernest's bridle reins and turned the horse's head toward
the east; he stroked its head, breast, legs, and back; put
some dust on its rump and stroked it off; then raised his
head and hands, and prayed for pony to be stout, quick,
take Ernest to northern tribes and make safe return.
Two of the young Indians then led the pony away to a
small log that had been chopped on, close to where we
were.

The boy that had been sent off now came back with
a rawhide rope. The old Indian bound it around
Ernest in such a way that to pull one end would make
it fall off; he took off Ernest's hat, stroked his hair,
prayed for him; then he took him by one arm, and led
him close to the pony, still wearing the rope, which had

been left on as a charm. Next the old man went to where Woki lay, took her by one arm, and using Indian words led her up to Ernest. Then he said, "Woki, Ernest heap talk straight; he no talk crooked. Ernest go northern tribes; he come to say good-bye. There is big tree where Woki killum deer. When leaves fall, you go there. Ernest come."

Woki walked up to Ernest and said, "Ernest, you said when flowers come we go agency get married. Now you say you go northern tribes; when leaves fall you come again. You go now. I never see you any more." She put her arms around his neck, kissed him, stepped back, waved her hand, said, "Good-bye, Ernest, good-bye," uttered as piercing a cry as I ever heard, and lay down on the skins.

Ernest stayed with us all summer. He was satisfied with our crowd; I don't think he ever aimed to go north. In the fall one of our boys stopped at Sand Hill's camp. He asked Woki if she was waiting at the big oak. She said, "I never see Ernest any more."

Spring Work and Deviltry on the T 5

It was at this time that the T 5 had a real Indian scare. It all started with a mysterious murder at the line camp on the Cottonwood, but one is at a loss to account for the panic that followed. Perhaps this was part of the plot – an old ruse of white criminals to divert suspicion to the Indians. Some hidden influence must have been at work to frighten these hard-riding cowboys out of their wits. But Oliver Nelson at home camp saw John Neal come to the ranch with no premonition of tragedy.

John Neal, former deputy marshal, came down from Caldwell one day in March with a message: a baby girl in the Carter family, red-headed. (They had a boy about three, black-eyed, smart; he would not play with children, liked to eat with me). Neal went to work as cook at Cottonwood camp. He was about forty years old.

Shortly after this – about five in the afternoon, April 8, 1883 – a boy came in to my camp bareback. It was Duval, the cook at the line camp on Sand creek. Soon three others came in: D. H. McPherson, who rode west from Sand creek, and the two riders from Cottonwood – one I named "Dan George" and another whose name might as well be "Will Adams," a cousin of Ben, also from Dogtown. They had a story to tell.

They said Dan came in off his line; turned his horse loose, which went into the bank stable; and he went into the dugout. There John Neal lay on his back on the floor, the back of his head broken in by the pole of a hatchet; his watch and forty silver dollars gone. Dan rode out and met Will coming in from his line. The two went in and looked John over; then rode east to the Sand creek camp and told Duval. Duval started at once – bareback – for home camp, thirty miles away. McPherson soon came in off his line. When they told him the news he wrote a note to Charley Noble, who rode the east line –"John killed. All go to head-quarters." Then the three pulled for home camp.

As we found afterward, Noble came in late and read the note; but he had ideas of his own. He got a bite to eat and rode to the Cottonwood camp after dark; he went into the dugout and fell down on John. He felt him over, found his hair wet and a hole in the back of his head. He wiped his bloody hand on John's coat, struck a match and looked things over good, rode back to camp, and went to sleep. The next morning he rode his line.

Ben Adams, the boss, and Watson, from the west camp, came to headquarters soon after the alarm came in. It seemed safest to call all the boys in from the south. So after we all ate supper, Ben, Watson, and McPherson rode out to notify Byron Long and Jim Mathews, who were camped on the Cimarron holding the cattle south of the river. When they got there, Long had come in. Soon Mathews' horse came in without a saddle. That really looked bad. The four started back to home camp with this new scare.

Meanwhile at headquarters the boys had put all the horses in the corral, but they overlooked one mule that should have been put in the barn. The night was dark and cloudy, and we were all nervous. About nine in the evening the mule began pawing at the barn door. Someone sung out, "The Indians are tryin' to break down the door!" I didn't take the Indian part strong, but said I would go out and see. I went out the north door of the cabin and started around the east end just as Dan George and Harry Carter (the manager's nephew, a boy about fourteen), each with a shotgun, stepped out the south door. When I came past the end of the cabin, one of them hollered, "Throw up!" I dropped down behind a pile of posts, and Dan said, "You come here!" I said, "You go back in the cabin, you damned fools." They went in, and so did I, and stayed in.

About ten the boys came back from the river camp with Long. Dan and some of the others wanted to make *them* throw up. I don't know why they were so foolish – they knew this bunch was coming – but they were all jumpy. If they'd started a gun play, we'd have had a real battle. But some of us said, "You fellows let your guns alone and stay inside," and the south bunch came on in. We got to talking about Will Adams' brother, Alec, who was riding the line for Quinlan – rode west to meet Noble going east. Ben said, "If a brother of mine was in danger, I'd go to him or break a trace." But Will lay down on the bed – seemed unconcerned – said, "He'll get along."

We decided to guard the camp, two at a time. The guards sat at the long table reading James and Younger history[2]. They would have made a good target – two lamps, windows open on three sides. When Watson and I were called to stand guard, I blew out the light and we slept till daylight. When the boys woke up, they said, "We might've all been killed."

I got breakfast for the bunch. Then Carter rolled in

[2] Jesse James had been killed in 1882. The T 5 boys may have been reading *Illustrated Lives and Adventures of Frank and Jesse James and the Younger Brothers* by J. A. Dacus, published the same year.

from the north. He asked, "What are you all doing here?" We told him John was killed. "What! Throw your lines open? Just a bunch of damned cowards." He hollered to several to go back to their lines. Duval said he didn't have a saddle. Carter asked, "Did you get up without one?" "Yes." "Well, get back the same way." In ten minutes I was alone.

They got to the Cottonwood camp. John was still dead. Forty dollars in paper was in his pocket. They rolled him in a blanket, took him to the top of the rise, and buried him

> Where the wild flowers bloom
> And the butterfly rests.

They met Noble riding his line. And nothing had happened to Mathews. He had got sick, and took off his saddle and turned his horse loose, aiming to walk to camp when it got cooler – which he did. He had got there just as Long and the other boys pulled out; called to them, but they did not hear him.

Later Will Adams took sick, and went to the Leland hotel at Caldwell. He had a high fever, and was perhaps delirious. McPherson went to see him there. He came back all out of breath and told us that Will, expecting to die, confessed that he and Dan George had killed old John and divided the silver, and he sent word for Dan to pull out. Dan got worried some, but Ben and Billy Smith said, "Stay right here. If you run, we'll know you killed him. If you stay and keep still, no one will know. And nobody cares. You're safe here." Will never came back, but went home to Dogtown.

The next September two men came in a spring wagon with a casket – an undertaker from Caldwell and a brother of John Neal from Boston. They went down to the Cottonwood camp after John's remains. When they came back late in the evening, I passed Neal and said low, "Meet me outside." He didn't seem to take any notice; and the next morning he called Dan out instead. Then he and the undertaker left pronto. Dan came in and told us, "He accused me of killing old John. I've a notion to plug him." I believe the man did the right thing by leaving.

One night Ben Adams came in from Caldwell, another man with him. He called to Billy Smith, who was in bed, "Come out, Bill. Here's a man you'd like to see." Billy rolled out, came to the front of the cabin, and said, "Well, Jesus Christ, Cal. How did you get here?" Cal said he was just huntin' new grazin', come up the trail with the 4 D. Billy asked, "How's them Jones boys?" "They got to brandin' cattle and had to fly." "Well, Jesus Christ! How's Big Jim Smith?" "Well, he got caught pullin' horses and they strung him up." "Well, Jesus Christ!" A third had left with another man's woman; a fourth had pulled out after killing a Mexican. It seemed like all Billy's chums were either hung, shot, or had run away. Ben said, "Bill, you been keepin' bad company."

Cal was on the dodge himself. Billy also was on a hide-out. It seemed a good many south Texas boys were up to ward off lead poison. Still they were all good hands.

Just before the spring work began, the boys brought in the saddle horses – about three hundred. When they started to ride them, we had a real rodeo. One boy closed the bars so as to ride his horse in the corral. The horse pitched half circle, threw the boy, jumped the bars, and ran off. The fellows all hollered and laughed. The boy said, "You can holler, but I tell you I'm hurt."

Another boy on a young horse went over forward,

caught his leggins (leather chaps) on the saddle horn, and hung on the side. The horse made a whole round, the boy hollering "Whoa." The horse made another circle. Then Carter said, "One of you fellers that's got a horse saddled, rope that bronc and bring it in." Potts got his rope, rode out and caught it, and led it in. Two of the boys took the rider off and stood him on his feet; when they let loose he fell flat and lay still about ten minutes, then got up and went back to work.

About the time the spring roundup began, a rough duck rolled in looking for a job. He was ragged and dirty, had fuzzy whiskers, brindle-red hair, and buttermilk-blue eyes. Just no good. The boss would not put him on. But he was always willing to take hold, so we called him "Ruff and Ready." We gave him an old saddle and a broke-down horse, and sent him south to hook in with the roundup. He hung up at the Sand creek camp.

Indian ponies were scattered around not far off. Some of the boys told him to spy out a lead, take several ponies, and move north; that it would beat punching cows. He layed in the jacks a few days, getting his grub at camp; took hold of several head, and pulled for Kansas. He sold at Anthony; then dressed up and went to Caldwell, took in the dances, got sweet on a widder, and hooked up – had a good time till his money ran out.

Oscar Mayes had spent most of his winter in Kentucky. When he returned he was leading a little black mare that had cost him four hundred dollars, freight and all. She could fly for four hundred yards; after that, she was done. Oscar headed for the south camps. He outrun all the Indian ponies he could hear of; got blankets, tanned hides, rawhide ropes, and quirts. Finally some new Indians came in with a long blue paint (spotted pony) with white eyes. They wanted to "run long way." Distance was nothing to Oscar, so they set the goal out a mile. The Indians piled up all the stuff they had. There was about forty punchers on hand betting for Oscar.

Oscar mounted his mare with a heavy stock saddle. An Indian brought up the blue paint; a small buck dressed in a G-string got on, with a quirt in each hand. One of the Indians pulled the bridle off, said, "Go!" – and the race was on. Oscar said later that when he got out about a quarter of a mile he glanced back and it seemed the paint was about half way; but from then on, it looked like his mare just stood still. The paint passed the judges fifty yards in the lead, and run on into the sand hills out of sight. Jim Hudson said, "He won't get back 'fore sundown." After that the boys called the Indian horse "Sundown." The Johns sure collected on their bets.

A few days after the race, Old Ruff rolled in with a pard – a kid about seventeen – and stopped at the Sand creek camp. He was shy on money again, and his honeymoon had sort of dimmed till he could pick up some more. The boys told him of the blue pinto and advised him to stick around and annex it. He watched a while and got Sundown and several others; then he and the boy moved to their hide-out for a lunch and a night ride. But they forgot to take up their tracks, and a bunch of Indians followed them up. Ruff and pard had to leave their lunch, and the kid dropped his gun, but they *moved*. Ruff on Sundown kept a little behind and turned up a dry run, aiming to draw the Indians his way. The kid hit high ground, seen a camp on the Cantone trail, and pulled for it. It was old Buffalo King with a freight outfit.

Just as the kid got to King's camp, an old buck hung a rawhide rope on him, and turned to take up the slack; but King hit the rope with a butcher knife and pointed to Ruff – who was just turning a divide – saying, "Go hang *that* man." The boy got in a wagon and covered up with a sheet. King's men all had guns, so the Indians took after Ruff. The freight outfit pulled to Caldwell, and told of the kid's narrow escape and the bad news about Ruff – killed by the Indians. The widow took it pretty hard; her home had lost its charm. She sold out, married a third husband, and moved to Hunnewell, ten miles east of Caldwell, to begin life from a safe angle.

The Johns and the cowmen fought their own battles, for the War department no longer had a garrison at Cantonment. That spring Castleberry and three other boys went to the south roundup on the Bickford, Dickey, and Day ranges south and west of the old post. On the way back with about three hundred T 5 cattle they'd gathered, they passed through the place and crossed the North Canadian. Just north of the river about fifty Indians ran through the bunch, cut out a steer, and took after it, shooting till it fell; then they returned, scattering the cattle, and cut out another. Two had guns, the rest bows and arrows. The boys pushed the cattle as fast as they could, but the Indians followed a couple of miles, killing about nine head.

The Scotch company became uneasy over the short dividends received from their interest in the Texas Land and Cattle company and sent secretaries over from Glasgow. We got a raw Scot, a young fellow about twenty named George McIndoo. He came one day about 3 p.m., said he was going to keep books for the company. He was well dressed and bleached out. I

never thought they would mix a dude of his caliber
with a bunch like us. The Carters were living in their
own house again, and I sent him over there. But the
missus sent him back, so I started to fix him something
to eat. The boys were dressing a beef.

I went out and cut off a slab of steak; then I fried it,
het the coffee, and put bread, plate, knife, and fork on
the table. Some of the boys were coming in. When I
went to take up the steak, I found Billy Smith had
poured several pounds of marrow gut on top of it. This
marrow gut is fresh unwashed entrails cut in about
four-inch lugs. I used to cook it with sage and plenty
of pepper and salt, and it always went strong with the
boys, but I never ate any; it is tender enough, but has
a low-down, cow-lot flavor – sort of a hound-dog relish.

I gave Smith a calling down, put the steak on the
Scot's plate, and said, "Now fly at it." Then the boys
got a dishpan, poured their mess into it, and set it on
the table; got themselves some tin plates, and started in.
The Scot just stood plumb locoed. Finally he asked,
"What is that?" Someone said, "Guts." Scotty said,
"You eat guts?" Then the whole outfit went to roasting
him and I could not stop them. But he stood his ground,
and when he did start eating he showed up for a good
feeder.

Some time before this – I do not remember just when
– Martin had put up picket walls to close the sides of
the buckboard shed so it could be used as a feed room.
Now he set in to build Scotty a picket room about
twelve feet square, with a dirt roof and floor, six feet
south of the cabin. He had as helpers a little Creek
Indian boy named Billy Culver, and a heavy fellow
about forty that he'd brought down on the same trip as
Scotty.

This last man claimed he'd chummed with the Youngers and James boys – let on he was pretty good material. The Texas boys didn't take to him strong; they did little bragging themselves. Finally Carter paid him off and warned him, "You'll be lucky to get away from here alive." He walked away northwest carrying a fairly good saddle. Soon Billy Smith came to camp from the same direction, said he'd met him at the Elm Mott and had a talk with him. I said, "He'll round up at Ule's camp"– this was twenty miles northwest on the Kiowa trail – but Billy said, "He won't round up nowhere." I never heard of the man again, but for a long time his saddle hung on a limb in the elm grove.

The boys didn't take to Scotty either. Soon as he got settled, one day when he and I were alone he hung on his riding habit – knee britches, derby hat, claw hammer coat, and cane. I said, "This will do for us two, but don't pull it off before a crowd." But one rainy day when twelve men were in camp, he went out to his room and hung it on again. As he came back in, several drew their guns. I took his derby and tossed it across the room, while the boys shot it full of holes. He turned to go out, and two bullets went through the tail of his coat. I followed him outside, and said, "What did I tell you?" He said, "Dash it to hell! This is a hell of a country."

I got to thinking ours was a hard crowd.

South Texas Moves In on the T 5

In June Ben Adams, Billy Smith, John Potts, and some of the others seemed interested in something. One day a buckboard rolled in, and a brother of Ben – I'll name him "Jim Adams" – got out. I never seen such a pow-wow. Later I learned that Jim had killed a Mex near Dogtown, and was in limbo, and the bunch was planning to go down and bail him out by force. But when he came in on his own power it saved them the trouble.

As soon as Jim arrived, business began to liven up. He was dangerous and crooked, but he went to work on the south side. He and one George Gordon soon rounded up at Harper, Kansas with a bunch of Cheyenne ponies, and were taken in by United States marshals. Jim got away, stole a horse, and rode back to camp bareback. But Gordon pled guilty before the federal court at Wichita, and to help the law along, implicated three outfits joining the Cheyenne country, including everybody on the T 5 – which no one believed. We were respectable then; the stealing was just starting in with our outfit, though the time was to come when it was the only thrill we had. They gave Gordon four years at Leavenworth to start on a new line. Some of us was mighty near heartbroke over his bad luck.

Several of the "Adams" family came in about this time: besides Jim there was Henry and Jeff, cousins to the others. Henry was good-natured, Jeff distant, Will sneakin', Alec middlin', Ben the best. Henry was about the only one that said much. I would tell him of the north, and he would tell of Texas.

He said that when the Civil War broke out, the able-bodied men joined the army, leaving the old folks and young folks at home to care for the stock, tend a little patch of corn and beans, and watch out for Comanche Indians, greasers, and renegade whites. The people lived close together in colonies on creeks or branches, in little log houses with rock chimneys. If trouble got to spoutin' they'd yell a couple of times, and help was a-comin' in a high run. They kept a few tame branded cattle, and the country was full of cattle that had gone wild. There was no market for beef: a cow hide on a fence was worth more than on a cow.

When the men came back, they reported they could sell cattle up in Missouri, so each settlement went together to catch the wild stock. They would select a good place down a brushy dry run, and build a pole corral about two acres in size with several ketch pens on the sides and a branding chute. It had a broad gap at the upper end, and a funnel-shaped lane leading into it from up the run.

The men would take a bunch of tame cattle and run them as fast as they could go down the lane and into the corral and let them out at one of the side pens, repeating till they learned the way. Then they would ease a bunch of wild cattle into a good position, and work the tame cattle in among them. When the wild stock got restless and began to run, the tame would lead them into the corral, and the men would close the gap with poles. The tame cattle would go into the side pens and out to graze. The men would brand the others, turn them into a side pen to bawl several days, then drink 'em and graze 'em with the tame herd, and shut them up to bawl again.

When they got the pen all full, thirty or forty men would take a wagon and some tame cattle and drive them to pens on clear land, and hold them there. If they got stock they could not handle they would make a slit in their eyelids, cut a string out of their ear, and tie up the eyes for a few days so they would stay with the herd. Sometimes stock that would not tame down would be "kneed"– a cord in one front leg would be cut, so they couldn't run.

When they got about two thousand head, they would take about forty men, some of the best tame cattle, plenty of horses, and two chuck wagons, and start the herd north. Of nights they would select high, level land free from badger or dog holes, and bed the cattle down about one hundred yards off from the wagons. They divided the night into three guards. Usually someone had a watch; if not, they measured the time by the stars, or if it was cloudy they went hit or miss. Eight men were on guard at a time, riding around the herd equal distances apart, singing all the while with a good strong voice, the bells on their spurs keeping up a jingle as the horse went on a slow trot. (They used spurs with large loose rowels and steel lugs on, called bells). They aimed to stay about twenty-five to fifty steps away from the cattle all the time. Of stormy nights nearly all the men would be out; and if the cattle began milling (going in a circle till they wound up and packed in the center), half the riders would turn back and circle the opposite way to spread them out.

When the cattle got trail broke, about fifteen men would take the herd – a foreman, a horse wrangler, a cook, and ten or twelve herders – with part of the tame cattle, one wagon, and six or eight horses for each man. The rest would turn back and begin to harvest another bunch.

When wild cattle got scarce, men would watch the glades of moonlight nights, and rope and hog-tie (all four feet together) them when they came out to graze.

Sometimes one man would catch four or five in a single night. Other men would follow with large tame cattle, fasten the wild critter's horns to the tame one's neck, and thus bring them into the corral. There the tame cattle would lay down; the men would turn them loose, and throw the wild ones into the branding chute and slap on the iron. If they were already branded, it was slap on another and fight if you had to.

They began the northern drives in April when the grass started with the spring rains. When they came to a flooded stream, they pushed the cattle in and guided them across. The cook would pile things up in the wagon as best he could, and several men would tie their ropes to the tongue or side and pull by the saddle horn. If things got wet, it was the cook's job to dry them when the sun came out. The cook usually kept dry, but all the others got a bath with their clothes on. During these spring showers it was apt to sleet, and then a bath in red creek water was awful refreshin'. If it rained at night, the cook had a dry bed in the wagon; the boys sat on their saddles, leaned against a wheel, and dreamed of the good time at the end of the trail.

On the drives the men were not very talkative; arguing was discouraged, and so was whisky, because when one boy was put to rest under a fresh mound and the other took a good horse and rode off, it left the herd short-handed. But one would pass a good many such mounds on the trails, with boards forming a cross – sometimes standing, sometimes laying down – with the name of some unfortunate boy inscribed in pencil or grease from the wagon hub. We had a song that said,

No mourner is sighing above him
But the soughing of winds as they blow
Through the grass that shades the dead cowboy
Alone chants his requiem low.

Henry never mentioned buffalo, but others have told me that when they went to catch the wild cattle they found buffalo mixed among them. When they started to run, the buffalo would pull for prairie land out of the way, while the cattle would break for the brush and be caught in the corrals. And Carter said that when he came up the trail in '72 it took more men to push the buffalo back than it did to hold the cattle. If they got together and started to run, the boys would follow till they came to an upgrade; then the cattle would slack up and the buffalo would get ahead, and the boys would ride in between them. I have been told that in central Texas in the early '70's the buffalo bulls would sometimes follow the milk cows right up to the settlers' corrals, and they'd have to drive them away.

I enjoyed the talks with Henry, but he soon rounded up at the Cottonwood camp, and took to riding a line. When he left, a good milk cow I had came up missing. In looking for her – she was branded T A R with letters ten inches high – I struck his trail, back-tracked it, and seen where he'd turned off to get her. When I saw him again I told him I knew he had her and just how and where he'd picked her up. But he wanted her milk, said he'd shoot her 'fore he'd let Carter bring her back; and whenever Carter was down at their camp he kept her tied out in the brush. (I had one milk cow with a horn spread of over seven feet. She wasn't friendly, so I let 'er go.)

Henry was hard on horses. He weighed a hundred and eighty pounds and the saddle thirty-five. His mount got weak. On his line there was a bog fifty feet wide where he crossed a draw; he could have missed it by riding a hundred yards to one side, but he went in. His horse could not make it; so he took hold of its ears, shoved its head in the mud, and held it there till it lay still, then carried the saddle to camp. When he got in, he told what he'd done and took a new horse. He left three horses in that bog before he finally went back to Dogtown. Soon after he left, word came back to us that he'd been killed down there by one of his cousins.

The boys often had to pull cattle out of bog holes. The Cimarron was always full of quicksand. Sometime in the spring of '83 Billy Smith passing the mouth of Eagle Chief heard a call, "HELP!" Billy shot off his pistol to show he was coming, but it took him an hour to locate the call. Finally he found a boy – I don't know where from – who had tried to cross the river afoot and bogged down till only his head was above the sand. Smith told the fellow to hold still so he wouldn't work himself under any further, and he went to a wagon camp and got help. They threw the man a sixty-foot rope, which he tied around his wrist, and pulled him out by the saddle horn, but it nigh displaced his arm. He set in with us. We called him Arkansaw.

That spring Martin was told to plow a fire guard on the west side of the range. Joining us on the northwest was a bunch styled the Wildcat Pool or Eagle Chief Pool. (In a pool several cattlemen held a lease or interest in a range, but the cattle were owned individually and each owner had a different brand). When our boys set the stakes, the Wildcats sent word we'd marked the line too far west and we better not try to plow it. Just then Martin happened to take a trip to Caldwell, and it seemed everyone sent for ammunition.

Then several boys loaded up and rode the sand hills, and Martin plowed the guard with no bother from the Wildcats.

Quick as these bands of armed retainers were to fight for the interest of their brand, they had their own code of chivalry. A free heart and an open hand was the pattern of intercourse with the outside world. If anyone failed, he learned the hard way.

Four boys stopped with us one night. They'd come from near Dodge, and were on their way south to take in with the roundup. In the morning one of our boys asked one of them for twelve .45 pistol cartridges, and paid him twenty-five cents for them. Another of the four found out about the transaction, and asked their pard if he took pay for the cartridges. He said, "Yes, I did. They cost *me* twenty-five cents. What of it?" The other said, "Nothing, only you're goin' to get a damn good lickin'. We stay here all night free, and then you won't give him a few cartridges. We'll learn you." They stretched him across the hind hound of the wagon, and hit him about twenty times with a two-inch cinch strap. I went out and said, "You fellows ought to be ashamed to whale that poor devil that way." One said, "*He* ought to be ashamed." They gave him a little more, and told him to pull back up the line to home camp – over a hundred miles.

The roundup working north passed our range in June. I baked up three sacks of flour the day before, two sacks the day of the roundup – five sacks in all – and had a big pile of fried bacon and lots of coffee, and told the boys to invite everyone to stop in and get a bite. It was awful rainy weather. That day it rained from ten o'clock in the morning till 2 p.m.; so the different outfits could not cook out of doors at their wagons. When anyone came by our cabin, some T 5 boy would holler, "Come in and fill up." No one refused, and the supply was nearly all gone when the day was over.

This hospitality of the cow camp was liable to abuse. Of the many men passing through – all accepted without question – there were some whose business was less than doubtful. To make matters more embarrassing, some of these were former T 5 hands who had reverted to earlier trades. It was the cook's duty to see that the place did not become an outlaw hangout.

About July Tall Horse and his brother, Dick, rolled in from the south with several good horses, which they parked off in the sand hills. They seemed to be on the dodge: Dick hung his belt and pistol on the end of the ridge log, hammer resting on a cap, pistol well loaded, and Tall Horse would mount the house and look around. I learned they had five "wet" horses they'd picked up in Texas. In the fall they went to Kansas, supposedly to shuck corn. They'd spot several horses, then wind up their work and leave; soon they'd return unbeknownst and get the horses, and on their way south they'd drop in on my camp. I finally told them a Kansas man had been down looking for them, and they quit coming my way.

Billy Smith traded in horses, and wasn't particular where they came from. He would get some from the north cheap and sell to some one going south; then get south horses and send them to Kansas. It was pretty safe. Once a fellow from Sun City came down showing a bill of sale for a horse Billy had. He stayed overnight. Billy talked with him all evening about things in general. Then in the morning he asked Billy what he was going to do. Billy said, "I'm not goin' to do nothin'.

You've got a bill of sale, and you're satisfied with it, ain't you?" The man said, "Yes." Billy said, "Well, I've got the horse, and I'm satisfied. Jesus Christ man, what more do you want? We're both satisfied. You might as well stayed in Sun City." Kansas horses were lost when they got down with us, and when our horses got up in Kansas *they* were lost.

In July a herd of company cattle was brought up from the King ranch. They were branded Laurel S S. I went south to meet them and point out a camp site. There were twenty-six men, two of them Mexicans. One Mex would not take his sombrero off. After supper when all were sitting in a circle a boy about fourteen, with the herd, went behind him, tipped the hat forward, and said, "Look!" There was a white spot on top of his head. The Mex took after the kid with his dirk and ran around the wagon twice. The kid sang out, "Stop him!" and several drew their pistols. The Mex stopped in his tracks, gritting his teeth like a hog.

The crew stayed at our home camp two nights. The boss told me to not let the Mex get hold of any knives or guns. Then Martin rigged up two trail wagons and took the men back to Wichita Falls, Texas to the railroad – leaving their horses at the T 5. On this trip the Mexican was not allowed to have his knife, and he got so mad he walked all of two days.

This outfit came from the fabulous ranch started in 1852 by Captain Richard King, now noted for its racing champions and hardy new breed of cherry-red Santa Gertrudis cattle. It still controls nearly a million acres of south Texas land, ranging from shifting coastal dunes to brushy plain. Now it is completely mechanized, with electrically lighted shipping pens and electric prod poles; especially designed jeep-like cars

*dashing across hills and ravines or following a many-
branched system of hard surfaced highways; and fleets
of huge trailer trucks transporting herds from one
grazing place to another. But it still requires the services of hard-riding Mexican vaqueros, who know how
to swing a lariat and patrol the fences for cattle rustlers.*

*Strictly speaking, the cattle brought to the T 5 came
from a tract temporarily alienated from the King
ranch. Mifflin Kenedy was Captain King's closest
friend and business associate. In 1860 he bought an
interest in the great ranching enterprise, but the
partnership was dissolved seven years later, and in the
settlement Kenedy retained the Laureles division. It
was this section that he sold to the Texas Land and
Cattle company in 1882.[3] It was soon apparent, however, to the T 5 cowboys that the stockholders were
becoming worried about their investments.*

The Scotch company got to thinking the divvy
wasn't showing up just right; so in September a man
named Davis, an old fellow about fifty, from Glasgow,
came to size up the range condition. He put up with
the Carters – stayed about two weeks – had his little
nine-year-old girl along. He would talk with one man
at a time, trying to find out things; but when several
were in, he would tell stories or the girl would sing
Gaelic and dance. He told us he had been at the King
ranch; said he rode a pitching horse down there, and
found it thrilling – was thrown but not hurt.

On the King ranch Davis with the help of the men
counted 67,000 head of Kenedy cattle and two thousand
horses. Then he went to the Horseshoe in the Panhandle, and they counted 22,000. At the T 5 he counted

---

3 For Mr. Nelson's account of this transaction see *ante*, p. 100. This tract
was eventually bought back by the King family, and now forms an integral
part of the ranch.

43,000 and three hundred horses. But this count was short of what the company was supposed to have, so his report riled the top men of the American interests, and there was quite a shake-down in wages and management. All this came later; for a time things drifted along same as before.

The shake-down came too late. The shortage was not the fault of the ranch managers or their hard-working cowboys. The fact was that the investors had never owned as many cattle as they supposed. Their purchasing agent had bought cattle here and there — perhaps at a fair price and a true tally — and then shuffled them around and "bought" them again. Thus the number mounted — on paper. When his tangled bookkeeping was finally unwound, it revealed discrepancies of hundreds of thousands of dollars between what the actual sellers received and what the company invested.

All this of course was hidden from J. Will Carter and the T 5 cowhands. It was their business to take care of real cattle, not statistics. Carter's integrity is apparent throughout Mr. Nelson's narrative. If he made any mistake it was in employing "Ben Adams" as range boss, thus increasing the influence of the Dogtown contingent. Nobody was expected to inquire too closely into the morals of a good cowhand, but the time was to come when the T 5 boys branched out into other business than ranch work. That, too, was in the future. A present problem was the remoteness of medical care. Two exciting trips that fall grew out of the infrequent illness at camp.

Trips to Caldwell

Mrs. Carter got sick. Oscar Mayes went to Kiowa, forty-five miles away, and brought down two women: a Mrs. Ramsey and Mrs. Chatham, the hotel matron, who later married Dennis T. Flynn, territorial delegate in congress from Oklahoma. Dr. Noble drove eighty miles from Caldwell and stayed overnight.

In the morning when the doctor was ready to start back, we saw that a fire had broken out about six miles southeast, with a heavy wind blowing from the south. It got almost as dark as tar. His trail would cut across the Spade range north of the fire, and we felt sure it would jump our plowed guard and catch him there. But he insisted on starting, so Carter told him to get some matches. He asked me for a few. I gave him a caddy. He said he would not need so many, but I said, "You must take them all. Use a handful at a time; strike on your boot sole, and when burning good, string out about ten feet. Then light another handful. But before you start using the matches, better wait till the fire gets to the guard; it might possibly stop there."

Later he told Carter that he did wait, but the guard did not check the blaze at all. Then he struck several matches, and the wind blowed them out. He then took a handful at a time as the cook told him to do, fired a strip about fifty yards wide, and followed behind it as it burned a lane north. When the main fire caught up, he took one lead strap and the driver the other to hold the horses, and they lay down on the ground as it passed by on both sides He said they could hardly breathe. After it passed, they took a good trot, but it traveled so fast they never saw it again.

The Spade (Bates and company) range, which the doctor crossed on the way to Caldwell, lay northeast of the T *5. The ranch had been established in 1877 by Frank Bates and a partner named Payne, both of Elmira, New York. The headquarters were ten miles northeast of the* T *5 camp, and the boys of the two outfits frequently met in friendly intercourse.*

One morning in October two men came in from the Spade camp. They said a little fellow inquiring for me had stayed there the night before; he rode a bad horse – it would pitch and throw itself backwards – but he'd be along after a while. Brother Charles, now eighteen, soon came in on a paint pony. He had a note from Aunt Mary, seventy years old; she had come out from Indiana, would be visiting my folks a week, would like to see me. I showed the note to Carter and asked if he could give me a week off. He said it would be just to his advantage. Fred Creigh was sick – was never rugged, and had been eating sour plums – and he would let me take him to the doctor; also would give my brother a job. He asked me which team of mules I would rather drive – three teams of Spanish mules had been driven up the trail with the King stock. I said the little black ones. They had been turned loose over two months – not gentle on the start. They were in the sand hills; had to be hunted up.

The next morning Carter came over to help. I roped one mule; it pitched and bawled. Carter caught the other; it did the same. We got the bridles on, then tied rags over their eyes to blind them, put on the harness, got Fred in the buckboard, and hooked up the tugs.

I got in and took the lines, and two fellows took off the blinds. Then we began to move. I turned them east in a dead run about a quarter of a mile to the creek crossing; then took a southwest road about the same distance and circled back to camp. I made this run twice, and got them down to a trot at the creek bank, so I turned in; they pitched all the way across, loosing one tug. Fred wanted to take one line, me the other, but I said, "No." They ran about three miles pulling by the lines; then I got them stopped and tied the tugs.

The trail had been changed since I came, for the north side of the T 5 was now fenced. It was fenced some time that year at a cost of $150 a mile. I had nothing to do with it; just knew it was being put up. An opening of about one hundred yards had been left for the trail. Fred was supposed to know the new road, but he didn't. We just followed one trail after another most of the day. Then I quit his directions; I knew the lay of the Spade camp, so I drove to a high hill, and there it was below us.

I drove up and several boys came out. I had them blind the mules, then tie the lariats. We got out, and I unhitched and put the team in a shed stable made in the bank. They had a frame cabin about sixteen feet by twenty, with a board floor. (A board floor had to be swept or it was dirty; at the T 5 I would sprinkle my dirt floor heavy, scrape 'er down with a shovel, and it was always clean.) There was two dugouts, which I didn't visit, some corrals, and a hitchin' post or two, no shade trees close. The place *looked* like a cow camp, but we had uncommon stuff to eat for supper – potatoes, onions, and canned goods.

Next morning I fixed for the good drive. One feller went ahead to open a gate. I got Fred in the trap; I wanted to sure take him along. A boy blinded one mule; I blinded the other with my silk 'kerchief, saying, "You hand it to me as I pass." I tied the tugs and got in. They took off the blinds, and I left in a dead run – missed my 'kerchief about six feet. When we got to the gate, the boy hid behind the fourteen-inch gatepost, but the mules wouldn't pass till he went off about fifty yards; then they took it in a high run. In about twenty miles I came to another gate. Fred opened it and went off a ways, and I drove through. But they wouldn't let him get to the buckboard. I finally had him hide in a buffalo wallow; then I passed close as I could and he slipped up behind and climbed in, and we went galloping on our way. At the next gate I had a foam on the mules, and they were not so timid. We got to Caldwell, seventy miles from the Spade camp, at about 3 p.m. We had passed through four gates.

The number of gates shows how rapidly barbed wire was enclosing the open range. It had been only two years since Chase and Sanborn had started to fence the Frying Pan in the Texas Panhandle, only one year since Oliver Nelson driving the chuck wagon out to the T 5 found the whole country open.

I put Fred in at the Moreland restaurant in care of Dr. Noble, then drove to a feed barn to put up the team. At the barn door stood Henry Brown, the marshal. I said, "How do you do, Henry." He just stood and looked. I passed on and he followed about ten steps behind. Somehow it seemed suspicion would loom up whenever a T 5 horse came to town. I learned later they had it in for us all, and he'd said he would make them T 5 men lay off their guns or kill every damned one of them. But I didn't have a gun – seldom carried one. Some boys didn't carry guns all the time.

Henry Brown had been serving about a year as marshal of Caldwell. Strong, fearless, vigilant, he was one of the few peace officers who ever brought the turbulent elements of that wild town under control. Law abiding citizens were too grateful to inquire into his past. They would have been deeply shocked to know that he had served as one of Billy the Kid's most active lieutenants. They were to be even more deeply shocked less than a year after Mr. Nelson's visit when at Medicine Lodge, Kansas he made a dramatic reversion to his old career of crime. But he was briefly an honest man in '83, apparently disappointed because he found nothing on Oliver Nelson during the night he stayed in town.

Next morning I hooked up, headed away from the business center, and left in a high lope. When I drove in home, I told the folks to stand back while I got out, blinded the team, and unhitched them; then we had a big handshake. Ad Sweney, a little cousin from Indiana, said, "Where's your gun?" He was plumb disappointed.

The fourth day I borrowed a saddle and rode one of the mules to Caldwell; I let Fred have a little money, and got the camp mail. The next morning I started back to the ranch. My youngest brother, George, opened a gate a quarter of a mile south; I blinded the mules and hooked up; then father took off one blind, George the other, and I left in a high lope. Father said, "I wouldn't have such a--" That was all I heard. When I came to a gate I would tie to the fence, open the gate, run through, tie up again, close the gate, and run on. When I got back, Carter said, "I never expected to see that buckboard roll into camp again."

I fixed up a mess wagon, and the outfit started to round up beeves to take to Caldwell. They would gather from the west side of Cheyenne creek, then Sand creek and Cottonwood. My brother worked on this roundup. Coming in to the camp on the Cottonwood on a wore-out horse one drizzly night, he struck the creek below the camp, and thinking he was above camp he turned down the stream instead of up. Finally his horse would only walk. He got off to lay down, but he saw two pair of bright eyes following. So he rode a little farther, then lay down anyhow, but held to the reins. At day when he got up, two catamounts were off about twenty steps.

After a bunch was gathered – about one thousand head – they aimed to drive them off the range the first day. It would take about ten days to gather that many, which was about the time it took to drive to Caldwell and back, so when the boys returned there was another bunch ready to go. The number of drives was governed by flesh and price. We had four in '83. The last one was in November. Then we settled down for winter.

Plots Hatched in Winter Camp

After the last beef drive they began fixing the winter camps. That year they'd put up only a little hay. Brother Charles and Fred Creigh were set to freighting for the outfit. I had only the horse wrangler as a steady. But men would drop in that I did not know. They did most of their talking outside of camp; it seemed they were restless.

Late in November a Reverend Mr. Lee came down from Anthony to survey the range.

The preceding March the cattlemen had got together at Caldwell and formally organized a "Cherokee Strip Live Stock Association," with constitution and bylaws, incorporated under the laws of Kansas. Then they made a five-year agreement with the civilized and constitutionally-governed Cherokees, leasing the entire Outlet – more than six million acres – for $100,000 a year. The Association surveyed and determined the boundaries of the ranges, and collected the rental – one and one-quarter cents an acre semi-annually for the lease and other expenses – from the individual members. The great ranching corporation functioned with surprising smoothness; but apparently its surveyor sent to the T 5 did not possess the robust type of piety that might have commanded the cowboys' respect.

Lee was about six feet tall, sixty-five years old. He didn't mix with the crowd much, had little to say, and would squint at a feller with a six-gun in his belt – which they all had. The boys didn't take to his style.

And he didn't take anything from us. Well, he might have taken a few graybacks, which were always in stock in the south camps.

Several of the boys were to go along and help him, and I fixed up a chuck wagon for the outfit. But it happened to be Saturday when he came, so he didn't start out next day – would not desecrate or something the Sabbath – just sat on a box and read the Holy Bible. He asked one boy how we observed the Sabbath, and the boy said, "We just do what we damn please." Later when settling up, he wanted his ten dollars a day for every day after leaving Anthony, but after Carter talked to him a spell he rubbed his Sunday charges off the bill.

When Lee and the boys went out on the survey, at first they all slept on the ground close together. But the boys would tell rough stuff, so he got to camping off out of hearing. And he would say a prayer every time 'fore he would tackle their slumgullion. When the next Sunday came he said, "This is the Lord's day. I will not go out." Potts said, "I don't give a damn what you do. Me and the compass is goin' to travel." Lee didn't take that day off.

He went next to survey the Quinlan range. It seemed them fellers didn't have the discipline we had, and they had a jug of tiger milk to help steady their nerves. After supper they got Lee to offer a prayer; then they began to sing, Lee leading at first, then when he rung off they sang on their own. They took a pull on the jug for a sacrament; and they hollered "Amen," and shot into the ceiling of the dirt roof with their .45 Colt pistols. Lee told me he took a corner on the floor without any blanket and lay there all night; and he finished their survey just as soon as he could. Later when all the surveys were finished they made a regular map of the Strip.

When Potts got done helping Lee he went to work on the south side. One afternoon in late fall he came in to my camp. It was a cloudy day and he was sour. He said he was going to quit. I gave him a message from Carter –"If Potts comes up, tell him to lay over till I come in." He said, "I don't care what Carter says." Then I gave him a message from Billy Smith at the west camp –"Tell Potts I want to see him." He said, "I don't care what Smith wants." Next morning it was drizzling from the northeast. I said, "It's goin' to be a bad day. You better lay over till it clears up." He said, "I'm goin' to shake the T 5 mud off my feet for good."

He saddled up and put one foot in the stirrup. I said, "You're going?" He said, "I'm going." I said, "Wait a minute." I went into the storeroom, got a slicker and slicker leggins that belonged to me, and said, "Put them on. If you can send 'em back, do so; it may help some-one else. If you can't, it's all right." He looked them over, said, "I never expected that of you," put them on, and rode off.

McPherson rode a line from the Cottonwood camp. In December he started for Caldwell, riding a slim gray named Chicken. He left home camp at sunrise, and got there 'fore sundown. At the Leland saloon he took on a little cat oil and started to yowl; offered to be one of ten men that would each give one hundred dollars for the scalps of Marshal Henry Brown and his deputy, Ben Wheeler. Someone soon brought his horse back of the saloon, and told him to ride for camp and stay there. This was about nine o'clock in the evening. He got to the Spade ranch in time for breakfast, and reached my camp at 9 a.m.– 160 miles since the morning before. That afternoon he rode thirty miles to the Cottonwood camp, and Chicken kept up his regular turn on the line.

The boys got it in some way for McPherson – I never knew why. One day they got to talking of laying out on his line and shooting his horse, and they hinted they might aim a little high. I thought well of McPherson, and so the next time he came to camp I told him, "You'll live longer if you tear out from here." He went right out, got on his horse, and hit for Kiowa. His leaving caused some guessing and a little disappointment.

Dick Broadwell, who was later killed with the Daltons at Coffeyville, hung up with me a couple of weeks that winter. He was a real nice fellow. His dad stopped and penned cattle with me two different times. I noticed he had several J D stock – my uncle's brand. I asked who he got them of, and he did not remember. I had brother Charles see my uncle to get the right to hold his brand; but uncle said when he wanted a *boy* to tend to his business he'd turn it over to us. Then I told Carter. He said he didn't want the camp to be a hide-out, so I told the old gent to hunt a new line on his next run.

Poor Dick! With those antecedents he had little chance to go straight. It was in 1892 that the attempt of the Dalton gang to rob two banks at once in Coffeyville, Kansas precipitated the most famous battle between outlaws and citizens in all western history. Four of the bandits, including Broadwell and two of the Dalton brothers, were killed. And Broadwell was "a real nice fellow" when he stopped at the T 5. The men who came to Oliver's camp represented a cross section of frontier life.

Billy Culver, the Creek boy, came in to camp one day, discarded his worn-out shirt, and bloomed out in new clothes. Harry Carter told me he was lousy. I said he had just changed clothes. Harry said, "He only took off the outside shirt." I said, "Billy, I got to look you over." I seen he needed some renovating. I cut his hair close, gave him a clean change, and said, "Throw all your clothes in the creek, scour up, put on this stuff, and leave the lice out."

Some time during the winter another Creek came and called for Billy Culver. I said, "He'll come in 'fore long. Stay overnight." When Billy came in, they had a talk and the next morning the boy left. Carter asked Billy what it was he wanted. Billy said his uncle had run afoul of the Creek law, was to be shot in a few days, didn't have time to come to see him, and wanted to send a farewell message. Carter asked, "Do you want to see your uncle?" Billy said, "No." Carter told him, "You can have a horse, and your time will go on." But Billy said, "I won't go."

The Creeks like the Chickasaws and Cherokees had a constitutional government and written laws. Their code imposed death by shooting for murder, theft (third conviction), and rape (second conviction). But lawlessness was serious in the Creek Nation at this time because it had just passed through the civil disorder known as the Green Peach war. Meanwhile transients continued to stop at the T 5.

A new man hung up with me a couple of days – I never found out who he was. When he got ready to leave, Smith held his horse and the two rode off together. I got my opinion. Sometimes I would hear a few words which indicated lots of business on the south side.

One day Carter met some hunters west of camp and gave them orders to get out. They came in and asked for enough provisions to take them to Kiowa; said they'd pay for the things. I said, "I can't sell you any, but if you'll take the Kiowa trail and agree not to shoot on this range, I'll give you enough bacon, flour, and coffee for four meals." They said they would not tell on me. I said, "If anyone asks, tell 'em, but do tell it all."

I got two boxes of .44 cartridges, paid for them myself, and asked them to shoot with me. We went to the shed stable. I used a rifle, and hit center at sixty feet. One of the men said, "Shoot again." I shot through the hole, and he, not seeing any mark, said, "Missed the board." I told him, "Go put a cartridge hull in that bullet hole;" then I shot, and knocked the hull out, not enlarging the hole much.

They soon left. Carter headed them off, and asked if they got grub and if they paid for it. Then he came to me, and I told him just what I had done. He said, "You know my orders against hunting." I said, "Yes, I do. But them men was hungry. They know the rules and will observe them." Still Carter didn't seem satisfied, so I said, "Mr. Carter, if I can't feed a hungry man and get his word that he'll respect our rights, you get someone you like better to do your cooking." Carter smiled, and that was all.

When snow was on in winter, the boys were supposed to hunt out the hunters. But Mrs. Carter was in Caldwell again, and Carter came down only about once in six weeks; so a hunting outfit with a little hooch and tobacco was perfectly welcome to the T 5 riders. They would hide them up the canyons and tell them to keep out of sight and have no fire in the daytime to create smoke. Scotty tried to clear them out, but a boy would ride ahead and warn them, so they could take their stuff to another spot. Once when he was looking for hunters, they shot his hat full of holes.

The boys spent much time in target practice. Oliver – even now able to read without glasses – had the combination of keen sight and steady nerves that made him the best shot in the outfit. One day he had a contest with one of the Crew boys, twin brothers known throughout the Territory for their dashing good looks, gorgeous trappings, and sure marksmanship.

A boy named Cliff Crew dropped in one day. He had a pearl-handled gat, a snakehide hatband, silver conchas on his spurs, fringed leggins, lugs in his ears, long hair – all togged out. Besides, being bad, he showed off swell, claimed he couldn't be beat with any man's gun. About ten men were in camp. They took him to the shed stable for target shooting. Ben soon came back and said to me, "We want you to come and shoot." I said I hadn't time – it was about eleven o'clock and I had to get dinner. Ben said, "You shoot first." I said, "Fix the mark, and I'll be down." The mark was sixty feet. I took a pistol, put the bullet as near the center as you could put your finger, and went back to my cooking. After they had fired several shots, Ben came to me and said, "Don't shoot again. He's beat now, and I want him to go away beat."

When they came in for dinner, Cliff said to me, "I'll bet you ten bucks you can't make that shot again." But I told him, "You beat *that;* I haven't time to play with you fellows." He foamed all through dinner, then went back to practice. He and Ben were to go south at one, but he stayed. All the other boys left, but he entertained himself in the shooting gallery all afternoon, getting farther from center all the time. He took supper, bed, and breakfast at my camp. In the morning he said, "I'll bet ten dollars I can beat you." I said, "You never have." He fired six more shots and left. He had tried every gun in camp.

Carter came in one day and asked if I knew what Potts was doing. I said, "He's broke at Medicine Lodge." Carter said, "Send him word to come and take care of the horses." So I soon got word to him, and in a few days he came. I went out and said, "Hello, John. I'm glad you're back." He came up and we shook hands, the only time I ever seen him take anyone's hand. This was about Christmas time. (But we were short of hay; so a little later the horses were taken to a place on the Kansas line ten miles west of Caldwell for the winter).

For Christmas that year I sent to Caldwell for some extras – lemon flavorings and such. I roasted two turkeys, which the boys sent up from the south camps, and I baked two cakes sixteen inches across and four inches high – baked them in the Dutch ovens. But a heavy storm set in Christmas eve, and all hands went to the south line to keep the cattle from drifting into the Cheyenne country. At noon a Greever man stopped in, and we ate Christmas dinner alone. Five days later a boy came up from the south, and I filled a gunny sack with the stuff and sent it down to the camps.

The boys at the line camps worked hard during the storms, but in nice weather they hadn't much to do. They sat in their dugouts and read up on Wild West history, especially gun men, and figured out the best way to steal Indian ponies and be plumb safe. Once in a get-money talk Billy Smith told how the U.S. pay-master used to come down the Cantone trail when there was a garrison at the post, and how he and another T 5 boy and two from Quinlan's layed out for him, aiming to shoot the guards and make away with the money. A bad storm came up, and they were afraid to have a fire and nearly froze. Then on that trip the paymaster went down to Reno first – taking the Chisholm trail – and the boys layed out two days for nothing.

It was common talk at the west camp that to rob the bank at Medicine Lodge would be an easy job. At the time I did not take their talk serious; I took it all for fun, and in a way it was – just deviltry and love of adventure – but there wasn't a thing those boys wouldn't do. And a prominent member of the Wildcat Pool, a treacherous windbag, was interested in the pony stealing and was helping them frame the bank robbery.

When the spring thaw came, life began to show signs of breaking out. Smith took on a boy named John Wesley and rode the range. I was not out much, but it was no trouble to find a bunch of split-eared Cheyenne ponies in the sand hills southwest of the home camp. The boys would hook a few, cross the Cimarron, and follow with a bunch of cattle to blot out the trail. If the Indians followed, some of the boys would be laying on the trail to shoot at them. A well-known citizen of Medicine came down two times, and drove a bunch of the ponies back. Smith let him take a little bay race horse, saying, "I won't sell him. If anything happens to me, Oliver here will be a witness to that."

Every night while the pony deal was going good, the boys would set a box at each door of the cabin with a bucket or can on, so that anyone coming in would wake the crowd. The guns were all full loaded. In the morning I was supposed to go out first and look around. During the day a pole with a white rag on was leant against the north side of the cabin, and I was requested to knock it down if anyone hove in that didn't look plumb safe.

One day Carter came down and said, "It's damn funny I can't meet anyone out from camp. What does all these Indian ponies mean in the sand hills?" When I told him, he said, "If they're stealing them, they'll drive them back." Then he went down to the Cheyenne country and told Buffalo to come and get his ponies. I told Smith the Indians were coming, and he said, "They won't be up." I asked why. He said, "There ain't been an Indian come across that river on the T 5 in the last five years and got back alive." (That may have been true; I know when I came I was told several Indian skulls lay near the lone butte south of the river[4]). But that time the boys did drive the ponies back.

Buffalo himself went to the Happy Hunting Camp before the spring was over. In April, Sam Horton, a horse trader, passed Cantonment with a bunch of horses. After they left the North Canadian, old Buffalo tangled with one of the Horton men and followed the herd to shoot him. Horton rode up behind the chief and shot him in the back with a Winchester. The Johns began to bunch up, and the herders said, "Let's pull for Kansas." Horton said, "No." But when about four hundred Indians lined up, the herders made a break for Cantone, and took refuge in one of the vacant stone buildings. Jim Kerwood, the bull whacker, was with the bunch; another was a man named Sam Pierce. A courier was sent to Reno for help, and the next morning the men walked out between two lines of troops. They were taken to Fort Smith to be tried before Parker, the hanging judge.

---

[4] Perhaps it is ominous that on some modern maps Cheyenne creek is named Skull creek.

Judge Isaac C. Parker presided over the federal court for the western district of Arkansas at Fort Smith from 1875 to 1896. He established a record for exterminating Indian Territory criminals, sentencing to death 172 men, of whom eighty-eight were actually hanged. But these drovers may not have been guilty of any crime. According to a contemporary newspaper the trouble originated when the Indians demanded toll for crossing their reservation; and Horton was obliged to sacrifice half of his herd to pacify them.

According to Pierce, Parker wanted to string them all up, but they got a change of venue to Wichita. Horton was held for a while, but turned loose later.

They Left Him There on the
Lone Prairie-e-e

*Nothing else in all his life on the range is etched so
deeply on Mr. Nelson's memory as the killing of John
Potts. As he presents the story in exact circumstantial
detail, it becomes a case study in human motives, of a
great waste of human capacities. It was completely
unnecessary. "I always thought it all happened because
Potts had been drinking," is Mr. Nelson's explanation.
But back of the drunken quarrel was an artificial and
highly romantic code, born of blood and violence and
nurtured by "western" thrillers. These boys were required by every book in their "library" to shoot by
certain rules and to die in a certain way.*

It was March 5, 1884. Ben Adams rode up from the
south side about noon. At about three the supply teams
came in – Fred Creigh and brother Charles driving.
Charles brought a jug of whisky Ben had sent for. Ben
asked me for a flask; I gave him one, and he and Potts
rode off together. There was a rule against gambling,
cards, and whisky on the T 5, and I generally managed
to enforce it at home camp; but nobody paid much
attention outside.

When Ben and Potts came back, I seen Potts was
feeling good, so I said, "Now Johnny, be careful." We
had supper by lamplight. Then Ben asked for the key
to the storeroom, and the boys all left. I was late in
finishing my work; it was about ten when I went to the

storeroom to get my provisions for breakfast. There Ben, Potts, and Espey sat on the floor. They drew a blanket over their laps when I came in. I knew it hid cards, but said nothing; Ben was range boss, and I knew about how far I could go. I got my stuff, and went back and was covering the coals. The others had bedded down: Charles and Fred in their wagons, the rest on the floor in Scotty's room. Potts came in and said, "I wish you'd fix some coffee." I seen he was badly teed, so I said, "I'll soon fix 'er, but John, you be careful." He drank the coffee, then went into Scotty's room. Scotty must have been up, and the lamp still burning. Even when Potts was sober, he didn't like this Scotch boy.

Just then Ben and Espey came into the cabin from the storeroom. They were talking. I heard Espey say, "I thought Potts was goin' to shoot you," and Ben said, "I didn't have my gun on, but I got 'im by the collar and could have handled 'im." I gathered the quarrel was over a bet Potts had refused to pay. While they were talking, I heard Scotty's lamp go to pieces. Scotty came into the cabin all worked up, and said, "Ben, Potts is in my room raising hell and tommy. He just shot out my lamp. I wish you would go out there and break him in two." Ben said, "I'll break his damned neck," and he and Espey went out to Scotty's room. I followed.

Dan George, who had been lying on the floor, had got hold of Potts and pulled him down to his knees, trying to quiet him; but Potts was cocking his pistol. He had his back to the door. Ben, coming in, reached down over his shoulder and took the gun out of his hand. Potts said, "Give me back my gun; don't shoot me in the back you son of a --." Ben started to hand it back, but Espey took hold of it. Ben tried to jerk it away, saying, "Leave loose, leave loose;" then as Espey held on, "I'll get another, and you won't take *it* away."

Then Ben came into my cabin, got a pistol from the box under the west window, and went back. By that time Potts was asleep. So Ben, Espey, and Dan came back to the cabin and talked a short time. Ben took Potts's pistol, knocked the loads out into his left hand, said to Dan, "Give him back his gun, and in the morning give him the cartridges. Or I don't care--" loaded the pistol again, "give it to him now and let him come in if he dares; I ain't afraid of him." Dan took the pistol and went out to Scotty's room. Ben and Espey talked a little longer, Ben saying, "I'll see what kind of leather he's made of; I'll make him fight or run." It was nearly one o'clock by now. Espey finally went back to Scotty's room; Ben slept on my cot by the south door, I on the pole frame in the northwest corner.

It was day when I awoke. Ben was still sleeping. I already had the bread made up in an oven, the bacon cut and in another, the ground coffee in the pot, and a bed of coals; so I soon got chuck started. When I was setting the table, Potts came in. He looked down at Ben, then at me, winked and smiled, then got a pan of water and went outside to wash up. I followed and said again, "Watch out; be careful." By this time Ben had waked up; he slipped on his trousers, buckled his belt, and pulled on his shoes and coat in no time at all, and was coming out. I went back inside. There was George McIndoo (Scotty), Harry Carter, Fred Creigh, Alec Adams, Dan George, and Ernest Espey. I said, "You boys that have been with them most, go out and keep down trouble." Potts said something to Ben I did not quite catch, though I know he did not want to fight. But Ben said, "If you say fight, fight goes." Alec and Espey were looking out the south window. I said, "If you won't go out, I will." I stepped to the door, and Dan followed. Brother Charles, who had been in the feed room (the place formerly used as a buckboard shed), had also heard Ben, and came outside at the same time.

Ben had drawn his pistol; it had a short barrel, and hung at his side. Potts was slower; he had a long-barreled pistol, carried well back, and his coat buttoned at the top. So he said to Ben, "We can settle it better than this. We've been raised together and friends. At least give me a show." And Ben dropped his pistol back in the scabbard. Then they drew together. I was just behind Potts. When I saw his coat move back, I stepped to the left, but I could see Ben over his left shoulder.

Potts got in the first shot, cut off some of Ben's right eyebrow. Ben's first shot hit Potts's pistol wrist, breaking one bone. Potts cocked his pistol, and Ben's second shot cut the wrist close to his hand, so that *his* second shot went almost straight up. Then Potts took his 'kerchief from his left coat pocket and laid it over his broken wrist, with his pistol hanging on one finger of his disabled hand; he took one step to the right, looking at Ben over his left shoulder. Ben fired again, a more careful shot, striking him in the left side, in front of his left arm. He fell flat, face down on the ground. Dan went up and caught Ben's wrist, saying, "You've murdered him. Don't shoot him any more."

Dan and Espey then went to Potts. He said, "I'd give a thousand dollars for a drink of water." So I brought him a drink, and we carried him into Scotty's room. As we picked him up he said, "If any of you boys write to my folks, tell 'em I died game. If he hadn't broke my arm the first shot, I'd a got him the next."

Ben went over to Carter's house and told what had happened. Mrs. Carter cried, but she never came to see Johnny. Carter came over and roasted us all good; he told Dan to go to Kiowa for an M.D. Dan cried; Brother Charles drank a cup of coffee; I ate breakfast, but no one else did. Espey waited on Potts.

At 2 p.m. Ben called Espey out of the room, and said for him to tell Potts he'd like to talk to him. But when Espey delivered the message, Potts did not answer. Again Ben called Espey out with the same request. That time Potts said, "Tell him to come in." Espey came outside, and Ben went in alone. When Ben came out and Espey went back, Potts told Espey, "Ben says he's goin' to Caldwell and give himself up. If he does, he's a damn fool, for if he skips now, he can get away."

The M.D. came down, a doctor from Ohio out on a visit. He gave Potts a dose to clear his throat, and Potts spit it at him, blood and all; had he not side-stepped, it would have gone into his face. Then he probed the wound, but gave him no more medicine. He charged forty dollars for his services, though we hauled him both ways.

Potts would swear at us at times; then he would say, "If I cuss you boys, I don't mean it. I won't be with you long." He died at 4 p.m., March 8, 1884. We buried him before sundown on a gentle rise about one hundred and fifty yards southeast of the camp house, about one hundred yards east of the present north-south road. There was no funeral – just five or six of us went down and put him in. When we were filling the grave, Carter said, "It looks like you boys wanted my wife to see that mound every time she stepped out of the front door." But the marks we placed there soon disappeared. I had Potts's knife, pistol, and four silver dollars; he left a saddle, a horse worth $175, and an unmarked grave.

I thought a good bit about things he had told me. He had been with me during most of February, and he had talked of his early life. He said he was raised in the brush country in Texas; was schooled in a picket cabin by a teacher that carried two pistols. He had a pard with a small pistol, who would shoot at anything passing the schoolhouse window, but they got afraid of the teacher, so after about a month they quit school. Potts then got a saddle tree and a cowhide; rigged up a saddle, bridle, and leggins of rawhide with the hair on; picked up a poor horse somewhere; and went off with the men.

He hired to an outfit on the Sweetwater, where a larger boy, the son of the owner, would run it over him, and draw a pistol on him when he'd show fight. One time he and the boy were alone at camp. The boy would make him kneel down, then jab him in the face with the pistol. After about half an hour, the boy turned to go away, and Potts picked up an iron coffee-grinder, throwed it, and struck him in the back of the head. The boy went down. Just then the boss rode up; he dropped his reins and went to the boy with a bucket of water. Potts crawled the boss's horse and started to increase the distance betwixt him and camp. The boss got in a couple of shots with a Winchester as he turned over a sand hill. Then the boss crawled Potts's poor horse to chase him, and some of the boys with the herd started shooting his way. But Potts took the best opening, got behind a hill, and gave them the slip. Night soon overtook him, but he struck a slow gait and rode till morning; slept till noon in a draw with water and good grass; then rode till late at night, when he came to an outfit going west, and got a job with them.

He started several stories of death and violence; then smiled and changed the subject. He had a bad cut on his left arm – could hardly use three fingers; he told me how it was done, then smiled – did not tell it all. He told a lot about Billy the Kid – gave the impression he had worked with him.

He told of a sheriff in the San Antonio country being shot, and his son, a boy of eleven years, vowed at his father's grave that he would trail the man and lay him down. He described the boy as having a rawhide outfit and a poor horse. He went to the neighborhood where the man lived, and met up with a horseman going the same road. They rode along together. The boy told his name, and the man said, "I knew your father." The boy said, "I'm hunting the man that killed him." The man said, "Now you're hunting big game. Better put it off two or three years." "No sir; I'm goin' to shoot 'im whenever I run onto 'im." After a while, a man came in sight on a side road. The boy's companion said, "That's your man. I'll ride past the crossroad, and you fall behind and take a shot when he comes out ahead of you." The boy dropped back, and when the fellow started to pull into the road ahead of him he shot and missed. The fellow then turned and drew his pistol, and the man ahead shot him in the back. Then the two rode together for a short distance; but the man soon turned off, and the boy rode on.

I always thought that was Potts's own story, that he was the eleven-year-old boy. As for his companion, I do not know. Once a man stopped at my camp; we got to talking of Potts's life and I told him that story. He said, "They never could pick out that third horseman. He ought never to have told you that story. But his name is not Potts."

In August, 1941 I talked to a "Steve Adams." (He was eighty years old; and said all the other "Adams" boys were dead). He told me the boy, Potts, was an orphan raised around Pleasanton, and that his real name was Billy Scrug. That was what Dan George told me once at the T 5 camp, that his name was Scrug. Dan said that he had a sister. He must have had some folks because of the message he sent when he was hit. I never knew whether the boys wrote or not.

Ben Adams wasn't present when Potts was buried. After the shooting he went to the Cragin camp northeast of us, and got what money they owed him on monte; and he got some of me on a debt Billy Smith owed him. The third night after Johnny's death I was out late. Seeing a horse and saddle going south I ran to it. Harry Carter was leading Ben's horse, T Diamond (named from its brand); he said he was going to feed it and that Ben was going to leave on it that night.

I just wondered how Ben felt when he took that long, broad, and lonesome trail. He rounded up at Miles City, Montana in '86. He and a soldier got into a row, and were parted by the law, agreeing to settle when they next met. Later when Ben was playing pool, the soldier stepped up behind and stuck a knife into his neck. By the time Ben was out again, the soldier was standing trial. Ben said, "Turn him loose; I would have killed him if I'd got the drop on *him*." I was told that always after that Ben rested his chin on his breast; that he finally died at Woodward, Oklahoma, sleeping in an unmarked grave.

I Quit the T 5

There wasn't much friendship in the crowd after Potts was killed. Most of us had a sympathetic leaning to him, while the Scot seemed pleased that he'd got lead poisoning – which didn't take very well with us. Then Alec Adams had been drawing boss's pay and helping Ben; now with Ben gone he kept on as boss, Scotty elected himself, and the two tried to run it over the rest of the outfit.

One cold day in March Alec asked me for some coal oil. I asked what he wanted it for. He said to put on Chicken – the horse had the scab and was very poor. I said, "Alec, go shoot Chicken if you want to kill him; but if you want to kill the itch take a little carbolic acid and tobacco juice and lots of water, only wait till a warm spell. And I'm not goin' to give you any coal oil." But at dusk he asked for the key to the storeroom, and he soon came back with an empty oil can. I said, "Did you oil Chicken?" He said, "Yes." I said, "I'll warm some water for you, and you take soap and water and wash it off and blanket the horse; I haven't time to do it." He said, "You go to hell." I said, "If I was boss, I'd fire you." He said, "I'm boss." I went over to the house and told Mr. Carter, but he said it wouldn't hurt. I said, "If you don't wash it off, you'll never lead him out of the stable again." The next day Chicken could not walk; and the second day they drug him off. Carter said, "There goes seven hundred dollars." Chicken was one of the best cutting horses we had.

There were two horses on the T 5 that would do nothing but pitch. Carter told two colored boys, called Balaam and Frank, to ride them or kill them. At a through camp one morning they put their saddles on. The horses pitched till noon. At dinner Frank said to Balaam, "No use us killin' ou'se'ves. We gotta have rest. You take you' regulah mount, and Ah'll ride mah outlaw. At fo' o'clock you take 'im. And jest leave de bridle 'n' saddle on de uddah, and tomorrow we'll take turns ridin' *him*." So they changed about, riding one bronc one day, the other the next. And the horse that was standing would not eat with the bridle on. After about the third day Balaam rode one of them down to my camp. I said, "Balaam, you're going to kill that horse." The darky said, "Lessen he quiets down, one of us is suah goin' to die." In about a week both horses were dead. The boys were slow for a few days, then good as ever.

Carter had bought plows, and in April he had Creigh plow a fire guard on the west side; then seven of us went to burn it out. (Brother Charles was sick, so he held camp and I went with the fire outfit). There were two strips of plowing thirty feet apart, and we burned the place between. Then we aimed to burn off the west side of our range, but the guard was supposed to keep the fire off the Greever range west of us.

The north guard had already been burned, so we began at the north end of the west guard. We did pretty good all day, working south against a south wind. At evening we were in thick bluestem about six feet high, where half the time the plow hadn't even touched the soil. I suggested going a couple of miles to short grass to camp, but Alec said, "No, we'll camp here." We staked the mules and two saddle ponies we had along, and bedded down. About midnight a high wind came from the north. The smoke got heavy. I felt pretty sure the gale had livened up the fire and was bringing it right down on us. I waked the crowd, but someone said, "Lay still; don't be so damn scary." The smoke got worse, and I could feel the heat. At near day I made up my mind to pull out. I hitched the mules up to the wagon. I thought the boys could shift for themselves, but I aimed to save the horses; so I saddled them, and tied them to the mules. Then I hollered, "Yay, fellows! I'm pullin' for sandy ground. If you want your beds to go, pile 'em on. The fire has already got past us, east and west." They jumped up in a hurry. Someone said, "Why in hell didn't you tell us before?"

We struck a high lope on a dim track south. Polecats got in the trail – strung out all along it. They made the mules pitch and snort till I had to drive outside. Deer showed up on every sand hill. When the fire surrounded them they would run back and forth, jump across where the blaze was lowest, and run north where it was already burned. The fire was on all sides of us, and on Greever, too. But we got around some sand hills, and made it to camp.

Carter asked Alec if he'd held the fire. He said, "Yes." The others all said the same. He came to me and asked, "Did you hold the fire in the guard?" I told him, "Mr. Carter, there was no guard at that end. And the wind changed on us. There was no way to hold it." Then he asked, "Where did the fire go?" I said, "You see that heavy smoke? That's the fire." He asked if Greever was burning off his range. I said, "He wasn't yesterday. He is now." It seemed I was getting in bad.

While we were burning the guard I heard Alec say that Charley Nelson would get fired pretty soon. So I told Charley, and Charley told Carter he would quit. But I don't know whether Carter intended to dismiss him or not. It seemed like Scotty and Alec had plumb lost confidence in Charley and I.

Charley had brought up some cedars to plant at Potts's grave. After he left, Carter set them in his own yard, saying, "I'll tend the grave." But he never did, and it soon leveled with the prairie. A few years ago a man living on the site of the old headquarters camp took up a body from a marked grave four hundred yards *south* instead of an unmarked grave 150 yards *southeast,* and buried it in a cemetery with a lot of fuss as the remains of Johnny Potts.

This man, of course, was Mr. McAdoo. His daughter says he was working on another part of the range when Potts was killed, but he, like the other T *5 boys, seems to have been deeply shocked by the tragedy. Apparently it was a great satisfaction to him to feel that he gave the lonely wanderer a decent burial. But when did two old-timers ever agree on exact locations? Here is Mr. Nelson's last word:*

I think likely he got the body of a boy named Clarence Pratt, who was shot a couple of years later. Anyhow it was not John Potts. Direction is pretty hard for an observing person to forget.

Scotty asked me for the things I held belonging to Potts. I said, "Only on Carter's order." But he said Mr. Carter told him to get them, so I turned them over. Then I told Carter to get a new cook. When my successor came to take my place, Carter happened to be on the south side and I wouldn't sign the payroll till he got back. But then he left the settling up to Scotty. Later I decided he did not know of our dispute and the division in the crowd, but at the time I was too mad to think. I just signed the payroll, took my check, and pulled out.

After I crossed the creek I heard three pistol shots. I looked around, and there was Carter on the cabin roof waving his hat. I was nearly on the prod, but I turned back and went over to the house. Mrs. Carter came to the door; she said, "Mr. Oliver, when you're leaving we want to say good-bye." The boy, Del, about four, said, "Mr. Oliver, when are you coming back?" And Carter said, "Oliver, I want you to understand that whenever you make up your mind to work for the T 5 your time begins right then. I don't mean when you get here or when you start back, but when you make up your mind. Just drop a card, and your time begins."

Then I regretted leaving. But there was general ill feeling and deception, and if I had stayed I would have had trouble with the Scot. The outfit was on the downgrade. All the old hands left in a short time. The next year Carter was put in as inspector for the company at Kansas City, and Hank Siders took his place as manager of the T 5. Then in '86 the company went broke, and the ranch was sold to Major Drumm.

It was about May in '84 when I quit. I rode a horse I'd got about nine months before from Billy Smith; a stolen Indian pony with a hole in each ear, from the Chilocco neighborhood.

Chilocco was on the eastern edge of the Cherokee Strip, close to the Kaw reservation. A boarding school for children of the Plains tribes in the western part of the Indian Territory was established there in 1884. It is at present the most important school maintained by the Indian service in Oklahoma.

Billy said he'd follow me home and leave sixty dollars for me and twenty-five for Charles, which we'd let Ben Adams have. Billy had business up that way. He and John Wesley and Marshal Henry Brown and his deputy, Wheeler, had been running through the Fall creek timber shooting at trees as they passed, fixing to hold up the Medicine bank – not telling it of course. I think Potts and Ben had been in on it, too, before Potts was killed and Ben had to skip.

When I got home Charles and George said they had a job for me. The settlers along the Kansas line had been letting their cattle run on the Strip lands south, but Treadwell and Clark claimed the range and fenced it. A little bunch of cattle belonging to my folks were enclosed in this pasture, and Treadwell ordered them out. The settlers were all cowards, but Charley and George made up their minds to cut the north fence along the state line as soon as I got there to help.

Treadwell and Clark had a lease – with the privilege of fencing – from the Cherokees, through the Cherokee Strip Live Stock Association. But pioneer settlers of course always felt free to occupy Indian land, and resented any leasing agreement between the tribal owners and the cattlemen.

Late at night we went to work, going east along the fence. We saw four horsemen coming toward us from the east, so we lay off the road till they passed. One man in the bunch looked to me like Billy Smith, but they did not stop. We went back to cutting the fence. It took us most of the night. Next morning the Treadwell and Clark stock came up into Kansas. A boy came up after them, and found someone had played hell with their fence. They offered a five hundred dollar reward for the culprit. We rode down and said, "Plank down the money if you really want to know." But nothing showed up.

Brother Delos had taken a job plowing, so I set in to help. While I was at work Ben Garland rode up. He said, "Oliver, they're killing all your friends." I asked, "Who's got it now?" He said, "Brown and Wheeler of Caldwell and Wesley and Smith of the T 5 went to rob the Medicine bank and killed the president and cashier; the citizens took after them and hung all four." So that was where they were going when they passed us riding west.

It seems their confederate in the Wildcat Pool held a bunch of Indian ponies Smith and Wesley had left for him to hide, as did several other worthy citizens around Medicine. They must have figured that if the boys passed out, the ponies would stay with them. Anyhow it was this confederate that warned the bank, and the town was ready.

The four rode up during a rain. Smith and Wesley kept the crowd away while Brown and Wheeler went in. Brown shot the president, and Wheeler got the cashier just as he closed the vault. Then they ran to their horses, but were slow untying the wet reins; so a bunch got ahead of them and run them up a blind road. Wheeler had one finger shot off, and dropped his pistol. Then his horse gave out – he was riding a large horse that had been winded. He said, "Leave me," but they all stayed together, took up a gulch, and got under a cliff in a hole of water. When the town people got there, three ran out and were captured, but they had to pull Smith out. They identified Brown by his gun – a Winchester with his name inlaid in silver, given him by the grateful citizens of Caldwell.

They cuffed Brown and Wheeler together, Smith and Wesley ditto, and put them in cold storage. But after dark the jail was opened by a mob. Brown and

Wheeler managed to get separated and made a run; the crowd fired on them and put out Brown's light and wounded Wheeler. Then they took all four down on Elm creek. Brown was still dead, so they hung him first. Wheeler didn't like to go, but he did. Smith asked them to send his money to his mother, then walked up under the limb. Wesley just said, "Let 'er rip," and took his place. It was believed that he was a nephew of the Texas outlaw, John Wesley Hardin; and Smith and Brown, like John Potts, were said to have worked with Billy the Kid.

Henry Brown's connection with the legendary Kid is well established. Johnny Potts and Billy Smith are not known to have been members of his gang, but it is possible that they were called by other names. The relationship between John Wesley and the notorious John Wesley Hardin may easily have originated from the similarity of names.

Brother Charles went to Medicine and put in a claim for what Billy owed us, but the judge and sheriff were insulting. The four should have left some property. Smith was riding the little Kentucky mare, which he had got some time before from Oscar Mayes, and two of the others had good mounts. They had four good saddles, four rifles, four pistols, and about three thousand dollars. But something happened to their money; not enough cash showed up to pay the grave digger.

When I finished plowing, I started for Comanche county, where settlers were going, aiming to take a homestead. As I crossed Barber county, I called on the judge at Medicine with my claim against Billy, but got no satisfaction. Then I stopped to see the man who had come down after Cheyenne ponies when I was at the T 5, and looked over his bunch. Seemingly he knew

Smith would go wrong, for he had a bill of sale to the little bay Billy had let him have, and to twenty-seven split-eared ponies. He was sewing up the ears, so they couldn't be identified. I got nothing.

From Medicine I rode on west. Southwest Barber county is all cut up with canyons. For about ten miles I followed a ridge road, very crooked but nearly level, with gulches on each side about two hundred feet deep; in some places this divide was not over twenty feet wide, never more than four hundred yards. That summer of '84 several men were killed on that road and rolled down the gulches, and their teams were driven west to Colorado.

But I rode on, keeping my smoker hid, and nobody bothered me. I reached Comanche county. Here the country was getting advertised, and towns were springing up promiscuous. I passed through Nescatunga – a church town, no booze, and a glorious future. Next I came to Coldwater. The town consisted of one tent with a keg of wine and a keg of whisky and the sign:

SNAKE PROOF HOTEL, Bob Cameron, Prop.

I was told Red Bluff, fifteen miles west, was the place to go. I got there one cold rainy day. The creek ran around a red bluff. There were stakes, but no people; so I turned back toward Coldwater.

Even though Oliver was "aiming" to take a homestead, he had small patience with the ways of settlers. He was disdainful of their land booms and townsite promotions. Fundamentally he felt that the sod was the right side up in the first place. He was repelled by their poverty. Most of all he missed the open-handed hospitality of the cow camps – the invitation to every passing horseman to " 'light and fill up" at the owner's expense.

Ten miles west of Coldwater, just at dusk I ran onto two wagons, belonging to one E. B. Peel and a fellow named Manning. They were what I would call broke-down nesters – people who just got to driving around looking for a place to settle their families. There was no other camp near and no houses. When I rode up, they were fixed for lunch. I got no invite, so got off, saying, "Well, fellows, just help yourself," and dove in. I got a dough cod, a hunk of bacon, and a cup of coffee, and began eating. I felt lots more at home than they seemed to. When it came to beddin' down, Peel, my chum (I took him on 'cause it was his coffee I got) said, "You can't sleep under my wagon." I said, "I can sleep any place you can." He had an overcoat; I had my slicker and saddle blanket. I said, "Hell, man! You ought to be proud of a bed like this." I seen we was gettin' plumb sociable. It drizzled all night; mercury about 40°.

Next morning the sun came up bright behind a cloudy sky. And without a start-in or take-off, I got my pard's coffee and some bacon and bread. He was gettin' so he didn't care, but the others looked at me sideways like they wouldn't want to form a habit on my style. On leaving I asked what they charged for the accommodation. Peel said, "Nothing, only I don't like to see a man so damned independent." I said I didn't like to have to be so damned independent –"but it's all owin' to the crowd you meet." Later on Peel was elected county clerk, and Manning put up a hotel at Protection – another new town, west of Coldwater.

Well, I got back to Coldwater, which now had two house frames up. I took the second claim north of town, but it was sandy, so I scouted around several days and finally located on Cavalry creek, seven miles southwest. I stopped a few days with Wood Fields and Al Mealy, just east of me, till I had a dugout fixed. Fields soon moved to a town named Reeder, six miles north, and Mealy hung up most of the time at Coldwater; but I stayed on my claim.

Holding Down a Kansas Claim

Living among nesters I saw some queer things. It seemed strange to me how little they knew about horses.

One evening Al Mealy came down to my place from Coldwater, and told me a mover's team had got away and there was a ten dollars' reward to bring it in. He said it was a farm team, had come from Arkansas, been gone two nights. Coldwater was in the Arthur Gorham pasture; the east gate was five miles east of town. The mosquitoes were bad and the wind was blowing from the south. I knew the team would have to follow horse nature. They would start back home, come to the closed gate, then turn south toward the wind, one following the other.

I told Mealy to ride to the gate and examine the tracks to be sure they hadn't gone through; then if they hadn't, to follow the fence south. I would work the country southeast, and turn north to meet him. I started at daybreak, and there near the southeast corner of the pasture I sighted them. I drove them back north; we met, and got the horses in by eleven o'clock. Mealy got the reward – which turned out to be five dollars in cash and five dollars in promise – and gave me half. In a few days he rode down and reported another team gone – this time twenty-five dollars' reward. We did just as before and got the horses in by noon. No reward. Soon there was a third team gone. Same result, same reward. They said, "Nelson is stealing teams and hiding them out." So for three runs I got $2.50 and the name of horse thief.

I never bothered again with stray stock except once when I was sorry for the mover's wife. She came and asked me to look up their team – a blind horse with a wild pony tied to its tail – that had been lost for seven days. She said they would gladly pay me if they could, but they had no money. I knew the horses wouldn't be along the east fence, because the blind one couldn't lead out; so I went down and found them in some red breaks with good grass and water, not more than four miles south of town – just where I knew they'd be. I put my saddle on the pony – which had never been ridden – and came back in good time. But a good many teams that got away were never brought in; they were driven west by rustlers and sold in Colorado.

A strange epidemic broke out that summer among the new settlers at Coldwater. Western travelers knew of a deadly disease that infested certain isolated sections of the Rocky mountains. They did not know that it was carried by a tick on the body of an animal, and thus might be brought to the plain. Widely scattered outbreaks within recent years testify to the truth of this danger. One can only speculate as to how it was brought to the tents and wagon camps and sod dugouts of the pioneer Kansas settlement.

A lot of people in Coldwater took sick with mountain fever. Seventeen died in August – just like sheep with rot. A lady was sick in a tent on a corner lot. Diagonally across someone set up another tent and started a saloon. It seems a dog had got a wolf bait and died, and every night the owner would come into the saloon to tell about the good traits of "Old Ketch," and call all the bums up to free tiger milk. Then they'd all roar and howl their sympathy mixed with forked lightning. I knew most of the town people, so one day I stopped at the tent to inquire about the sick lady. She said, "Is that the cowboy? If so, tell him to come in; I want to talk to him." I went in, and she told me she got no rest at all; during the day she could not sleep for the heat, and at night she was kept awake by the noise at the saloon. I said I would speak to the fellows.

I went over and told them of the lady's condition; I said if they would be quiet a few nights her folks would move her away as soon as she was able to travel. But 'fore I got through, several bums started in, "Of course we'll keep quiet; come over and have a drink, and help us keep still." I thanked them for the promise, told them I was sure the lady would get a good rest.

A canyon set in about seventy yards south of the saloon. I got some round stones a little larger than quail eggs and piled them up there where there was an off-set or bench about four feet down. I went to a lumber yard, got a soft pine stick, and cut out a rock thrower about three feet long. Then when it grew dark I tied my pony about one hundred yards down the canyon, and took my position.

The rounders soon started in: "Anyone that would poison a dog--" I began on my end of the program. At about the fourth stone I heard somebody say, "Look! There it went, right through the tent." The light went out. I don't think I hit it; I think the barkeep decided it was best to put it out. Anyhow the saloon got quiet. I waited about an hour, then went to my pony and rode back to my claim. Next morning I came in to see the lady. She said she'd had a good rest and was very thankful; to tell the gentlemen how grateful she was. I went over and told them what she'd said. A red-

muzzled guy with a pistol belted on said "Ye-ah!";
but they kept quiet. The dog was still dead.

A lot of fellows wanted plowing done, would pay
three dollars an acre for breaking sod. I went to Caldwell and bought three yoke of cattle and a twenty-inch
plow from my oldest buddy. But I didn't know nesters;
they run without a governor, nothing to check their
enthusiasm. I got only ten acres of plowing, and only
fifteen dollars in pay.

Next I turned to putting up hay. I had a little money
to hire a hand, so got Mealy to help me. We cut and
stacked about twenty-five tons. Brother Charles came
out to Comanche county about that time. He still had
the white-eyed blue paint he was riding when he came
to the T 5. Once Mealy tried to ride it, but it fell back
(threw itself over backwards) and he didn't care to
get on again. I took the reins and swung into the saddle
with no trouble. Charley could ride it; if handled
wrong it would pitch, fall back, bite, or kick, which-
ever was easiest, but it worked O.K. if the other fellow
worked right.

Charley settled on a claim joining mine. He was too
young to file, but he held it by bluffing. Then sister
Anna came out and took another adjoining claim.
Charles took my three-yoke team of oxen and began
hauling freight from Kinsley, fifty miles north. But
soon Anna and then Charles took down with mountain
fever. I took the oxen and freighted in Charles's place,
hauling lumber to Coldwater. (I remember there was
one yoke that hauled from Kinsley that could keep up
with horse or mule teams).

On my second trip I took to ailing, coming down
with the fever. I could hardly keep track of my cattle.
My brother Delos, just getting to Coldwater with three

yoke of his own, was told of my condition. He headed north, met me out a few miles, and spiked the teams. He was a good hand with a whip. I think every man in town was down on Main street to see the only six-yoke team that ever passed through Coldwater.

After Delos brought me in, I stayed with a family in Coldwater. I never gave up, but walked up town every day to see the M.D., a man named Tincher. I soon noticed that when I went into his office several would be there watching, and someone would take my arm and help me. I was told later that when I would start off the doctor would say, "This is his last trip." I lost forty pounds, but I finally started to mend. As soon as I was able I stayed with Charles or Anna, and Delos looked after my claim.

Dr. Jennings at Reeder waited on Anna and Charles. He had several boys who could not control their steam. They would ride to Coldwater, get stewed up, and leave town in a high run – gathering wild oats to sow later. One of them, Al, got to holding up trains and was sent to a federal penitentiary. Terrible Teddy turned him out. Later he ran for governor of Oklahoma. Then I lost track of him.

For a number of years Al Jennings has been living in California, writing moving picture scenarios and speaking to church groups as a lay evangelist. He was not exactly "turned out" by "Terrible Teddy." According to his own account he was released from prison by President McKinley through the influence of Mark Hanna; then several years later Theodore Roosevelt restored his rights of citizenship. It was in 1914 that he sought the democratic nomination for governor of Oklahoma, and he placed third in the primary election. Oliver Nelson seems to have had a genius for crossing the paths of picturesque Western characters. But it all came in the day's work.

When we all got well again, Delos and Anna returned to Caldwell and I went back to my claim. One yoke of my oxen had wandered off while Delos was keeping the place. Seventy-five dollars gone! Next, range cattle began destroying my hay. Brother Harry was with me by that time – I think he came out in November – so he helped me haul it to Coldwater to sell. The price was six dollars a ton. (I could have got seventeen dollars if I had held it longer). I kept only what I needed for my own pony. When we finished hauling, Harry started back to Caldwell taking along my two remaining yoke of oxen.

I was putting in a bank stable. The ground froze three inches deep, so I had to finish with a grub hoe. Charles had come up to my claim. We put the two ponies into the stable, and that night it snowed – five inches deep. It was December 17, 1884. We holed up for the winter – all underground. We had a stack of hay, some shelled corn, a pile of cow chips, flour, coffee, bacon, beans, and a fireplace. It just kept snowing about once a week.

Southwestern Kansas was still a range country. John M. (Dock) Day held cattle on the west half of Comanche and Kiowa counties and two other counties west, and about the same area south of the line in the Cherokee Strip. The Arthur Gorham range was in the south part of Comanche county and also in the Strip. There were several small ranges east.

The cattle were fat in November. With the snow they came to low ground. It rained twice between Christmas and New Year's, then snowed and froze; six inches of ice covered the ground, then more snow on top. Sometimes a ball of ice would form on a cow's nose – a ball five inches across, with two small holes made by breathing. The poor things just walked the creeks and bawled. The mercury got down to 17° below. In February their feet, and then their legs froze. When it would turn warm, the legs would break at the ankle or knee. Sometimes they would rest on the pegs a day or so before they would lay down. When down, they could not get up. They died by thousands. Then in March the snow went off. There was plenty of grass under it, so that the cattle that hadn't died soon got stout again. But the spring roping nearly always took off their horns. This was the winter that broke the stockmen, though most of them managed to hold on till '86.

After the snow melted, I went with several men on a twenty-five mile hunt down into the Indian Territory. We got a shot at some antelope bunched up on a hillside and wounded one, but the crowd did not want to go after him. We drove to the salt plain on the north side of the Cimarron, just across from the mouth of Buffalo creek.

This is the Edith salt plain, a few miles northwest of Freedom. It is a strange and desolate place, especially in summer with mirages playing over it and merging with the gypsum-capped bluffs across the river. It has changed very little since Mr. Nelson saw it.

This plain was about a mile wide and three miles long. A small stream of green water came out from between two hills to the north and crossed it; it was bad tasting stuff, but worse if you swallowed it. Croton oil! Another stream ran across the plain, of clear water, thirty feet wide and six inches deep, with an inch and a half layer of salt on the bottom. I was told that in dry seasons salt six inches thick would form in these crossing streams. And it was said that on the south side of the river, salt could be found under the sand of Buffalo creek. The Cimarron was only about two feet lower than the plain; it covered it all in times of high water.

In April father came out and filed on the claim brother Charles had held. Charles then started out for the Texas Panhandle. It was two or three years before I saw him again. He followed the drives to Wyoming, Dakota, Montana. I let him take my pistol with a bone stock, also my pony that I'd got from Billy Smith, and he let me have his blue paint. I had made proof on my claim in February – one could preempt government land in six months with the privilege of buying it at $1.25 an acre – but I stayed to fix up for father and sister Anna. We built a sod house on each of their claims. But it was not long before I was back on the range. This time I followed the roundup.

Following the Roundup

In the range country the roundup was for the purpose of gathering the cattle that had drifted south with the winter storms. It usually began with good spring grass. It started in south Texas and worked up through Texas, the Indian Territory, Kansas, Colorado, Nebraska, Dakota, Wyoming, and Montana. The cattlemen of each district formed an organization. They elected a captain, who ate with the bunch, slept on the ground wet or dry, took no favors, carried a Jane Gunter[5] with a walnut stock, and only told you once what to do. He kept a pretty good tab on what was ahead; sent on word, "Will work your range in three days."

Say a range was twenty-five by thirty miles. The day before the roundup, the range outfit would work their cattle toward some central point, where there was a good level tract – usually bottom land – free of dog or badger holes. Then the roundup lead would pull in; probably ten or fifteen outfits, each camped with its own chuck wagon; and perhaps some extra men riding alone.

At 2 a.m. on the day of the roundup two men started from each camp for the outside of the range; then separated and went in opposite directions, circling the range, till they met circling riders from other camps, all the time hollering as loud as they could and in rough country firing pistols, to drive the cattle toward the

[5] Mr. Nelson explains, "We called our gats Jane Gunters because we used them to smoke our adversaries with. A Jane Gunter was really a pipe."

center. When these outside riders met, they turned back on their circles, this time looking for any trails leading off the range; if they found any, they followed and brought the cattle back. Meanwhile at the camps, other pairs of riders started out later to form a smaller circle, to turn the cattle in closer. By daybreak several were out from each camp; at good daylight, perhaps forty men were on circle. By about eight o'clock cattle – or clouds of dust – could be seen coming from all directions down the slopes toward the level place selected as the roundup ground. The chuck wagons would begin to move in close by 10 a.m.; also the remudas would begin to string in to be convenient to change mounts at noon. By twelve the cuts would be near by; these were bunches of cattle belonging to other ranges that had been picked up farther south and brought along following the roundup.

The men would eat dinner; then all would take fresh mounts. Some horses were taken along only for separating or cutting out. They knew just how to go into the herd after a cow brute, and follow it up, turning and twisting till they got it out. A good cutting horse might be valued at $1000. The usual herd had three or four thousand head of cattle. Some ranges had as many as fifty thousand head, which was too many to work, so they would cut into five or six bunches.

The captain would ride through the herd and notice the predominating brand; then tell the boss of that outfit to put in three or four of his men to work the bunch, cutting out their brand. The rest of the outfit would be holding their cut-out bunch close to the main herd; so the cattle gave little trouble, walking from one bunch to the other. After one brand was all cut out, the men representing the next most prominent brand would go in and get their cattle. And so on till they were all separated. It was the rule that all unbranded calves followed the cows.

Some ranges would have a lot of old bulls, which would have a terrible time finding out which was best. No one would ride out to part fighting bulls, but sometimes they would drive the herd off to another ground. Here is something strange: no bull with horns can handle a muley. The muley gets between the horned bull's fore legs and throws him; whips him every time.

After the brands were all separated, the home cattle were held only long enough for the calves to find their mothers. Then they were scattered over the range. The others were driven away by the owner or his representative. Nobody else was allowed to take them. Nobody could claim fresh-branded stock without a satisfactory bill of sale; otherwise they were left on the range. Mavericks (unbranded stock, not calves with their mothers) also belonged to the range. Stray beef steers with nobody representing their brand were shipped to market with the shipper's own cattle. All the large stock yards, like those at K.C., had licensed inspectors who settled for these strays, giving five dollars a head to the shipper, and all above the expense of shipping, yardage, and selling (which totaled about fifty cents a hundred) to the owner of the brand.

I was told there were seventy-five wagons in the roundup at Ford, Kansas in '85, with an average of five men to a wagon, and six horses to a man. Some boys following the roundup would be four hundred miles from home camp. (A man was a boy till he quit the range). They worked in all kinds of weather – hot, dry, wet, and cold. Nearly all had good blankets and slickers, Stetson hats, and guns. Boys going long distances alone usually had tied to their saddle a plug of tobacco and a piece of bacon – if very thirsty they held a piece of bacon in their mouth to keep it moist. When they got away from their wagon, they took their meals at any place that was handy.

The beef roundup, such as we had in the fall on the T 5, was different from the general roundup. It began in July or any time when stock was fat. The boys just worked their own range, and collected the cattle that were ready to drive to the railroad.

The roundup in Comanche county began in May. I followed it several days on Old Paint, hoping to find my yoke of steers, but I never did; I figure they were butchered by local talent. We run up and down half a dozen creeks: Coldwater, Cavalry, Bluff, Kiowa, Satanta, Rattlesnake, and others. I seen dead cattle everywhere, all over the range. There were thousands in the forks of streams bearing south – carcasses just pushed together, covering twenty acres. The smell was awful.

Seemingly there was no system to the roundup in Comanche county, no director; supper and breakfast all right, but dinner whenever one found a chuck wagon. One day eight of us came up to a wagon. The boss told us, "I've got grub, but this boy is new, and I don't know how to cook; that's all there is to it." I said, "Send the boy after chips"– B.S. coal –"and you set out the plunder, put coffee and water in the pot, and cook the bacon; and we'll fix something to chew on." I made bread, the man fried the bacon, I fixed flour gravy, and soon we were each feeding his face. When I started to clean up the pans, one of the boys said, "I'll take your horse and leave my fresh one, so you can catch up." Before I got done, ten more men were in sight. I told the boss, "Send the boy to the coal mine and put on the coffee, and I'll help you out." In a few minutes I had the same as before, and plenty of it. As the men 'lighted, I rode away.

My horse was getting jaded, so I concluded I might as well ride other men's stock and get paid for it. The next afternoon I rode up to a Day wagon with ten men, and said, "Can any of you fellows give a man a job?" The boss turned out to be John Edgar. He said, "Can you cook?" I said, "No." (Cooking on the round-up is hard work, so I preferred to work as a cow hand). He then said, "If I send you with a wagon, you can show a fellow how to cook, can't you?" I said, "Yes, I can do that." He said, "Go down to camp and turn your horse out, and come back and start in." While I was fixing my saddle I heard one of the boys say, "Now he says he can't cook; how in hell is he goin' to show someone else?" Edgar said, "I'll risk that." He had been in the bunch that rode up to my chuck the day before.

The Day camp was on Day creek, about ten miles southeast of Ashland, in Clark county, just west of Comanche. There was a white six-room, story-and-a-half house facing the south, with a wide hall cutting across north and south through the center. There was a board fence around the house, and two hundred yards east was a corral of two by six pine planks, enclosing about an acre. The land east was level, sand hills south and west; a mile south was the Cimarron. Several cottonwoods grew on Day creek.

The Day brand was D Cross, later changed to D D D, on each side. The horse brand was D Cross on the left hip. (A horse's skin is not as thick as a cow's, so was given fewer brands, and the brand was smaller and not burned as deep). Day was in hard straits; the settlers were pushing him off his Kansas range, and then came the hard winter. I was told that at K.C. in December he had set a price on his holdings, but at the next talk he had jumped the price up twenty thousand dollars. The buyer asked a few days to think it over. Then the December 17 storm set in, and they waited for it to let up – which it never did till March. That winter broke him, though he held on for a year longer before he gave up.

That evening I helped Hank – the cook I was supposed to train – fix up his mess wagon. The next morning we pulled south for the R Bar S on the Beaver, six miles west of Fort Supply. There were four of us – the other two were Leroy Bowman, the wagon boss, and a man we called John Whiskers. We stopped that night at the R Bar S (Red Odum,[6] boss) and turned our horses in their pasture. Whiskers started to show Hank how to perform on chuck mixing; I told him that was all I came along for, so he backed off. Later I learned he was sweet on Hank's sis.

We camped near the R Bar S several days. Hank was quick to learn. I had him stand back and watch me, then try out. I told him one thing was to be on time; then correct proportion, mixed right, and not overcooked or underdone. We had flour, coffee, salt pork, soda, a few country dried apples with a lot of dog hair in, and sugar for Hank and Whiskers.

The three of us left Hank with the wagon, and went to tie in with the roundup down to Reno. On the way back a bunch of us stopped at a canteen in Supply. Amos Chapman, chief scout, and Sim Holstein, our roundup captain, met. In their talk our captain said, "If them Indians kill any of our boys, I God, I'll hold

---

[6] Red Odum's real name was Bill Meadows.

you responsible for it." Amos growled something I did not catch. I just thought of two bulldogs. Some Indians dropped out (shot by cowboys) but no boys were bothered. Every cowboy carried a Colt pistol, and the Indians just stayed in their camps and didn't show up around us.

When we got back to trailing our wagon, Hank was putting up choice bread. He told us, "Bring some one in to try my biscuits." His dinner bunch began to grow. One day about twenty rolled in. He just blowed up; said, "That's too damn much work." The next noon in came a full bunch, but the bread had no rising, no shortening, not one hole in two sinkers – one of the boys said, "squatted to rise, and baked on the squat." After that Hank was much by himself at noon. I got so I would eat at another wagon when I could.

From Supply we worked northwest up the Beaver. The Y L outfit, which held a range in the west end of the Strip, had bad horses and most new boys. The boys would catch a horse and tie up one front leg, then put on the saddle; or they would rope and throw him, and roll him into it. If they couldn't pry his mouth open for the bit, they would take the bridle apart and slip it in at the side. All the horses would pitch; some would bite, kick, and fall back. Some of the boys just fell over forward; it didn't seem to hurt or bother them much.

The Y L Ranch had been established in 1880. It was capitalized by Webster, Hoare, and company, an English syndicate, which floated $500,000 in preferred and $500,000 in common shares. Its headquarters were on Kiowa creek near the present Laverne, two or three miles from the west line of the Cherokee Strip; and its cattle ranged in the Cherokee Strip, the Texas Panhandle, the present Oklahoma Panhandle, and southwestern Kansas.

The Y L *brand is still burned on cattle in the Okla-home Panhandle. When the great ranch was forced to sell out before the crowding of homesteaders, R. A. (Bob) Maple acquired the brand and set up on a small scale in the sand hills northeast of the present county seat town of Beaver. When he died in 1935, his capable wife took over the active management. She raises registered and commercial Herefords — about 350 calves a year — and uses registered Arabian horses alongside motorized transportation. The pastures are fenced and cross-fenced, but the cattle are worked at the headquarters on Timber creek, where a large square two-story house, a beautiful pond stocked with bass, and a grove of huge cottonwoods make an oasis in the expanse of grass and sagebrush. All this was far from the experience of the Day cowboys.*

We followed up the Beaver into what is now the Oklahoma Panhandle, then called the Neutral Strip or No Man's Land. It was 168 miles long and thirty-four and one-half wide. It had no government and it didn't belong to anybody. It had been left out some way when Texas and Kansas were formed, and it hadn't been given to the Indians.

The historian will remember that in the Compromise of 1850 Texas relinquished all claim to the land north of latitude 36° 30′ in order to maintain the division between slave and free territory established by the Missouri Compromise; then the Kansas-Nebraska Act of 1854 fixed the boundary of Kansas at the parallel of 37°, and Colorado was formed on the same line a little later. This left a strip half a degree wide between Texas on the south and Kansas and Colorado on the north. And the same Compromise of 1850 fixed the eastern boundary of New Mexico at the meridian of 103°;

while the grants to Indian tribes, which brought about the segregation of land known as the Indian Territory, had been made in the 1820's and 1830's when the hundredth meridian was the western boundary of the United States. Thus the ends of the tract were bounded by New Mexico on the west and the Indian Territory on the east. It was literally a No Man's Land, completely outside laws and courts and any legal system of land tenure.

Across the country lay the famous Jones-Plummer trail, first used for the buffalo hunting traffic of the Texas Panhandle in the early 70's. Ed Jones and Joe Plummer, two hunters turned merchant, had opened a trading post near the head of Wolf creek selling hunters' supplies and buying hides, tongues, and cured meat. Their freight trains had made the first track across the prairies to the railroad at Dodge City. South of their place the trail was extended to another supply house and hide market on the Sweetwater, maintained by Charles Rath and Robert M. Wright, well known hide dealers of Dodge City; then on to a post called Rath City, near Fort Griffin on the south Plains. This section was often called the Rath trail. In No Man's Land just south of the Beaver a southwest fork branched off from the Jones-Plummer trail to follow up the Beaver and Palo Duro creeks to another Panhandle trading post known as Zulu Stockade. But the hide business had vanished before Mr. Nelson's time, and the frontier highway now carried the trail herds and freight wagons and stage traffic of the ranching industry that succeeded it. The southwest branch led to the riotous cow town of Tascosa on the Canadian, and the south fork to the equally riotous Mobeetie and near-by Fort Elliott in the vicinity of the old trading post on the Sweetwater.

A few people were living in No Man's Land. Where the Jones-Plummer trail crossed the Beaver was a stage station – wire corral, hay-covered shed stable, sod cabin in one corner – and a sod house with a dirt roof, where Jim Lane kept a supply store and post office. Cowmen were using the range. One was Colonel Jack Hardesty (brand, s Half Circle) with headquarters on Chiquita creek, which comes into the Beaver from the south. They had two sod dugouts with doors on the south side, and a shed stable west.

We went away up the Beaver, then drove across to the Cimarron, came back to the Beaver and followed it well up toward the west end of No Man's Land. Then we turned back east with cattle we'd gathered, and joined in with the roundup further down the Cimarron. The lay of the country up the Beaver was fairly level, but in some places there were sand hills on both sides.

When the roundup was above Palo Duro creek on the Beaver, we run onto about twenty-five buffalo. Nearly all of the men – seventy-five or so – took after them. The buffalo had a mile the lead. The land was solid and level; then they struck an upgrade and outran the horses. A few of us stayed and held the cattle; we knew if we let them scatter we would lose two days. When the buffalo hunters came back, their horses were completely fagged. But they had caught one calf. I rode to a camp a mile or two away to get a piece of the meat, but was told it was still further up stream. So I asked for some beef and forgot it.

The cowmen of the Texas Panhandle had built a fence along their north line to keep cattle from drifting in from No Man's Land. Some of the cowmen in No Man's Land had started to fence their ranges too, but in 1884 U.S. marshals had cut the wire. Then came the bad winter and the cattle drifted all the way across with nothing to stop them till they came to the Texas fence. When we were working that country I saw drifts of dead cattle along that fence sometimes four hundred yards wide, just like they had bedded down. There would be some vacant places, but not many; carcasses were pretty much all along. A few buffalo had died with them. Some bunches of antelope also lay dead on the flats, and along the creeks the quails had nearly all died.

Working these ranges we finally got a bunch of about three hundred D Cross cows and about one hundred calves. Most of the calves had wolf bites on their backs; some had a strip of hide three inches wide hanging from hip to knee. We would catch them and cut these strips loose. Some cows had half the bag eaten off, and one yearling had its tail eaten off, but I never saw any that had been hamstrung.

Thus Mr. Nelson is skeptical of the assertion sometimes made by old-timers that wolves would disable cattle by cutting the large tendon in the hock, before they closed in for the kill.

Most of this damage was done by the big gray wolves called loboes or "loafers." Following the cattle they would make tracks as big as calf tracks. But once I run onto two coyotes attacking a steer, which was trying to fight them off; they had cut a hole in its flank, and pulled out a piece of entrail about ten feet long. When I came up, they ran off and the steer lay down to die.

We started to drive this bunch of cows and calves from the Beaver to join the roundup that was working down the Cimarron. It was about a seventeen mile drive – too far for one day. It would take the stock a week or so to get over it. But that was how the Day outfit worked. Day was no cowman.

It was early in June and the cattle were in good flesh. We started about noon. There were five of us. The drive went very good till 4 p.m.; after that it was a drag. We got so we couldn't holler; then we took down our ropes. Bowman would say, "Don't whip 'em, boys; holler," but his own holler played out 'fore sunset. We had no trail. When it got dark we went by guess; once in a while I could see a light farther on, and we headed for it. We hit the roundup bunch about midnight. I can't tell yet how we made it.

Soon we gathered another D Cross bunch and started northeast for the roundup on the Cimarron. We were between the Cimarron and the Beaver, quite a ways up. It rained all afternoon. We pushed the cattle as far as we could, and camped after dark on high ground. The bunch drifted some before the rain, then stood with tail to the storm; we all sat on our horses in front, ready to hold them. The rain turned to mist. The night was heavy, foggy.

Mr. Nelson's careful description of the close, heavy night is important, for he was about to experience one of the strangest phenomena of the High Plains. Old-timers of that region still tell of trails that glowed with a dull light a considerable time after the herd had passed over, of balls of fire hanging on the horse's ears, of streams of sparks flowing across a break in the wire fence. But apparently atmospheric conditions had to be exactly right for these electrical displays – just such weather as Mr. Nelson remembers.

A ball of dim light about ten inches across would come with the wind, roll along the back of a critter and then on to another; if it came to a vacant place it would drop to the ground, then mount and roll along the next back. The boys said I didn't see it, that I was sleepy and imagined it. But a ball rolled that way across the herd and fell in front of a calf, and the calf bawled and jumped. About twenty head followed. I took after them in a dead run. In about fifty yards my horse went into a gulch about ten feet deep, with four feet of running water at the bottom and the calves coming in from all sides. I jumped off and led the horse, following the water till I found a path; then I rode back to the herd, the calves following. I said, "Boys, if the cattle run, don't follow. We're on the breaks." It was a very dangerous country; daylight showed red breaks straight down, some as much as forty feet. My horse was no good afterwards on night herd.

Several other times that summer I was lucky riding in rough ground. One day on circle I was riding a clumsy horse. When we came to an old trail he fell, and I flew off ahead. When we picked ourselves up, there was dirt on the horn and cantle of the saddle. At another time on the side hill my mount stepped in a badger hole and went down. I fell on the low side, my leg underneath. I caught the cheek of the bridle and held the horse down till I could work myself free. It took me an hour.

When we got the country all worked, we started bringing our D Cross herd, near three thousand head, down the Cimarron. We had ten men, nearly all kin. At noon the right way is for half the boys to go to camp to eat and change mounts, then come out to take the herd, and the others go in to eat and rest an hour while the cattle graze. Then when the second bunch comes back with fresh mounts they start the herd. But here the first noon all the lead men went in; the others left, one at a time; and I stayed on herd till two. Then the bunch came out, and I rode in. I found the wagon ready to leave. They had a fresh horse tied up for me, but the cook had plumb forgotten to save any chuck. I said, "That's all right, George," took a cold sinker and a drink of water, and let it pass; changed mounts and rode off.

Next noon it was the same thing: all go to camp, lay under the wagon two hours, and forget me. I said, "Now George, you're goin' to form a habit of this; then when someone goes to change your way you won't like it at all." And sure enough, next day when it happened again he acted like it was my fault more than his. Edgar lay under the wagon – he carried a pearl-handled gat. He said, "Bolivar,"– that was my name on the range – "Bolivar, you was howling yesterday." I said, "And you and seven others lay under the wagon from eleven till two, and knew I was on herd alone." I told the cook, "I won't bother you, George;" got in the wagon as he was hitching up, throwed out a sack of flour and a slab of bacon; went to his mess kit, took out half he had; then said, "Now George drive on; this won't happen again." The next day I rode in with the lead, and Edgar sent a cousin out to hold the cattle.

Soon we got our bunch down to the Day range. We aimed to work the home range last.

Working the Day Range

When we worked the home range, we gathered 3,300 coming yearlings. (Some calves were born in the fall instead of spring). Many were not weaned. One would get away from the herd and bawl; then a quarter of the bunch would tear out in that direction. They would run one way, then another, then try to follow the rider. It was hard work. We changed mounts every two hours. We set this bawling bunch about eight days.

We were eight miles from headquarters. Nearly all the men were kin. It seemed Day had married all the Edgars and Herrons and a lot of others I never heard named. When anyone came out to the herd, a lot of kin would follow; then when some of them headed back home, the rest were apt to trail along like they weren't weaned. Two or three of us would be left holding the calves. Sometimes they all went home at noon, and pulled the mess wagon in, too. Bowman said, "Do they expect us to live on scenery?"

One evening a transient fell in. He said, "I'd like to stay here tonight; if anyone will let me have a slicker, I'll stand his guard." A boy said, "There comes Bolivar – he's been in the saddle a week – take his." The truth was these transients usually didn't aim to stand guard – just wanted to get someone's slicker. But I gave him mine and he took my night horse and rode off, while I ate a bite and lay down on my back between the mess kit and the wagon. George, the cook, slept in the wagon.

The cattle were bedded down about one hundred yards away.

The next morning when I woke up, my blankets were soaked and I saw a pool of water a ways off. I said, "George, did it rain? And where is the cattle?" George said, "You damn fool," and a bit of other nice stuff. (Cook and I were gettin' real intimate in our converse). Then my relief – the transient – came up. He said, "Well Bolivar, you are alive. When I came in last night it was raining like the devil. I had a notion to cover your face with your slicker, but you was already wet and didn't know it, and I didn't want to get wet too, so I just let you go. The cattle ran – passed within ten feet of you. I wouldn't think any live man could lay like you did."

Day was selling off his cattle – sold nearly all he had that summer. A man named Berry from Montana bargained for 3500 two-year-old steers, which were on the range of Tony Day – J. M. Day's brother – below Supply. The Days were short-handed, so Berry's men went down after them. When they came up, J. M. went out to look them over.

Day wore long whiskers, a starched shirt, and a diamond as big as the end of my little finger. He drove out to the herd in his buggy and met the Berry foreman, a tall scion of the north border, with a keen eye and a bad taste in his mouth. But Day was a wise guy. He said, "You are out cattle." The Berry boss said, "I know it." Day said, "You are out three hundred head." The boss said, "You're a liar." Day said, "How many do you think you're out?" "I *know* how many I'm out; I'm out three lame steers." Day said, "Are you hired to string cattle over the country?" The boss said, "I'm hired to take care of them." Then Day picked up a monkey wrench, and the boss hauled out his gat to tap him on the conk. Several boys rode between them and stopped it.

Later I was asked what I would do if a fight broke out. I said, "I'm hired to punch cows. If Day finds a fight let him settle it. If he wants me to join in his rows, we better talk it over before he starts in." But it seems the Berry boss *had* left only three lame steers to be picked up by the next roundup; so they just let it pass.

We were still holding our calves. But after several days of drinking with a prospective buyer Day got rid of that bunch, and we turned them over to drive north. Then we went into headquarters camp at 2 p.m. to catch up on sleep. Day asked us, "Who's got the best horse?" A half dozen hollered, "Bolivar!" like they thought they might not be heard. Day said, "Here's a telegram I want you to take to Ashland. It must get to Dodge 'fore the stage leaves. Here's half a dollar. Now ride." It was a hard ride, but I made it. When I gave the telegram to the operator he looked it over and said, "You damn near killed your horse; did you read the message?" I said, "No." "Well, read it." It was to a bar-keep in Dodge telling him to put a jug of whisky on the stage. Well, I wished I had read it on the start.

I got to camp after dark. A rain had set in from the east – no wind, just a good summer rain. I turned my horse loose and walked in. Day asked, "Did you get the message in on time?" "Yes." Then he said, "Eat your supper. Then you'll find a fresh horse tied up at the corral. Ride to the three cottonwoods. Bowman is up there. He'll tell you what to do."

I ate, saddled, rode east about two miles. This was in a fenced, three-mile square used for a horse pasture. Bowman was warbling a lullaby to a herd of four thousand two-year-old steers Day had bought from Andrews. (It may have been J. V. Andrews, who held the range east of Supply. It seems to me the cattle were branded with a v Bar, almost the same as the Garland brand). They were to be turned over to us next day. I said, "Leroy, what's up now?" He said, "I don't know. You take 'em; someone'll come." And he rode away saying, "My bed's at the three trees."

Cattle are not apt to scare during a calm rain. I set them till past twelve; then I rode up to the Andrews wagon, about eighty yards off, and asked, "How you got this guard thing fixed?" A fellow said, "Day said you fellows would hold the cattle." Then I knew the way Day managed things that meant I could hold them all night. So I said, "Well you come set 'em till I get back." He began to crawl out of the wagon. I left in a good trot, singing pretty loud. He hollered, "How soon'll you be back?" I never heard him. By the time I passed the herd, I was in a lope and singing louder. He called again, but I didn't hear him this time either.

I rode down to the cottonwoods, about a mile south. It was dark as tar, but I found Leroy's bed, tied my mount to a tree, slipped off my boots and slicker, raised the tarp, and slid in. Bowman rolled out on the other side in a hurry. I said, "Come back; you'll get wet." He said, "I thought it was a pole cat." I never slept better, never had less on my mind. The next morning we rode down to headquarters, and lined up at a twenty-foot table, me at one end. A long hungry-looking guy at the far end of the feed trough asked, "Which one of you fellows asked me to hold them cattle till you come back?" Nobody spoke. It looked like the guilty man wasn't in.

In J. M. Day's dealings in cattle one glimpses the

growing importance of the northern ranges. The south, with its mild climate, was becoming a breeding ground; the north, where the animals grew larger and heavier, a maturing ground. Thus many thousands of young steers, like the herd purchased by Berry, were trailed to the Wyoming-Montana-Dakota area to finish growing. At the same time some of the northern ranchmen, believing it practicable to breed in the north, were stocking their ranges by buying cows from the older ranching area of the southwest. Day's sales reflected this traffic also.

We began to gather a bunch of cows to drive to Cheyenne to sell. We worked Willow creek, Snake creek, and a creek on the other side, and got about two thousand cows and some calves. Before sending the cows north we branded the calves. When we penned the cattle, some of them got on the prod. One day a three-year-old bull got auger-eyed, and the boys began climbing the fence. But Bill Herron and I stayed inside. I seen an old cow makin' faces at Bill, so I hollered, "Don't take the fence; fight 'er off with a club." He turned and took a fling at her head. Her horns raised the club toward the top of the fence where Edgar sat; he fell back and hollered, "Open the gates." So the cattle got out and we had to pen them all over again.

When we were branding, my helper was a little fellow about sixteen with a nice suit and a white shirt — what we called "bald-faced." When he got the iron warmed up, he crawled the fence and began, "An iron! Here, Bolivar, here's an iron! Hurry up!" It looked like it would get chronic. I remonstrated — advised him to come down, or I would press *him* with the iron. He came down, but was soon sent to camp. Another novice took his place. It seemed like our bunch was getting plumb sour, but I saw the work was about over, so decided to stick it out.

I think we branded nine hundred calves in 1885. The year before they branded about ten thousand. No wonder the winter of 1884-85 broke most of the stockmen. Not only Day and the Texas Land and Cattle company but a good many others folded up in '86.

Edward Everett Dale, the historian, cites another factor in the disaster that overtook the range cattle industry in 1886. In the summer of '85 President Cleveland issued a proclamation – with General Sheridan at hand to enforce it – ordering the removal of all cattle from the Cheyenne and Arapaho reservation. This meant the displacement of about 210,000 head at a most inopportune time. The owners threw them on already stocked ranges of the Texas Panhandle and the Cherokee Outlet, or sold them hastily on a low market with heavy loss. This order had interesting repercussions at the Day headquarters.

While we were working at home camp we got the *Kansas City Star*. One day Bob Edgar, John Edgar's brother, read how Phil Sheridan was ordering all cowmen out of the Cheyenne and Arapaho reservation. He said, "Who's Phil Sheridan? If it had been Major Drumm or Arthur Gorham we'd a knowed who it was, but who the devil ever heard of Phil Sheridan? He's the unpopularist man I ever heard of."

When we got the calves branded, I told Day I'd boss the drive to Wyoming for forty-five dollars a month and a return ticket on the railroad. But he got a twenty-five dollar foreman – and I didn't go.

Next we cut out 4500 steers, three years old and over, to take to the Barton pasture above Cimarron station on the Arkansas. They were to be kept there till fall, then shipped. I think we had seven men on the drive, besides the cook and horse wrangler.

The first night we camped in a corner of the horse pasture a mile from the fence. The night was stormy, and the cattle were unsettled. By eleven o'clock all hands were out. The cattle would swing out, and we would push them back. A boy got up to the herd at one place, and about a quarter of the bunch swung out around him, and they all started to mill. Bowman said, "Boys, we got to get that fellow out. String in and follow me. And don't let any of 'em come in behind *us.*" The cattle's horns began to light up. It looked like the boy was higher than we were. We pushed in, cutting off a lot of them, and got him out. He told us they'd crowded him so his horse had been raised up off the ground half the time.

Then the ones we'd cut off swung back, and they went into a heavy mill. The center must have been ten feet high; the horns were tipped with dim lights. A heavy stroke of lightning caused them to break and run with a roar that shook the ground. We took after them. I was getting near the lead when they hit the fence – four wires and cedar posts. They struck with a crash, and sparks followed the wires over a hundred yards. They broke off about a dozen posts and went through. I slowed down till I was sure I was past the fence, then I moved. I finally headed them in the sand hills and got them turned. Bowman and one other boy came up, and soon the cattle began to lay down. But they were shaky for the whole drive.

We started northwest without a trail. We drove up Crooked creek, past Meade Center, to where there was an unfenced space close to a large white church.

Bowman said, "This is mow land; I got permission to cross, but not to graze." But he got mired in the creek and in helping him out we lost some time. A boy we met told us, "You fellers will ketch the devil. That's Old Hell Roarin' Brown's mow land." But we pushed the cattle together and strung them out, and soon left the place.

Cattle properly handled on the trail are kept headed toward their destination, just grazing along, not driven much. There are men at the "lead" who point them in the right direction, but hold them back so they won't get too far ahead. Then men at the "swing" or "flank" aim to keep the center moving. This makes it easier for the men at the rear or "drag," who drive the slow ones. Men generally prefer the lead because it is easily handled, but a cowhand is supposed to fit himself in where he is needed most. On this drive it seemed that the whole bunch would stay in the lead close together. I was working the drag. Sometimes the cattle would string out three miles, and when they turned off to graze I would be an hour behind.

We got to where there was more settlers. They lived in half-dugout, half-sod castles, with a line plowed around the claim and a dog on top of the castle as a lookout for stray stock. We aimed to stay away from crops, but the dogs didn't know that; so they would tackle the lead, and the whole bunch would be back at my end. They soon got so most anything would start a run. We didn't dare shoot, but I finally learned to go out and meet the dog, put my string on him, and lead him a quarter of a mile in a dead run. After that he was easy to turn loose. I got to riding close to the lead to be ready for them.

When we got to the Arkansas slope, about six miles

from the stream, a shower came from the north. The cattle were thirsty; they broke for the water and we could not hold them. But after about an hour the wind changed, and they quieted down. Then when we got to the river the water was high, but they plunged right in. The boys had to swim out ahead of them and turn them back. One thing we saw here on the Arkansas was interesting to me: a company fixing to irrigate was damming the river with sacked sand. It looked foolish.

We drove west up the valley, south side of the river, got to the Barton pasture about 10 a.m. Our wagon didn't follow. We aimed to scatter the cattle over the pasture; we would drop out a bunch and drive the rest on. Once a stray sheep got among them, and we had to rope it and drag it away. At 2 p.m. we met a roundup wagon and asked for a little chuck, but the cook said, "Chuck! Hell, no." We dropped the last bunch at four. Then we started back down the river to our camp.

Two of the boys got funny and made my horse pitch. I wasn't looking for it, so I got riled and said several things they didn't like. Then after we got to camp, they crossed over to Cimarron, got tanked up, and brought back half a sack of bottled beer. They started again to have a little fun at my expense, and I thought if they got boisterous, things might go wrong. A dark cloud was coming from the north; so, knowing most western men were afraid of the hereafter, I said, "Would you fellows rather go to hell drunk than to stay sober till that storm gets through with you?" They said, "Aw, shut up," but they finally went off in the high grass and bedded down. Then the storm came; only a few drops of rain fell, but the thunder and lightning was as bad as any I ever saw. When morning came, the boys threw out their beer.

On the home trip we pulled south on a road going through sand hills. The two boys were still funny. They caught a sheep that had strayed away from a bunch an old man was driving, and put it in the wagon. That night we camped on the bank of Crooked creek, and the cook started to roast it. When chuck was about ready I heaved the mutton into the creek, and said, "George, let's have some bacon fried." No kick came of it, and that was the end of their imposing on me.

The next day our two funny men run onto an old man with a jug of vinegar. They roped him, and he fell and broke his jug on a rock. We were then going east, meeting a good many emigrant families going west; so the two boys started ahead, aiming to fasten a rope from one saddle horn to the other and drag the people out of the next wagon. We saw a wagon come up out of a sand draw as the boys started down, but one dropped his end of the rope. When the wagon came up to us, we understood why. It was a freighter with a six-mule team, a jerk line and a saddled wheeler, and a man resting on a pile of blankets with a Sharps rifle laying on top of the load and a .45 in his belt. When we caught up with the boys, one of them said, "We're pickin' our men." But they didn't try it again.

We soon got back to home camp. The range was pretty well cleaned up, and they were fixing to put up hay; so I pulled for Protection.

Back in the Indian Territory

When I got to Protection, there was an Indian scare looming up. Having no guns, the citizens got some split sticks at the lumber yard and marched up and down the streets. The more they drilled the worse scared they got. I said, "Learnin' how to die?" Several didn't like my style. They had meetings where everybody spread terrible reports of the danger. Then the next *Kansas City Star* came out, and it increased the commotion.

An Indian scare was a favorite cowboy stratagem for driving nesters away from the range country. But Carl Coke Rister, the historian, has found evidence that this scare in Clark and Comanche counties was fomented by a band of outlaws scheming to plunder the abandoned settlements. It was real enough, however, to the inexperienced settlers training for defense.

They called on the governor for guns and ammunition. Father said I could join the militia and shoot a few days, then hand in the gun and ride off; that was the way he did in '63. He joined the militia to hold Morgan back when he raided Indiana; then when Morgan crossed into Ohio, he set his gun down and came home. It was not until sometime in the '80's that he signed some papers and got released. He always had the idea one could join the army and just quit when he got tired.

Well, I thought I wouldn't mind having a little target practice while I was laying around home. So on Saturday I went to town aiming to sign up if they had guns; if not, I would pull for Supply Sunday morning to look for a job on the range. At the meeting that day several got up and spouted; told how the Indians were killing boys and driving off cattle down in the Territory – it was getting terrible. Nearly everyone was in favor of heading for Topeka. Then Old Man Ross, a neighbor of ours, got up and said, "Oliver, come up here in front and tell us where you have been, what you have seen, when you left the roundup, and what your opinion is of the danger."

I told them I had worked the country on the Canadian near Reno, all around Supply, and more than once up on the Beaver; that the Indians had stayed away from us; that there were reports of several Indians being shot, but no white man; and that all the bad news I got came from the *Kansas City Star* "just where these gentlemen got all the bad news they have." And to show how I looked at the danger, I was going to start for Supply in the morning.

They never got any guns. But Sunday morning a lot of them loaded up their goods and pulled for the county seat towns, and some drove to Topeka.

There had been a real Indian raid in southwestern Kansas in '78. The government had brought a bunch of Northern Cheyennes down to the Indian Territory. It seems they didn't like the country and broke back north. When they crossed the Day range they took on a bunch of horses. One fellow started to outrun them afoot and they got his hair. (He was buried on Cavalry creek six miles southwest of Coldwater). Then Day and his punchers headed them off and run them up a canyon. A cavalry troop came up. Day wanted to make a drive on the Johns, but no, the soldiers took charge. The commander sent a detail to Dodge to telegraph to

Washington, "We have surrounded the Indians; what shall we do?" Orders came back, "Capture them by all means." But while they waited, Day had run in and got his horses, the commander had got an Indian pass to glory, and the Johns had got away. But I'm gettin' plumb off my range.

Mr. Nelson is at a disadvantage "off his range," where he has to draw on other men's accounts instead of his own photographic memory. J. E. George, old-time Driskill cowhand who was present at this skirmish, says it was J. L. Driskill and Sons whose boys surrounded the Indians; and that they sold the ranch to Doc Day about four years later. He says that the commander who failed to attack lived to be courtmartialed at Fort Supply for cowardice; and Reginald Aldridge, an Englishman who was holding cattle in southern Kansas, but was not an eye witness of the affray, adds that the officer was dismissed from the service. But regardless of details, this raid was a recent memory in southwestern Kansas in 1885, when the settlers fled and Oliver Nelson calmly turned his horse toward the Indian Territory.

Sunday morning I pulled south. The first night I stopped at the Day camp. They asked me what I would do if I run onto a bunch of Indians. I said, "I'll plan that after I see 'em; it may be a small bunch." The next morning I started south, then turned up the Cimarron through sand hills, aiming to strike the Dodge-Supply trail. Finally I seen a bunch ahead that I couldn't make out. When I'd get a side view, they would be high in the middle. A cow slopes down, a horse slopes up, a buffalo runs up and breaks off square, but this was something else. In this country objects can often be seen five or more miles away, so it was a good time before I came up to them. Finally I rounded a sand hill, and a little burro came over the rise with a pack on as big as a bedtick – goat hides, sheep skins, old clothes, rags. Then out came two more burros, just loaded down with trash: coffee pot and fry pan, more sheep and goat hides. Next out came a man on a small pony; he had a Mex saddle with a horn as big as a plate standing straight up, a Mex hat with several air holes and brindle bristles sticking through, a mop of dirty clay whiskers, clothes hung on him lookin' awful rusty, and a pair of dreamy blue eyes. It sure was old Ruff and Ready!

When we got even, his horse stopped. I stuck out my paw and said, "Well, hello;" then drew back saying, "I thought I knew you, but I don't." He said, "You do know me." I said, "No, the Indians got the man I took you for." He said, "They didn't get me. You remember Old Sundown? And that fool kid. How did he come out?" I told him how the kid was saved by Buffalo King. Then Ruff took up his story:

"Well, they run us off from our bunch of ponies and they damn near got us. I tried to lead 'em away from the kid. Near dark I dodged 'em, and rode all night. I went to Las Vegas 'fore I let up. I'm in now with a big Mexican sheep man. He has a nice girl; he wants me to marry her, and I'm goin' to. Oh! – How's my poor wife?"

"Say, that little woman has suffered a thousand deaths over you," I told him. "They brought the news that the Indians had caught you." I seen the big tears begin to fall, bounce off the saddle horn, and spread out on the grass; and I just had to ride on.

Afterwards I heard that he went to Caldwell and later to Hunnewell to find his missus; but the new husband kicked him out of the yard and clubbed the donks away, and that's all I know.

Well, I rode on, crossed the Cimarron, and took a trail up Snake creek south. I seen a wagon coming with the team in a lope – an old man, old wagon, little team nearly winded. When they got close, the team slacked. The man said, "The Indians are just over the hill; go back." I grinned. He swore at me, flailed the horses with a willow about eight feet long, and increased his speed.

After I got out in the open on higher ground, it just seemed like things were not in their natural shape. It looked like a pony on every point, and here and there a wagon off to itself alone. I had been over that country several times, but this was new. When I got to where the creek prongs into three forks, I seen a man on a high point, standing by a horse, swing a blanket towards me. I knew it was an Indian signaling that something was in that direction. Then about twelve horsemen came in sight and made straight at me in high speed. It looked a little scary. I was about four hundred yards from the creek. I jogged up a little to get there 'fore they could get to me; then I put my horse down out of sight and sat on the bank. I just thought, "Any funny stuff, and you'll find what you're lookin' for." But they swung out of line till they passed me, then rode on. I felt plumb out of place.

Then I heard a bugle call. I was close to the military telegraph line between Dodge and Fort Supply; and soon I reached a flat and seen a square tent on this telegraph line with soldiers swarming around. I rode up and asked what the big show was about. They said they had Indian scouts thrown out to reassure the settlers; and the bunch I had seen were some of these scouts out after ponies that had strayed away. So that was what the signaling meant: the man on the point had located the ponies. And an Indian usually took his family along wherever he went, so the wagons I had seen were for the squaws and papooses. That was the end of my Indian scare.

Oliver Nelson then followed the Dodge-Supply trail down into the Cherokee Outlet. This was a branch of the famed Western trail, greatest of all cattle trails. Here the drives started from far down in Texas, cut across the Indian Territory with the tongue of the chuck wagon pointed – literally – to the north star, and came to Dodge City, where the fat beeves were loaded on the railroad, and the young stock were sold to northern buyers to take the trail again for Wyoming, Montana, and Dakota. Where the route crossed the Cherokee Outlet a lane three or four miles wide was reserved from leasing and fencing.

But the Western trail passed about ten miles west of Fort Supply, while the military road swerved to the east along the telegraph line to the post. This also was a busy thoroughfare with long wagon trains of military supplies and sutlers' stores, cavalry troops flashing by, and stage coaches hauling the mail and passenger traffic of the frontier. There was a stage station called Buffalo on Buffalo creek, not far from the present Oklahoma county seat town of that name. Apparently the stage keeper was a family man, for Mr. Nelson remembers a woman there and a boy about twelve years old. "The boy had a rope and a pup that would run by him and dodge; he would throw his rope and catch it every time." Then "some peelers rode up and showed off some, joking with the boy's mother and knocking each other around as young fellows will." Oliver, relying on the careless hospitality of the cow camps, joined them as they rode off across the country.

We took a dim trail for the R Bar S on the Beaver. We run onto a rattlesnake that crawled under a weed and we could see just its head sticking up. One of the boys took a pull at it and knocked the head to pieces. I stayed at the R Bar S overnight. Next morning Red Odum said the Apple outfit in the Cheyenne-Arapaho reservation was going to drive out of the Indian country – Sheridan's orders – and would need hands. So next day I rode to Supply and started down the Fort Supply-Fort Elliott trail.

Fort Elliott was on Sweetwater creek in Wheeler county, Texas. Two or three miles southeast was the place where Rath and Wright has established their branch trading house for buffalo hunters. This was first known as Hide Town, then as Sweetwater. It was a busy little settlement. A contemporary describes it as "a wild and woolly place," with a large dance hall, two restaurants, and three saloons; with Rath and Wright's great stock of hunters' supplies and "acres of high piles of hides"; and with ten or fifteen hunting outfits a day coming and going.

By the time the hide business ended, Fort Elliott had been established, so that Sweetwater had soldier customers. Then it fell under the displeasure of the military. Mr. Nelson was told that "soldiers going there by twos and threes never got back, so the army put a ban on it." Walter Prescott Webb, the historian, believes, however, that the sutlers at the post induced the commandant to make this ruling in order to monopolize the soldiers' trade. Whatever the reason, Sweetwater became "off limits." Then – to quote Mr. Nelson –"the Sweetwater people moved their frame buildings north and started Mobeetie, and the old trade ketched up."

Thus in Mr. Nelson's time Sweetwater was only a lurid memory. But its successor, Mobeetie, was not exactly distinguished by morality and sobriety. It was not only a post settlement but a cow town. It was located on the high land above the Sweetwater a little southeast of Fort Elliott. A modern Texas farm center about a mile north now carries the name, but a few buildings still stand in "Old" Mobeetie, and Western legends cluster thickly there. In its roystering heyday two trails connected it with the outside world: the Rath, or Jones-Plummer trail, cutting 175 miles north across the plains by way of Jim Lane's post on the Beaver to Dodge City; and the Fort Supply-Fort Elliott trail, with its military and civilian traffic and its telegraph line, down which Oliver Nelson was riding; a cowhand hunting work and stopping at ranches along the way.

The first night he stayed at the K H *camp on Wolf creek, still in the Cherokee Outlet. He remembers that Billy Button was the cook and that "he was quick; there was about twenty there for chuck, but he refused my help." The next morning he "joined up with two other boys" and continued down the trail, still following Red Odum's tip that the Apple needed hands. They rode up Wolf creek to the mouth of Little Wolf. Here a short distance east of the present town of Gage, Oklahoma they stopped at a stage station called Buzzards' Roost.*

The station was a two-room picket with a dirt roof and floor. The keeper was a man with a game leg, named Kluxton – a Civil War veteran, who aimed to hold his job till he got his pension. He told us of an accident ten days before. The Wolf was up and still rising when the northbound stage rolled in driven by Mani Leopard. There was one passenger, an Englishman full of booze and wind. It was about midnight.

They ate their lunch, put on two teams – the trail was heavy – and pulled out. At the Wolf crossing two miles north, Leopard got out and looked at the creek; then he came back and said, "Creek's up; got to turn back." The passenger said, "In England they pay no attention to high water, but drive right in. You Americans are such damned cowards. And I want to get to Supply." (At least that's the way Leopard told it afterwards). Leopard asked him, "Well, what do you say?" The Englishman said, "Drive in." So in they went. The stage turned over. Mani swam out. They found the passenger in a drift close by, the stage-coach and team half a mile below, and some of the mail. But Mani lost his job.

We pulled up Little Wolf still following the Fort Elliott trail; rode through sandy shin oak up to a high flat overlooking Commission creek, a string of clear pools twenty to one hundred feet long and fifty feet across, hung together by a stream about a foot wide. Rounding a fence corner we crossed into Texas, and the boys began to sing. It made an awful change – to Texas boys.

We left the trail and turned down Commission creek, back again in the Indian Territory. We saw many fish scales along the banks of the pools; later I learned that was an otter sign. About a quarter of a mile above the Apple camp we run onto a lot of young turkeys in the shade of some cottonwoods. They flew up all around us. There were thousands of them.

We got to the camp and put our mounts in a small pasture. Several buildings made of eight-foot cottonwood pickets were set under a high cliff to the north. I was told they had three other camps. The Apple range claimed forty thousand head.

This was the Cheyenne and Arapahoe (popularly known as the C. *and* A.*) Cattle company. It is said to have been organized by Texas cattlemen in 1878 for the express purpose of leasing land from these Indian tribes. It obtained control of one million acres extending about forty-five miles east of the Texas Panhandle line, and bounded on the north by the Cherokee Outlet and on the south by the Washita river. The rental was two cents an acre, paid semi-annually.*

Edward Fenlon, who became the ranch manager, had made the agreement with the Indians through the active cooperation of John D. Miles, United States agent to the two tribes; but it was the announced policy of the Indian Office that such leases were made at the lessee's own risk, and would not be backed up by the government. Thus the cattlemen had no recourse when President Cleveland issued his famous proclamation ordering them to evacuate.

It is known that the Cheyenne and Arapahoe Cattle company had two headquarters camps north of the Canadian. Besides the one visited by Oliver Nelson there was a camp on Turkey creek about six miles west of the present town of Camargo. Both these places were equipped with buildings and corrals, and served as supply stations for the line camps. The main headquarters camp, the business center of the great ranch, was near the Washita at the mouth of Quartermaster creek, about six miles south of the present rural center of Moorewood. But at the time of Oliver Nelson's visit the whole enterprise was in process of liquidation; according to a report made by an army officer the ranch hands were driving out the cattle and dismantling the camps.

The cook at the Commission camp was named Buford

Gillock. He was an artist, was making a sketch of the camp. It seemed they needed no hands on the Apple, but I did several little things to help the cook, while the two boys went to a room and lay down. The next morning he asked me to ride to the stage station two miles west and get the mail, and perhaps land a job there. "Those two bums don't want work." I rode down. The station was just inside the Indian Territory line two miles east of the present town of Higgins, Texas. It was a picket cabin lying north and south, about forty feet long and twelve wide with dirt roof and plank floor. The company agent, Charles H. Sawyer, who had charge of all the stations, was there alone. He had just fired the station keeper, and I got the job. I rode to the Apple camp and delivered the mail; then came back and started in. The pay was thirty dollars a month.

The stage line ran from Dodge, Kansas to Mobeetie, Texas. Vaile, Miner, and company was the owner, but I never knew much about it. L. P. Williamson was the president. I understood he was interested in several lines. He had been involved in the recent Star Route prosecutions, but got out clear.

The historian will remember that these noted trials were concerned with contracts by which the government was grossly overcharged for the carrying of mail on frontier routes. The scandal broke during the brief tenure of President Garfield, but the prosecutions were carried over into the succeeding Arthur administration.

The stage came from the north at 6 a.m. one day, from the south at 6 p.m. the next, making the round trip from Supply to Mobeetie. It changed drivers at my station; while one drove the other stayed with me, ready to hook on and finish the run. Happy Jack (Jack Elder) made the night drive to Supply, and Reno Jack

(George Hall) the day trip to Mobeetie. (Drivers and station keepers were generally called Jack). Happy was short and heavy-set, with an auburn crown; neat in dress; good-natured when in good humor, but plumb unmanageable when things went the wrong way. Reno was small, more of a man, better to get along with – so *he* said. Happy let you do most of the talking; some way he did not take strong to Reno, who handed out most of the information himself.

My job was to keep house and have meals for the drivers and passengers. I cleaned up the cabin – which needed it bad. It had three rooms, strung end to end, each with an outside door in the east. The north one had the cook stove. It had a west door, which was seldom used; so I fastened it shut, drove in several nails, and hung up some extra ovens and things and covered them with bran sacks. We ate in the middle room, and my cot was in one corner. (Everything was homemade; there was no furniture out there). The south room was the "parlor" where passengers waited and people came after their mail; also the driver slept there. It was about twenty feet long; had a weak ridge pole propped by a post in the center – later two side props were put in about three feet each way from the center prop.

The fare was not of the best, but I shot game to help it out. Reno had a .44 Marlin, which I used to bring in turkeys. Happy would go with me, but would not handle the gun, because he said Reno was ornery. I killed nearly all on the wing for practice. I don't think I ever missed one flying. Happy used to say that was good shooting.

After I had been there a few days Happy asked if I had seen a pair of blue trousers with a silk seam on the outside of each leg. I said, "There's no such pair here, but Reno is wearing some like that." Happy said, "If he has mine on, he'll pull 'em off first thing he does when he gets off the stage." That evening Reno rolled in with two lady passengers. He got off and began saying nice things to Happy. Happy said, "You get out of my britches and talk later." Reno started for the cabin to change, but Happy called him back. Reno said, "There's ladies in the stage," but Happy said, "You get out of them britches." Reno slid out of the breeches right there.

The station was in the Cheyenne and Arapaho reservation. One day a bunch of Indians with several head of cattle came along. They camped close to the cabin and killed a beef. They cut the paunch in strips and shook the fillings out of the guts; took forked sticks and held the casings over the fire a short time; had a good feed and lay down. North of us was a high flat that broke off in a steep cliff just above our cabin. That night a bunch of wolves set on top of this cliff and howled; it sounded like fifty Newfoundland dogs on our roof.

BeJesus Jack was the keeper of the stage station below me on the Canadian river. One day Sawyer held his camp and he drove to Mobeetie. He got full down there, and on the way back got sleepy. The day was warm, so he lay down on the trail to rest; and the mules, tired of waiting, moved on to camp. After a while a man driving past picked him up and took him in, too. When he got to the station, Sawyer met him with a Winchester in his hand. They had some words and he quit. I got his job next day. It was better than the one I'd held at Commission.

The Stage Station on the Canadian

The Canadian camp was in the Texas Panhandle, eighteen miles southwest of Commission. Sand hills stretched all the way between the two places, with tall bunch grass and bluestem and a few hackberry trees. The station was on high ground, two hundred yards south of the river, several miles east of the present town of Canadian, Texas. There were two old rooms – one log, one picket – with dirt roof and floor, and a frame addition built on. We used the frame for the station, and the old part, which was liable to fall down any time, for a storeroom. I got water from a well six feet deep, near the river. All around was plenty of sage brush but little timber. The C T camp was two miles north, the P O three miles west, the Horseshoe four miles east, Fort Elliott and Mobeetie thirty miles south.

When winter came, the frame room was about as cold inside as out. But I calked up the cracks with anything I could get, and calcimined with bran sacks, then papered on that with newspapers. I got a good many advertising pictures through the mail, so I placed the choice ones in groups on the wall. Besides this the company had printed orders tacked up all around. It looked quite neat. Ladies passing through would ask where my wife was. I would tell them, "I'm alone." Then they would say, "Oh, a family has just moved out?" "No." "Well, who fixed this place up?" It did not look regular. There was a persimmon patch across the river two miles upstream, and as soon as the frost

ripened the fruit I kept a supply on hand. Everybody
ate it.

The stage – with Reno driving – passed at noon, south
one day, north the next. The rest of the time I was
alone. I had three teams to care for, would have a team
harnessed and ready to change when the stage stopped.
Also I had a large white shepherd dog named Blitzen.
Then I had Old Tobe, a large, poor, buckskin horse,
which I used to pilot the stage across the river.

The Canadian is a treacherous stream. The banks are
of caving sand about ten feet high. The bed is about
four hundred yards wide, filled with very fine sand, no
rocks. It has been sounded down sixty feet, and still no
solid foundation. It has a heavy downslope from the
west, so that in spring freshets it comes down with a
roar. These rises wash channels in the bed, then fill
them up with sand as soft as mush. Once a flood brought
down a tree with a trunk three feet in diameter, the top
pointed downstream, resting on the soft sand and sticking up twenty feet above the water. It was in sight four
days, working its way down at the rate of 150 yards an
hour. The January before I came a thirteen-foot stone
abutment had been placed in the middle of the bed to
support a telegraph pole. They had set it six feet below
the sand and seven feet above, but when I got there it
had sunk till only about four inches projected. By
spring it was buried under three feet of sand, and had
moved downstream until it broke the wire.

The stage crossing was difficult, especially after one
of these rises. First I would ride across to find a solid
lane, then come back and pilot the stage over, riding
ahead to show the way. I got so I could pretty well tell
soft sand by the riffle of the water over it, but sometimes
I would strike a soft spot, and Tobe would fall down

and roll over on his side. Then I would tramp around to settle the sand a little, find a solid passage, and lead him out by the rein.

I also piloted travelers across, charging a dollar. One evening some men drove up with a team and asked how the crossing was and about staying overnight. I told them they could have meals for fifty cents apiece, but I could not feed their horses; that I could not tell them about the crossing, for the channel might change any time, but I would pilot them unless they waited till the sun got behind the ridge of sand hills to the west. Well, they took some time deciding but finally gave me a dollar to take them over. I went with them to the river, and the sun was below the hill. "Now listen," I told them. "This stream is dangerous. I won't go in unless you agree to wait on the other side till I get back out." They promised to wait. I rode in. Tobe went down once, but I finally found a lead and took them over. By this time it was dark, but they plumb forgot their promise and drove off in a trot. I had to find my way back to a place on the south bank about ten feet wide, but I made it with little trouble.

When the river was too high for the stage to navigate, I carried the mail across on Tobe. Sometimes waves would form as high as he was and push him downstream, but he would keep his head pointed upstream and move towards shore. When the water was too deep or the sand too soft for Tobe, I used a skiff. One time a cowboy had me take him across in this skiff, aiming to lead his horse with his rope. I told him to take the bridle off, but he left it on. Out in the stream the horse got one foot over the rein. We got the saddle, but the horse stayed in the river.

I kept the stage stock in a shed stable just east of the

cabin. There was a stack of hay there, and I also fed bran and oats. I gave Old Paint a little too, so he wouldn't forget where he belonged. I would throw a club at him if Sawyer was with me at feed time, and he learned to leave when he saw the agent. But Sawyer got suspicious. One evening he went out with a bucket of bran, and Paint walked right up and stuck his nose in; then he snorted, blowing out bran, turned, and kicked the bucket. It really looked like the horse and I were innocent. But I soon sent Paint to the Horseshoe.

A little fellow about ten years old named George Hakes used to come for the Horseshoe mail. One time he said, "The ranch people want to know your name." I said, "Oliver Nelson." Seems Siders and Hoos Hopkins had told the boss about meeting me on the T 5, for the next day Hakes reported, "Bee Hopkins said he'd give you forty-five dollars a month to set in whenever you want to, and seventy-five for the spring roundup." But I had things my way at the station, and did not want to change.

The Horseshoe folks got to sending me cake, pie, butter, fresh pork, some honey – they nearly kept my camp. About Christmas they sent me the hind quarter of a bear. When company came I would say, "I'll have to cut a chunk out of Old Rover."

Winter storms would cause the antelope to bunch up and come to the sand hills along the river, five hundred in a bunch. One day I went out and shot at some. They were spread out on the flat land like a flock of sheep, covering several acres. I shot only once – at 250 yards and close to dusk. One antelope ran up near me and fell; two ran off and fell; the others just ran around bewildered. I took in the closest one. It had the bullet. The other two I left. I used a Sharps .45 hammerless, which I had borrowed from a real nice U.S. teamster.

In November I got to killing deer. I would knock off china berries several times at a certain place so they would learn where to find them. About sundown I would take up a position three hundred yards from the trees, and when they came to pick up the berries I would shoot one. The others would look all around before running away, but they couldn't tell where the sound came from. They would find another place to feed, and a few days later I would get another shot at the same bunch. I had no place to sell them, so killed only to keep a supply of meat. During the cold weather soldiers would often pass with a load of deer for Elliott.

One night several wolves came to the camp. The next evening I put out a bait, then went to tie up my dog; but Blitzen had watched me put it out, and had already got it. I fed him all the tallow he would eat, but he died. I wasn't on to the antidote. Later I learned that a good drink of brine would make a dog heave up a load of wolf bait.

One day I saw a skunk heading for my cabin. I pulled out my .44 I'd been carrying all summer, and tried to shoot him, but it hung fire. The skunk went under the house and I throwed the gun down the hill. I didn't want to get disappointed again; a man's likely to make a fool of himself relying on an unsafe gun. It's a good rule to try your old smoker out about every so often.

There was a beaver dam across the Canadian two miles west of the station. It was three hundred yards long, and in one place seven feet high. It was built of green willow sticks about sixteen inches long, stuck in the sand and leaning slightly downstream; these sticks formed several rows across the bed of the river – not straight across, but bowing upstream – and grass and mud was packed between the rows. Passing drift caught on the sticks, and the sticks themselves sprouted and grew, forming a compact dam. Later other rows were placed on top to increase the height. In the pool back of this dam were several of their houses, just made of reeds, no mud on top.

Beavers have a forefoot like a cat's paw and a webbed hind foot half as large as one's hand. When they walk they make a double trail: the inner one of cat tracks, stepping about six inches; the outer one like a hand, stepping about twice as far. When running, they catch the ground with the front feet and jump with the hind; they go faster than a man can run. They have very heavy squirrel teeth. When they fell a tree they pinch out perpendicular bites several inches long all around the trunk; then the next row of bites is shorter, and so on, so the cut ends are pointed like a lead pencil.

I thought I would trap some of the beavers, but I never did. I finally told an old trapper about them, but he said he'd leave them for me. I also told him of the fish scales up on Commission. He went up there, and in a few days caught seven otter. Then he went to Dodge and had a glorious drunk.

I had not been at camp long before a livestock inspector stopped in – Bobby Nolls. He had quite a talk with me just about nothing, seemed to be trying to find out what I knew.

This man was probably employed by the Texas Cattlemen's Association of the Panhandle. The ranchmen had held a meeting in 1880 and formed a permanent organization the following January; and they kept inspectors at Caldwell, Dodge City, and other shipping points to examine the brands of cattle offered for sale; other inspectors rode the trails to cut out stolen stock. Nolls carried the authority of deputy sheriff of the state of Texas, and apparently it was in his capacity of peace officer that he began making discreet inquiries of the young station keeper. Finally he told Oliver his suspicions.

"A young feller kept this place shortly before you came. He never drew his pay, which was quite a savin' for the company. He had a good horse, saddle, and pistol. A driver up the trail got them, and a company man is wearing his hat, coat, and boots." I said, "And I have part of his bed." Bobby said, "Yes, and some day we'll find his bones in one of these sand hills, if he ain't in the river. You watch out when you're hunting; and if you find any old clothes or any place where someone has been digging, let me know." But I never found a mark; the case was never solved. The suspected driver had quit 'fore I started working for the company.

Reno Jack soon quit driving, and a man named Ben Steed took his place. Steed was about thirty years old, had Duroc hair and jowls, was about six-feet-six and weighed 165 pounds. He could hardly speak without swearing.

But Steed was leery about the hereafter, so was very pleasant when the river was up. One noon two Horseshoe ladies came for the mail. One said, "I do dread meeting Mr. Steed; he uses such profane language." I saw a heavy cloud in the west, so I said, "Steed's joined the meetin' house." Then the stage came up. Steed got out and in a real nice tone said, "Ollie, I'll give the ladies their mail. I wish you'd change teams. I want to get a soon start." The next time the ladies came they asked me, "What did you mean when you said Mr. Steed had joined church?" I said, "There was a storm up the river, and whenever Steed expects high water the next day, he won't swear. When the Canadian is up, most people use good language till they get across."

Steed got to ailing, so I drove for him several trips to Mobeetie while he kept station for me. Three miles south of camp I passed a hole about ten feet across and eight feet deep in the middle of the trail – an abandoned well where an old camp had been. A mile farther on I struck a high flat – level, hard land – that extended fifteen miles to the Washita; here was a little sand and a few scrub hackberry trees; then more flat, tight land to the Gageby, which was just a deep hollow, no timber; then another high flat to Fort Elliott, on the Sweetwater, and a mile east on high land again to Mobeetie. The flats were just landscape: buffalo grass, no prairie dogs, no game, no trees, no nothing.

The high plains of the Texas and Oklahoma Panhandles are crossed by several parallel rivers bordered with sand hills or flowing at the bottom of deep gorges. But away from these streams the land is entirely without drainage. One may drive for fifty or even one hundred miles without crossing the slightest watercourse; the surplus rainfall collects in saucer-like lakes.

Mr. Nelson's description of these "high flats" is surprisingly like that of the first white men who gazed with awe on their limitless expanse. In a letter to the king of Spain in 1541 Coronado told of crossing vast plains, "with no more landmarks than as if we had been swallowed up by the sea . . . not a stone, nor a bit of rising ground, nor a tree, nor a shrub, nor anything to go by. There is very much fine pasture land, with good grass," but wood was found only in "the gullies and rivers, which are very few." And Castañeda, the historian of the expedition, said, "I dare to write of them because I am writing at a time when many men are still living who saw them and will vouch for my account." He described the lakes, "round as plates, a stone's throw or more across. . . The grass grows tall near these lakes; away from them it is very short, a span or less. The country is like a bowl, so that when a man sits down, the horizon surrounds him all around at the distance of a musket shot."

The conquistadores found almost incredible numbers of buffalo grazing on the short, curly grass, where "the country is so level and smooth . . . that the sky can be seen between their legs;" at a little distance, where their shaggy bodies merged, "they looked like smooth-trunked pines whose tops joined." But in Mr. Nelson's day the gaunt longhorns had replaced the "crooked-backed oxen" of the Spanish explorers, and the cow town had succeeded the tepee village of the native hunters. And stories came up to the Canadian station of the riotous doings at Mobeetie.

Sometime in November a puncher roped a large black bear. They brought it to Mobeetie and tethered it to a post back of a saloon, intending to kill it for Christmas. One bright afternoon some dogs came around, and it broke its chain and took out for the colored district where there was lots of dogs. When they heard the commotion, the black population came out to see the show. A dog would come down the line and jump a palin' fence, the bear would crowd straight through after him, and each she nigger would grab a piccaninny and break for cover. A half dozen punchers rode down with their ropes, but could not make a go on account the horses had to turn the fence corners while the bear broke through the palin's. They ran it all over Africa, and headed it up to the main part of town, where it met the city marshal.

For me, I would rather face the bear. This marshal

was five-feet-six inches tall, weighed over two hundred, had ear bobs like harness rings, a hat like a parasol, and two gats in his belt; otherwise he was dark, not dirty – that's my notion. But the bear didn't know all this, so they met. The marshal set up a rat-tat-tat, and the bear went to sleep. But some of the coons didn't forget it till long after Christmas.

Well, I got to see the town when I drove for Steed. But he soon quit his job, and John Peterson set in. In a short time – this was January of '86 – a storm came, a regular hummer from the north; one of the coldest spells I ever seen. The river froze over. I cut poles to walk on, laid them on top of the ice like boards to keep from breaking through. I watched pretty close for the stage, which was long overdue. Finally about four o'clock the snow stopped, but the sand kept rolling. Then I seen the top of the stage coming north of the river, so I went down and started to slide across with my poles. The channel was all on my side of the stone abutment. John tied the team to the telegraph pole and came to me on the ice. I said, "John, are you cold?" He said, "I'm freezing." I said, "Can you make it to the cabin?" He said, "Yes. Let the team go."

But I took the team. I was afraid to try driving them across, for the water was four feet deep, and I knew if they broke through they would be lost; so I drove them back two miles to the C T camp. When I got there, two boys came out and took hold of me saying, "You go to the fire; we'll care for the horses." I said, "What's the big idea? I ain't cold." They told me, "When John came by, we had to help him off the stage." I said, "Then I'd better go back and look after him." I took a short cut through some tule, and fell in muddy water three feet deep; so I backed out and took the stage

POST OFFICE AT MOBEETIE, TEXAS, 1878

road home. John shivered all night. I always thought the reason I stood the cold was that I had been living on deer meat and eating lots of tallow.

A few days later another storm came along – about six inches snow, cold as the devil. (The stage crossed on ice ten days). A soldier had dropped into the station for cover. Peterson drove in from the north at dark, and went on towards Mobeetie. About nine o'clock he came back; said he had drove right into the old well on the trail. It was filled with snow and he hadn't seen it. I had given away my overshoes, but I started out. The soldier went along to help, too. We took two shovels and a pick.

When we got there we found the tongue had stuck in one side of the well. Peterson had cut the team loose – a heavy horse we called Punkin, and a tall, spry mule. The mule was standing up, the horse laying down. About thirty minutes of digging got the mule out, and it went to camp. Punkin would not move. We thought he was hurt bad. We tied ropes to his feet; then we would fill in one side with dirt and snow, roll him over with the ropes, fill in the other side, roll him back – thus working him to the top. My feet got so cold they had no feeling. I went to a canyon and tried to fix a fire, but failed. The two men told me to go to camp, but I stuck it out. Finally at daybreak we slid Punkin out on the snow. I said, "Slide 'im away from the hole." So we worked him off about twenty feet; then he got up and trotted to camp.

When Sawyer came down he said he ought to hold John for the cut harness; then he said something about "Poor old Punkin!" I said, "How about me?" My feet had peeled off till I couldn't get my shoes on; I was wearing a pair of overshoes I'd got from the Horseshoe camp. He said, "Well, you can look out for yourself."

About eight days later the stock came up at sunset – all except Punkin. I fed them, then took the trail after dark. I found that Punk had grazed out on a bog and got down. I let him alone, for I knew I could not get a team out to him in the dark. The next morning a C T man happened to drive up with a good mule team. I got a rope, got in the wagon, and asked him to help me. So we went out. Punkin was laying in a low place; there was a mud rim all around him, and his top side was white with frost. I said, "Dead as the devil." He raised his head and nickered. We hitched to his hind feet and pulled him out; then he got up and trotted to camp. Some horses or mules will just lay down and give up – won't help themselves at all.

Sawyer soon came down. He said, "Take warm water and soap and wash him off." I said, "You wash him," and Punkin stayed crusted.

Texas Neighbors

The winter of 1885-86 was not bad except for the January cold spell that almost froze Peterson; but that storm brought big losses to the stockmen. All the draws leading east or west along the Canadian filled with snow. The cattle drifted before the wind into these traps, and others behind pushed them in further. Then the snow covered them. Some died within two hours after the storm struck. Ten days later they were still standing, packed and frozen stiff, only the tips of their horns showing above the drifts. They stood that way till the snow melted away. One bunch was right north of my cabin, and others were all through the sand hills along the river. I went out and skinned a good many and sold the hides.

I heard reports of losses all over the country. Tom Hungate, foreman of the Hardesty outfit in No Man's Land, took several boys and followed his cattle south when they started to drift, aiming to cut the Texas fence and keep them from piling up. But before they got there they met a Turkey Track boy.

The Turkey Track, owned by the Hansford Land and Cattle company, had been one of A. H. Johnson's promotions. It controlled a range extending forty miles along the Canadian. Thus it contributed a forty-mile section to the erection of the drift fence and maintained line camps there to see that it was not cut. The Amarillo author, Laura V. Hamner, gives one instance

when the boys at a line camp humanely looked the other
way while Tom Hungate cut the fence and saved his
cattle. But apparently they were past saving in the
terrible blizzard of '86.

The Turkey Track boy told Hungate's bunch, "Turn
back fellows; the cattle are all dead." So they went
back. I don't see yet how they rode north against that
blizzard, but boys on the range were used to standing
hardships. That year finished cattlemen that had managed to hold out after the winter of 1884-85.

In the spring when the cattle were weak a good many
bogged down in the river. Herds would be driven across
and some would get in the quicksand, or they would
run in to get away from the heel fly. (This heel fly is a
small black bot-fly that lights on the heel of the hind
foot, causing stock to break for water to get rid of them.
Where there is no water, the cattle will lick them off
with their tongue). When cattle mired down, men
would ride up leading a harnessed mule or horse, throw
a rope around the animal's horns or neck, tie the rope
to a singletree, and drag it out; then loose the rope and
drive the brute away from the bog.

Thus cattle continued to be the dominant interest of
the young station keeper on the Canadian. All around
him were the great ranches, and cowmen and cow talk
came to his cabin on the trail. Most important to him
were his visits with his friends of the Horseshoe, the
neighborly contacts with the P O *on the west and the* C T
across the river, the news that drifted down to him
from the Box T.

The Box T *range was along Commission creek on*
both sides of the Indian Territory-Texas line, with
headquarters on the Texas side just west of the Com-
mission stage station. It was owned by a group of

*Canadian capitalists known as the Dominion Cattle
company. The first herd had been purchased from J. M.
Day, who started a ranch there about 1879, but sold out
to the Canadians and concentrated on his Indian Territory and southwest Kansas interests.*

*Frank Biggers, the tough, capable Box T foreman of
the 1880's, is well remembered in the Texas Panhandle.
Mr. Nelson, as usual, paints a vivid portrait.*

Biggers was six-feet-six, weighed nearly two hundred
pounds, seemed not to care for anything. One day when
the river was iced nearly across, he drove into it in a
buckboard, and his team broke through. I asked if I
could help, but he said they'd make it. The team would
mount the ice, break it and fall, and try again, finally
working their way over.

*The story of one misfortune on the Box T spread
through the cow country. Mr. Nelson is not sure of
the date – it might even have occurred the year after
he kept the Canadian station – but its effect was serious.*

One of their line riders left his campfire burning,
and it burned up his tent and set the range on fire. It
burned for three days. Some of the stockmen wanted to
stretch his neck. But Bee Hopkins told him, "Move out
till spring; I'll look after your cattle,"– he owned forty
head of steers – so the boy left. By spring everything
had quieted down.

The high flats between the streams were covered
with short, thick buffalo grass. It made good winter
feed; it didn't seem to rot, and the stock ate it all. But
when it was burned it was not much good for two years.
A fire might go for weeks unless stopped. Fire in daytime is too hot to handle, so they would fight it at night.
They would drive out a bunch of old cows and bring
along two wagons with several barrels of water. When

they got to the fire, they would shoot a cow, cut its head off, and split the body in halves; take one of the halves and fasten a wire ten feet long to the hind foot and another to the fore foot, a long rope to each wire, and a saddle horse to each rope; then drag the half carcass along the blaze, flesh side down, one boy riding the burned-off side, the other ahead of the fire. Right behind it came the other half, rigged up the same way. Then several men would follow on foot with wet gunny sacks to beat out what was left. They worked this way in two directions, one wagon following each outfit. A bunch of cows would be driven along with each, and a fresh one killed every two miles. That way they could put out about fifteen miles in a night, but it wasn't fun. And though they could whip out a back fire by this means, they usually could not stop the head fire.

South of the Box T and closer to Oliver Nelson's stage station was the C T. This ranch had had a bizarre history. In the early 1870's Jim (A. G.) Springer had come to Boggie creek, which flows into the Canadian from the north, to establish a trading post for the buffalo hunters. He built a stockade, with a blockhouse loopholed on all sides, and underground passageways leading to a covered, fortified pit and to his corral and stable. Here secure from Indian attack he bought buffalo hides and sold provisions, clothes, and ammunition. In the fall of 1875 – as soon as the Indians were subdued – he bought three hundred cattle from a passing trail herd and turned them loose on the empty range. Thus on a small scale he established what was probably the first ranch in the Texas Panhandle. Other business came from Fort Elliott. His place was on the military road from this new post to Fort Supply; a postoffice was opened there, and he kept a stock of whisky and a gambling resort for passing soldiers. It was through this last enterprise that he came to grief, when he was killed in a gun battle with some disgruntled soldier customers.

Two Dodge City men, Tuttle and Chapman, then bought the cattle and established the C T *at the site of the former roadhouse. Tuttle soon bought out his partner. He drove his cattle to Dodge City on a more direct route than the Jones-Plummer trail, thus establishing the Tuttle trail. But in 1880 he sold out to a wealthy Pennsylvanian named Rhodes and the Englishman, Reginald Aldridge. While still living at the old headquarters during the summer and wintering in England during the slack season Aldridge wrote his* Ranch Notes, *a lively guide to the range cattle industry published in London in 1884. Shortly after – as related by Mr. Nelson – the cowboy, Mose Hays, became a stockholder and the manager.*

The ranch has long since passed out of existence, but the site is still known locally as "Springer Ranch." Hays lived to be one of the cow country's old-timers. His sprightly wife died young, but gray-haired men speak her name with almost reverent affection. Here is the way it appeared to Oliver Nelson in '86.

A fellow named Rhodes ran the C T. Mose Hays, a hand about thirty-two, had set up a correspondence with a stocky, black-eyed girl, and they were married just before I dropped in. He built a cabin out on his line, a little off the trail, and they started in by themselves for a quiet winter. But the girl was good-looking, quick, sharp, had a disposition that took them all – also a good cook. It seemed that every cowpoke that came any ways near had to turn off, take dinner with Mose, and get acquainted with the missus. Soon the transients were eating more than Mose could haul in with his wages; but the missus said, "We'll fight it through, and do it free."

Before long the boys began bringing in flour, beef, coffee, and sugar – everything that could be used and more than was needed. At Christmas they brought several turkeys, and everyone went to Mose's cabin for a big time. It kept up that way till new grass came, without a murmur from Mrs. Hays. Then the boys registered a brand in her name, and when the spring roundup started, they slapped it on every maverick they run onto. Mose already had a little bunch and went into the company that spring, and the missus turned in 250 head. Mose became foreman and she did the cooking at the home camp; and the two drew down three hundred dollars a month.

On Oliver's side of the river was the P O with Tom McGee as foreman. This ranch had been started about 1878 with Robert Moody as half-owner and active partner. The year after Oliver kept his station, the Santa Fe railroad built down into the Panhandle and started the town of Canadian near the ranch headquarters, and Moody became one of the new city's pioneer bankers.

Bobby Nolls also came on frequent business to the stage station. And Oliver records one notable instance when he failed to catch a thief.

One Sunday Nolls drove up in an open buckboard. One of his horses had a nice white tail. I said to a man named Nels Peet, who was with me, "I'd like to have some of that hair." Nels said, "I'll go behind Uncle Bobby and start talking and get him to turn around; then you cut it off." Our scheme worked fine; I cut off about one-third of the tail and hid it in the woodpile.

When Bobby turned back, he said, "Just look at that horse's tail! I tied him up last night, and the calves chewed it." He should have shot me for that dirty trick – he might have, too, if he had known I did it. But later on I plaited a bridle out of the hair and gave it to him.

Uncle Bobby had better luck when a horse went with the tail. Oliver also witnessed an example of this.

From my north window I could see the stage about eight miles off; then after a couple of miles it would pass behind the hills out of sight, and not appear again till it got close to the river. One Sunday morning I spied a string of white ponies followed by a man on a brown horse at that clear place on the stage line, and coming my way. Uncle Bobby soon came in from the south. He asked, "You seen anything unusual this morning?" I said, "Not unless five white horses driven by a man on a dark horse is unusual." He said, "That's just unusual. Keep your eye on 'em." And he went to one of the ranches to get help.

After about an hour a young fellow rode up on a brown horse – no white horses in sight – and asked for lunch. I said I would fix him a bite. He tied his mount under a hill north of the cabin where it was hidden, too, and took a seat off from the door. I worked as slow as I could. Pretty soon Uncle Bobby rode up; he asked, "Say, Jack, has a herd of cattle passed here this morning?" I leant against the door frame and pointed with my thumb back over my shoulder. He whispered, "Hold 'im a while." He and a peeler he had got to help him hunted around and located the ponies hid about a mile west of the cabin. They went through his pack, and found he didn't even have a gun.

The boy soon left. Then I saw Uncle Bobby and his

pard bringing him back, one on each side leading his mount. It was near noon now. Bobby said, "I'm deputy sheriff, and the state of Texas gives me a right to call help. You get your horse and go"– he told me where – "and get the white ponies and bring 'em to the Horseshoe. We'll eat dinner there." I did as he said, and joined the trio at the Horseshoe camp.

We sat down at the table. Mrs. Bee Hopkins said, "We looked for just you, Uncle Bobby, so we saved only one dish of oysters." Bobby said, "Here's an old T 5 man. He never seen an oyster in a cow camp. Give 'em to him." I said, "Mrs. Hopkins, there's a little story that should go with this dish. When Mr. Siders was at the T 5 in '82, he said if I ever came to the Horseshoe I'd have oysters for my dinner." She said, "We'll make his word good." I said, "There's a little more to that story I expect I ought to hold back." Mrs. Hopkins said, "Let's hear it all." I said, "I told Mr. Carter, and he said, 'Oysters in a cow camp! That's just a lie.' "

Well, the boy and the ponies went back to Supply, and he got his reward – four years' rest. Seems he'd stolen them from the Indians up there.

Indians also came by the stage station, returning with the permission of their Indian Territory supervisors on peaceable visits to their old haunts. Some of their young bloods, spoiling for the lost excitement of the buffalo chase, found a substitute in running the cattle that had been issued for their food.

A bunch of Indians camped across the trail from me one afternoon. They had eight large steers, that had come as fast as they had, and were tired out. The Indians kept driving them around trying to get them to feed, but they would do nothing but lay down. The squaws went to work putting up the tepees. At the same time they het up coffee, and had a meal of coffee and persimmons, which they carried in square kerosene cans. In about an hour they had coffee and beef; later they had coffee, and bread made of flour and water. By the time the fourth meal was ready they had their tents up.

At dusk two boys and I went to the camp, and were talking with some young bucks. An old fellow came out of the center tent and said a few words in Cheyenne to the young Johns and they left us and went back to their tents. Then he explained to us, "Indian no obey order. Drive wohaw too fast. Government take money away, and put Indian in guardhouse if not careful." And he went back into his tepee. I wanted to talk some more with the young fellows, but they stayed where the old man sent them.

Soldiers also came by the station. To enlisted men, whether white or colored, Oliver showed his usual hospitality, but he had small respect for brass. Eventually it was a quarrel with his own superiors over a soldier that closed his tenure at the station.

A colored detail came in a snowstorm one evening after dark, and asked for a good place to camp where they could find wood. I said, "Put your tent close up south of my woodpile, and use what you want." The next day was bad, so I said, "Stay where you are." The third day they moved their camp across the trail west of me. They went out on the river and gathered wood; brought a load to repay me, but I wouldn't take it, so they unloaded at their camp. I also killed a number of deer for them, asking them to furnish the cartridges.

They had been sent to fix the telegraph line. Uncle Bobby had told me they were going to replace the cedar posts with iron, so I asked the sarge for some of the old poles to bolster up my habitation. He said his orders were to burn them, "but they ain't gonna be took out, 'cause they hain't no iron poles to put in." They hung up about ten days, not doing much because they had nothing to work with. By this time the abutment in the river had moved downstream with the sand till it snapped the wire; so they swung the line from my hill to the north bank, about five hundred yards.

One evening the paymaster – a major – came by on his way to Elliott, and stayed overnight with me. He traveled in an ambulance. He had along a clerk, and a lieutenant with an escort of four men. They brought in the money box – about three feet long, two feet wide, and a foot high – and set it on a tomato box in the middle of the floor. The major was pretty drunk, and not too serious about his job; he said he was hired to pay, not to fight. "If anyone tells me to raise my hands, up they go." He ordered the lieutenant to have the guard pass the door every so often, but make no noise. At about twelve the lamp went out. The major just snored like a hog and lay still.

He went down and paid the garrison and came back up the trail. When he got to the river the ice was softening and the ambulance broke in. The colored crew was still camped at my place, and I went down with them to see what was happening. The axle rested on the ice. The major asked me what to do. I said, "Chop a lane." But he put two niggers at each wheel – working in three feet of ice water – to lift it out. We tramped around to find ice solid enough to support it. I walked behind the major trying to break a place so he would fall in – failed with him, but managed to get the lieutenant in. After they had worked about an hour, the major ordered them to cut a lane, and they got it out. Then he got a gallon keg and gave each one a tin cup of whisky, he taking two drinks. He offered me a drink, which I refused; then he gave me a handful of cigars, saying, "You don't drink or smoke, but you have friends that can use these."

The telegraph detail soon went north to Commission and Supply, and then came back again on their way to Elliott, camping overnight close to my station. I was about out of cartridges, so before they left they gave me fifty, mentioning the favors they had received at my camp. An officer soon came down from the north to inspect their work. He followed the trail, which in some places was two miles away from the telegraph line. He had along a clerk and Jesse Robison, a packer, with a mule loaded down.

It was noon when they came to the station. I said, "Drop in for dinner." Jesse shook his head at me; the high chief didn't bat an eye. In a few days a note came up from the sarge of the telegraph detail, saying he was going to stand trial, and asking if it would be too much trouble for me to come down and make a statement as to his conduct while at my camp fixing the line. I sent down and got a copy of the charges against him. The document stated that the detail had been drinking with the station keeper and had allowed the station keeper to take the cedar poles, and that the line had not been put in good repair; it recommended a dishonorable discharge for the sergeant.

I tacked the charges up on the wall where I always posted important stage notices. Tom McGee, the P O foreman, dropped in and I had him read them – also Mose Hays of the C T and Bee Hopkins of the Horseshoe. Each said, "Drink with niggers! Hell! You won't drink with us. Every man we have will go down to the fort and tell 'em so." So I sent down a statement that no telegraph poles had been taken up near the Canadian, that for ten miles the inspector had not been in sight of the line, and further that I had even refused to drink with the major and the lieutenant; I gave them the foremen's names, and said I could get sixty men to refute the charges. Then the line was pronounced O.K., the nig was given an honorable discharge (he re-enlisted), and that ended the matter.

Two white cavalry troops came by from the north one day. They followed the stage trail to my door, then took the Horseshoe trail east – a single track, instead of the Fort Elliott trail south, which was fifty yards wide. When the first bunch tried it, I saluted and said, "If you're goin' to Elliott, take the south trail; this one leads to a cow camp four miles east." No one cracked a smile. The other bunch hove in, and I shot the same lead into them; then I asked, "Do you loose fellows know you're loose?" Some of them grinned. But both troops went on to the Horseshoe. Then the cap ordered a sarge to order a corp to order a private to find out where they were; and they went back to the forks and turned south.

Forces were even then at work that would make both the trail and the stage line obsolete. While young Nelson was at the station "some surveyors came out and put through a line of stakes for a railroad into Texas from Kiowa, Kansas." Construction began at Kiowa the following fall; and the road reached the townsite of Canadian in the summer of 1887. The road became important at once in cattle shipping, eliminating the long drive to Dodge City. It now forms a part of the Santa Fe main line to California. While the survey was in progress Nelson almost succumbed to the ever-

present fever of townsite speculation. If his methods
skirted a legal ban, they were condoned by the spirit of
the time.

Bobby Nolls spoke to me about taking a section of
land on the survey: him to finance, me to hold, later
sell and divide. He thought there was a chance of a
town on the south side of the river, a few miles west of
my station. He told me to find out the location. I was
handling the surveyors' mail.

We had been having rains, so the river was past
fording much of the time; the stage just came to the
bank, and I took the mail and passengers across in a
boat. One evening after a three-foot rise had come
down, a bunch of railroad mail came and laid up with
me overnight; the next morning I took it across. A
couple of days later Uncle Bobby drove up. He said,
"I want to know if you know where they're goin' to
locate the depot. I don't care how you found it out, but
do you know?" I said, "Yes, I know." And I showed
him a pretty good sketch. He said, "That's enough."
Later our enthusiasm died down, so we let it drop. But
I had the location of Canadian City, Texas before it
started.

About this time Harry, my older brother from Caldwell, came along with a bad case of Texas fever and
wanted me to share it. He had struck a wonderful
country a few miles northwest, in Ochiltree county; it
was on the Gilalieu[7], which runs into Wolf creek from
the north, on the Bar C C (Creswell) range. He was
going to Mobeetie to file on a section, and had selected
a section for me. I said, "I've seen the high land between
here and Mobeetie, and it's worthless. I wouldn't take
it as a gift. Look it over, and if the Gilalieu is like it,

---

[7] Mr. Nelson insists on this spelling, but some modern maps use the form
"Gilhula" or "Gilaloo."

let it alone." He said he would look it over careful; that was a habit of his. When he came back he said there was no comparison at all; the Gilalieu was the lost paradise with a little left over. He had a tail hold and a strong pull; could get a section for a dollar an acre, which in forty years would be worth $20,000. I argued against his scheme, but finally gave in, and hooked onto a section of Ochiltree gumbo, putting up seventy-five dollars as a first payment. Harry went back up the line to get ready to settle on it.

The Creswell Ranch and Cattle company, of which English-born Hank (Henry Whiteside) Creswell was the moving spirit, held a range of a million and a quarter acres extending from the Canadian river nearly to the northern boundary of the Panhandle. Few of these great Panhandle ranches owned the land over which their cattle grazed. Public land in Texas belonged to the state rather than the federal government; it could be purchased in large or small tracts, but was not subject to homesteading. Oliver Nelson's square mile lay south of the present Perryton. Close by were the ranch headquarters, at the old picket house built by Jones and Plummer for the buffalo trade. Here the prairie was littered with the remains of blacksmiths' tools, old wagon wheels, and hunters' equipment, and men still remembered the great cords of dried hides that were piled up for freighting to Dodge City. A scant ten years had seen the buffalo displaced by longhorns, but it required more of a prophet to see the land filled to the horizon with wheat.

Ironically enough, it was the visionary Harry rather than the steady, practical Oliver who more accurately gauged the future. Shortly after the turn of the century farmers began to settle the country, but land prices rose

Bar cc camp on Potts Creek, 1887

slowly — up to four or five dollars an acre at the begin-
ning of the first World War. Then the wheat boom shot
the price up to twenty-five dollars in 1920, and it rose
unevenly to about thirty dollars at the end of the decade.
Thus Harry Nelson's rash prediction of $20,000 for a
section (640 acres) in forty years came uncannily close
to fact. Prices dropped almost half during the drought
and depression of the 1930's, but in the inflation follow-
ing World War II land sold for $125 to $150 an acre.

The soil is rich, uniform, of unknown depth. The
country is an unforgettable sight when the wheat stands
high and the grain sorghums raise their rank, full
heads, every acre for mile on mile exactly like every
other acre. The only crop failure it knows comes from
drought. During the "dust bowl" years of the middle
'30's one could hardly distinguish grass land from
wheat field; all was a uniform desert of dry sticks and
drifts of dust. Small wonder that Oliver Nelson, know-
ing the uncertainties of the climate, made his invest-
ment reluctantly. Meanwhile friction was developing
in his job on the Canadian.

Sawyer, the agent, and Williamson, the president of
the company, came down in a buckboard one day after
a cold spell. The river had froze over; then the ice was
covered with sand and it flooded and froze again; and
now the ice was breaking and the water was boiling up
through the holes. A heavy wind was blowing from
the north. They wanted me to ride across and pilot
them, but it was dangerous and I stalled. They went
back to the C T; then they crossed the next day, both out
of humor. The next time George Hakes came for the
Horseshoe mail I told him to bring up my horse. It
looked like the time for me to quit.

Not long after that the stage hove in with a soldier

passenger. It stopped on the north bank, and the team was taken to the C T; I brought the mail and driver across in the boat. But the passenger was afraid to come along; he thought if I made the first trip O.K. he would let me go back for him. I said, "This ain't no pleasure boat; you can ride free if you come with us, but I won't go back under a dollar." I had to drag and push the boat across the shallow water, which was half way. Finally when the stage was ready to start south from the other side, there was the soldier on the bank wanting to be hauled over. I told Peterson to go on without him, but he said, "Go get 'im," so I made another trip to the north bank. Before he got in the boat I made him pay his dollar. He howled, but he paid.

When he got to Mobeetie, he hunted Williamson up and told his story. Williamson and Sawyer came back up the line, Williamson hot as the devil. He would not hold still till I could tell my part. We had a running talk for half a minute. He started to pull a Colt he had under his left arm, and Sawyer cocked a shotgun; I had no ammunition, so couldn't do much. Just then George brought up my horse. I saddled, gathered up my plunder, and rode away to the Horseshoe.

A couple of days later I rode to Commission. Sawyer was to be down with a load of feed in a few days, so I hung up there to wait for him. He owed me nine dollars. When he came, we had it around and around all over the cabin: he reached for his gun, but didn't quite get it, and heaved an ax, which buried itself in the floor; I grabbed an oven in each hand from where I'd hung them on the door in September, and chased him around the roof props in the south room. Finally he wrote me out an order on a merchant in Supply. When the northbound stage pulled in, he sneaked out the back way and climbed on.

The next morning I headed north. I stopped at Buzzards' Roost, but the stage keeper did not come out, so I stayed overnight at the K H. The next day I got to Supply. I stopped at Joe Mason's hotel, a three-room picket with a board floor and a shingle roof, and put my horse in the shed barn. I went to the merchant and presented my order, and he turned it down. Then I went to find Sawyer. He slipped out of a canteen as I went in; then we had some gun play at the hotel, and he pulled out. I never got my money.

Buffalo Bones

From Supply I rode on toward Comanche county, where father and sister Anna were still living on their claims. I stopped for dinner at a sod house on the Kollar Flats. A girl of sixteen was keeping the house. Her mother had just died, her father was broke down, her husband was out looking for work, and the flour, bacon, and coffee was all gone. I gave the lady three dollars, and they said they would go right to town for supplies. Many of the southwest Kansas settlers were flat broke – just hanging on.

Near Protection I met brother Harry with four ponies, a three-inch wagon, and a spring wagon trailer, all strung out together. He had enticed along Henry Parker from Boulder, Colorado; Jumbo, a big no-account Dutchman; and Jim Staton, with a good large team of mules. All ready for the Ochiltree Flats!

I joined them and we headed toward Ashland. The road was full of movers going west. Two wagons in our string contained the Weaver family from near Harper, in Harper county. What made the Weavers loom up so was like this. They were on land that someone else wanted. So at a dance the opposition jumped the two Weaver men and got a first class trimming, besides losing a couple of ropes they'd aimed to use as equalizers. The next day several men went in, claiming to be officers. They "arrested" the two, took them to a shed and hung them, loaded the wagons, and started the family west.

We got supplies at Ashland. Then we drove down into No Man's Land, and pulled for Jim Lane's stopping place on the Jones-Plummer trail. They called it Beaver "City." A very slow boom was on. I noticed a sod house or two that hadn't been there when I saw it during the roundup the year before. The trail here was loose sand so that freight teams had to double to pull down Main street.

About ten miles south of Beaver we struck the flat land: gumbo covered with buffalo grass, buffalo bones scattered around, no weeds, no trees except a few lone cottonwoods along sandy streams, some wavy ridges way ahead – all nice looking, but fit only for the natural covering. We turned southwest, crossed into Texas, and came to the Gilalieu – hard banks, clear water, and few trees. We drove out to my section; it was on the flat land three miles north of Wolf creek. I said it looked like seventy-five dollars throwed away. Parker said he would take it off my hands. Brother said if I quit I was the damndest fool in the world. I said I didn't like to throw away a year to show who the fool was, but there sure was a fool in the mix-up.

We put in a dugout. Then we piled up a lot of buffalo bones. (A railroad was bound to come right away just to get them). We found two shoulder blades with iron darts sticking through a heavy part; later Harry gave them, so he said, to the Jones collection at Austin.

Staton and I loaded up some of the bones and hauled them to Dodge. On the way we passed a freight outfit of five six-yoke teams belonging to Rath and Hamburg of Mobeetie. They dropped off a fifty-pound box of evaporated apples, which we stored away among the bones and forgot to mention.

The firm of Rath and Hamburg of Mobeetie was

apparently the successor to Rath and Wright of Sweet-water. Henry Hamburg of this firm became the partner of Robert Moody in establishing the bank at Canadian.

At Dodge we bought 200 feet of three-quarter-inch rope for a well. The merchant said, "If you don't have to get more, you're lucky." But when we started down, brother was sure we'd strike water at forty feet. The deeper the hole got, the more some of us would rather dig than crank the enterprise. We cut cups in the side wall to climb out, but it finally got so deep it took seven minutes to draw out a bucket of dirt. Digging was hot work; and we hung a blanket over the windlass so the wind would cause a draft. Finally we struck flint, had to go through twelve feet of it, making only a few inches a day. Under that it soon got sandy. We went into this sand forty feet, lining it with boards to keep it from caving. I was down digging and it started to slide. The boys hauled me up, but I said never would I go down into that hole again. We had got down 170 feet.

Later a family settled on the high flat south of Wolf, and I let them have my rope for their well. They dug to the rope's end, then got a drill and went down to 325 feet; then they quit. While they were digging, a hen fell in and hit the digger on the head. It killed the hen and damaged the man; help went down and tied him to the bucket, and they drew him out, but he was groggy for a few days. (They had chicken for dinner).

We made quite a business of gathering bones; we hauled water along for our team and picked up all over the high flat north of Wolf creek. A man could pick up a load (three thousand pounds) in about an hour, sometimes in twenty minutes. Twenty-one large skeletons would weigh a ton. Some of the bull carcasses still had the skin on.

I believe the bones were used in sugar refining, also possibly for fertilizer. We got $7.50 to $10 a ton. It would spoil a week to make the trip to Dodge. About '88 the railroad built down to Liberal, Kansas and we hauled there. Once the Liberal buyer offered me fifty cents a pair for all the buffalo horns I would bring in. I drove a day and picked up three hundred pair of good ones. The man just lost heart. I sold a few pair – one for $2.50, some for $1.00 – later took the rest to my folks in Sumner county, and they gave them away. I also brought back several pounds of bullets I'd picked up where the carcasses lay, and brother George melted them down. Now in the Historical building at Oklahoma City they have three bullets and two pair of horns – kept like something precious.

Buffalo trails six inches deep and twelve inches wide led for miles across the high flats. I never could figure out how such trails could be made in that gumbo. They always ran north and south. Old buffalo hunters told me the herds would go north in the spring, south in the fall, the bulls by themselves. They said that in '74 the grazing buffalo covered the country as far as they could see like wheat shocks in a field.

The main killing was done prior to '75. A hunter named Lew Hopkins told me how he worked. The outfit would camp close to water, and he would ride a horse out toward the herd and stake it as nearly out of sight as he could, then slip up afoot to six hundred or eight hundred yards. He would set up two twenty-inch sticks two inches apart, and tie a thong between them for a gun rest. Then he would take a long shot at the herd. When he hit one, its death struggle would attract the attention of the others; and he would take the chance to get a position close by, usually in a wallow –

A BUFFALO HUNTER

Billy Fox, Marshall, Oklahoma

any way to get hid – and start in. He would take a shot, run a cloth wiper through the barrel, put in a cartridge, take good aim, and fire again. It was good business after a few shots to look all around to see if an Indian was stalking you; and if a dark object was seen off a distance, take a pull at it, and be sure to kill.

Lew said sometimes after he fired a few shots the poor things would all lay down. The hunters called this a "killing bed." He would shoot all his outfit could take care of, then slip away. The live ones would leave, and the next day he would get another kill at them. But if they got scared, he would have to find another bunch. Sometimes he would follow behind a string on trail and pick off the hind ones. If they looked around, he would lay behind a dead one till they took the trail again. When we picked up bones we sometimes found thirty carcasses on less than an acre of land.

The hunters used a Sharps .50, called a Long Tom. They kept bar lead and black powder; molded their bullets, put the powder in the shell and rammed it tight with a wood stick and a small mallet, wrapped the bullet with heavy paper and pressed it in. When they went out to kill, they took two sacks – one for loaded shells, the other for the ones they emptied. They always aimed to hold back six or eight cartridges they had tried in their guns to be sure they fit, for any surprise by Indians.

One man in the outfit did the shooting; several others would do the skinning and cure the meat. Dried meat brought three cents a pound, hides fifty to seventy-five cents each. Good shots got five to ten dollars a day, or they were paid by the hide ten to twenty cents a head. They sold the hides to Jones and Plummer on Wolf creek, and Jones and Plummer hauled to the railroad at Dodge, thus starting the Jones-Plummer trail.

The magnitude of this traffic is almost unbelievable. In Dodge City, the Cowboy Capital, Robert M. Wright states that during the winter after the Santa Fe railroad reached the town he and his partner shipped over 200,000 hides, two hundred carloads of hind quarters, and two carloads of tongues; and he estimates that at least an equal amount was shipped by other dealers. The business was short-lived: the railroad reached Dodge City in 1872, the take began to fall off in 1875, and the herds were virtually exterminated before 1880. As Mr. Nelson says, "There was nothing left now but to pick up the bones." But he and his partners did see a few survivors in the fall of '86.

We hung up at my section most of the summer. Then in the fall we took a trip into No Man's Land. We were out larking anyhow, so we figured just as well see what there was. The country was perfectly level for twenty miles between Wolf creek and the Beaver. Six or seven miles away across this high flat we seen a bunch of buffalo. Brother said he would give fifty dollars to get another shot at one, but we had nothing but shotguns.

We stopped at a cow camp on Hackberry creek – a dry run that went northeast and joined the Palo Duro – a few hackberry trees along the channel, valley half a mile wide, wolf skulls scattered around. The camp house was made of odds and ends of lumber and planks. We asked how they happened to have such a fix-up, and a boy told us this story:

"We had a story-and-a-half house here, three rooms. Last year it rained up the creek when the sky was clear here, and the water came down in a ten-foot stand. I'd taken a bath and was dressing. Another boy was at the south window reading. All at once he looked up the valley, and called out, 'Come, look at the water.' I said,

'Likely it's a mirage; watch that tree and see if it moves past it.' Soon the boy said, 'It's to the tree! *It's over the tree!* RUN!' I jumped out the door, run 150 yards east, and up the hill. It caught the other fellow and washed him with all his clothes on against the corral, but I got him out. We never seen the house again; it was scattered all down the creek. We picked up what pieces we could find, and this is what we got."

We took a claim on the Palo Duro, aiming to sell when the boom got good. There was no way to file on a homestead in No Man's Land – just dig in and stay. We put in a dugout with sod walls, and took a two-day trip to Wolf creek for poles to cover the roof.

Harry soon went to Kiowa where he had a girl spotted he aimed to marry. Jim Staton and Jumbo pulled up cottonwood sprouts from Wolf creek, and left for the timber claim country around Boston, Colorado; they said they could sell them at two and one-half cents each. Parker and I stayed on the Palo Duro to hold the fort and keep the cow chips burning. I went to the Hardesty outfit on the Chiquita, four miles east of our castle, and helped them put up hay. We cut just small patches in the sand draws. Then Parker got a job driving a freight team for York and Draper, and I went to work for Sourdough Charlie.

I had met this Sourdough at the T 5 in '83, where he'd come near getting in bad with Billy Smith over a horse race. He lived in a dugout on Wolf near the head water, about two miles from the Creswell cow camp. He hunted, trapped, tanned hides and made gloves, sometimes cooked for a roundup, and was going to cut cedar posts in the Canadian canyons and haul them to Beaver City to sell at twenty-five cents each. We followed the trail from Wolf creek south: going up the Northup, a dry run, a branch of Wolf, several miles; crossing a high flat, about fifteen miles; and dropping down three hundred feet into Pickett canyon, which runs into the Canadian.[8]

In many places this canyon has perpendicular sides, with round buttes standing out, covering one to five acres. Rows of cedar trees ran in circles around these buttes, following certain rock ledges – some had as many as five circles. We saw side canyons filled with flint boulders five to twenty feet across; and some of these boulders had small cedars growing out of the top. We found shaped tepee poles, and the stumps where they had been cut, though the Indians had been out of that country more than ten years. And there were fresh-looking paths through the flint blocked by growing trees twelve inches through.

Soon I joined up with a man named Sol Bigham and we went to cutting posts for ourselves. We moved to the canyons west of Pickett. We would cut a lot of posts and then carry them out, sometimes up three hundred feet; we would cut steps in the rock – in one place we cut eighty steps. In another canyon we fixed up a sled, tied on the posts, fastened on four hundred feet of rope and a pulley, and hauled the loads out with a team on the flat above.

Bald eagles would fly low over us. One day after circling around me several times, one settled so close I killed it with a rock. It was so big I held the tip of a wing up five-and-a-half feet while the body lay on the ground. I set traps and caught several beaver. I followed bear tracks, but never got a bear. Also I seen lots

---

[8] Mr. Nelson's Northup creek is variously spelled on modern maps as "Northrun" or "Northrup." The map of the Bureau of Public Roads shows a Sourdough creek that seems to be identical with the one usually designated as Pickett canyon. It appears fairly safe to assume that this name perpetuates the activities of Sourdough Charlie.

of cat tracks, some four inches across, but never seen a cat. A trapper caught one in a trap – a large cougar. He had been offered ten dollars for a tanned hide with no holes in it, so he killed it with a trappers' ax (an ax with a handle eighteen inches long). When a cougar begins to yell, the cattle move out.

In No Man's Land

Oliver Nelson spent most of the next two and one-half years on his claim in No Man's Land. True to form, he happened along at the most exciting time in the history of that frontier that Washington forgot. For it was in those years from '86 to '88 that the country had its most active boom. Nelson felt at home with the cowmen who still lingered there; but his scorn for townsite promoters, would-be state builders, and starveling nesters was tempered only by his chivalrous courtesy to their women folk. He witnessed most of the lawless episodes that still live in Oklahoma Panhandle legend, and the region's most poignant tragedy — still told and retold after sixty-five years — touched him very closely.

The only land title lay in the strong arm of the squatter and the backing of voluntary associations; the only protection to life or property was the settler's own six-shooter and the uncertain support of a vigilance committee. Nelson, who felt perfectly competent to take care of himself and his land, stayed out of the organizations. Sometimes in the wrong hands they seemed to him instruments of tyranny.

The historian, George Rainey, has told how the ambitious town planners of Beaver "City" organized a provisional government and appointed Addison Mundell as marshal, paying his salary by voluntary contributions from the business men. It is uncertain whether this was before or after an episode described by Mr. Nelson:

I rode into Beaver City one afternoon – I suppose it was in '87. Civilization had hit it hard: a Main street running north and south, sod and frame houses going up and dugouts going down all around. One could find a saloon or a card game and not waste any time hunting.

I saw a lot of men bunched up on the west side, some sitting on boxes, some standing, all looking into the street. I tied my cayuse and went to find out. I soon seen that one Addison Mundell had a .45 drawn on a gambler named Thompson, making him do a stomp dance by a well curb in the street. Thompson had his gun on, but his hands were raised, and he was kickin' sand fit to kill. He kept it up quite a spell. Finally a mule on the east side rolled in the wire fence, and the stage keeper and several others started running for the corral, hollering "Whoa!" Mundell glanced over his shoulder to see what was taking his crowd; when he turned back Thompson had him covered – said, "Now it's time for you to dance, ain't it?" He made him get up on the well curb and jump out on the board walk a few times, then walk south out of town with his hands raised up. That's where Mundell got so he didn't like Thompson.

In '87 Beaver City was takin' on life – what you might call progress. Settlers were dropping in – special men with imagination and prospective money. They were ready to make a state of No Man's Land. Dr. O. G. Chase from somewhere, with a regular goat fleece hung on his chin, would take the governorship. There was another hot shot named Dale, and George Scranage would be satisfied holding all the land around town. There was other stars just a-peepin'.

The plans of these promoters indeed soared far above the prospects of the poverty-stricken settlement. First they made a constructive attempt to bring order into land titles. On August 26, 1886 thirty-five men met in a sod schoolhouse at Beaver and created a provisional organization to register claims to town lots and home- steads. The next year they formed a "Territory of Cimarron," with Beaver as the capital. An elected legislature met and enacted laws, a great seal was adopted, a constitution was drawn up, seven counties were formed, and rudimentary courts were established; Chase was sent to Washington to obtain congressional sanction for this provisional government. Towns were being laid out everywhere. Some attained a few sod buildings; others never progressed beyond rows of stakes in the buffalo grass. Newspapers were springing up to boost for territorial status with eventual statehood, even carrying titles like Territorial Advocate *and* Benton County Banner.

But congress failed to take action, a terrible drought in 1888 drove out the settlers and wilted the enthusiasm of the promoters, and the "Territory of Cimarron" died for want of voters and office holders. Two years later when the Territory of Oklahoma was formed in the heart of the Indian Territory, No Man's Land was joined to it to form one of its counties with Beaver City as its county seat. Thus for the first time it obtained a legal government. The federal census that year showed a population of 2674 in contrast to an estimated twelve or fourteen thousand in the spring of '88. It was this febrile activity of '86 and '87 and its subsequent decline that Nelson watched from his dugout on the Palo Duro.

By now sod houses were startin' in No Man's Land promiscuous. Every settlement had a vigilance com- mittee. The rule was that each member could hold all the unclaimed land he chose, provided he aimed to do some work on it; he could turn it over to some kin coming later on, or sell it if he could find a buyer. Nonmembers were just out of luck. The penalty for jumping a claim was hang by the neck till dead, DEAD, DEAD.

Scranage organized the town of Grand Valley on the Palo Duro, nine miles north of our dugout, and Optima, a good ways northwest. He held most of the land adjoining these places and had a committee in each to watch his interests. He was the prospective financier, top man, and overseer; would get a little money from somewhere, then have a grocery man move in, give him a small deposit to start his credit, and tell him, "Just let my men have what they want on me." When he went broke – which he did – it was the grocer's hard luck.

Oliver Nelson's contempt for Scranage could hardly have been greater if he had known that the speculator was advertising his land for sale in eastern newspapers –"Finest climate, best farms, purest water . . . titles clear and terms easy." Apparently a partner in Ohio was furnishing the funds to promote the scheme. Meanwhile other townsites were being laid out from Kansas.

About the same time a general town starter named Bill Kinneman (Meade Center Bill) laid off a townsite on the Coldwater, a few miles west of Grand Valley. Billy Bailey and Joe Cruse, who had helped Scranage start Grand Valley, got disgusted because Scranage wanted to run everything, so they moved over to the new location and opened a saloon. Someone put in a stock of groceries and a feed yard, and they had a town – about ten buildings, all sod. It was called Hardesty for Colonel Jack Hardesty, who had a cow camp just east of it, and the s Half Circle headquarters on the Chiquita near my shanty.

This town has long since disappeared. The present town of that name is several miles east of the old site.

Two other towns – Gate and Neutral – had been set up northeast of Beaver City out on the high level land. Each had a store, and one had a hotel. They were rivals, but the only rivalry I could see was which could play town the longest; because about every six months some ranny would stop in and demand all the cash and some grub, and if there was opposition the lady of the house was apt to become a widow.

One time I went up to Beaver to send out a money order for a payment on my Comanche county land. It was a cool day, a light snow falling. I got in there about four o'clock, and went to the Tracy feed barn. No one came out, but some dust fell from a crack in the loft floor, showing somebody was hid up there. I said loud enough for him to hear, "Well, I'll just put you here, Paint, and hunt the boss later." Then I went to call on a Mr. Miller, a nice old fellow who lived across the street. I thought he would give me the lowdown, but when I asked, "How are things coming?" he just said, "Everyone is keeping quiet." I went out on the street. It seemed deserted. Finally I met a bozo I knew, but all he said was, "Everyone is mum." I turned into Jack Garvey's saloon, said, "Hello, Jack; how's tricks?" He said, "There ain't no tricks, and you better hunt a hole and crawl in."

I went back to the barn. There stood Norton, who worked for Tracy. I'd met him on the roundup in '85. He was a heavy-set fellow, generally good-natured, but a little bull-headed when he felt that way. Now he was full of tanglefoot, and plenty brave. I said, "Hello, Norton; how's the town?" He asked, "Hain't you heard the news?" "I just hove in," I told him. Then he said,

"Hell's liable to break loose any minute. They done crippled Thompson, killed Bennett, then punched twenty-three more holes in Thompson. The cold-bloodedest murder I ever seen, and I ben in Abilene 'n' Hays 'n' Dodge 'n' Caldwell. There goes one of the murderers now." Addison Mundell with a Winchester was passing about twenty feet off in the middle of the street. I said, "Norton, he'll hear you." He said, "I want 'im to hear me."

I noticed four other men with Winchesters stop under a porch in front of a house on the other side of the street. I said, "Norton, them fellows are fixing to shoot you," and I got him to step inside. Then they left. I went to Mr. Miller's house again, and he told me, "Don't be at the barn after sundown. They're going to kill Norton tonight, and they're asking questions about you." I went over to feed my pony and told Norton, but he said, "There ain't no danger." I stayed at Miller's overnight, slept by the front window. At daylight I raised the curtain at my head and looked out. Norton stood in the barn door with a shotgun in his hand.

In the morning I went to the post office and got the postmaster, L. N. Hodges, to make out my money order. I asked several round-about questions, but found out little. At about eleven a.m. I was standing in front of the Miller house. I saw a wagon coming down the street drawn by a yoke of steers, a boy named King driving. It was guarded by five men with Winchesters – the same five I had seen the night before. Two walked on each side, and Addison Mundell followed behind. There was a boy staying with Miller – I found out later they had marked him for death, too, but Miller had agreed to stand good for him till he could get him away. I asked him, "What's that coming?" He told me,

"They're goin' to bury the dead men." I said, "I'll go and help," and started out. One of the guards, using lingo, said, "Come on; we'll bury you on top of the boxes." I said, "Say fellers, I just made up my mind I won't go," and turned back.

Later I learned that George Scranage had bought a claim joining the south edge of the townsite from Noah Lane, Jim Lane's brother, for $1300 — three hundred in spot, and a thousand in mebbe so tomorrow. Three men decided to jump the claim: Frank Thompson, the gambler; Charley Tracy, who ran the feed barn; and O. P. Bennett, who owned a store. Thompson put up a tent on the land and started living there, and the others were financing him — all to divide the profit. The vigilance committee met and voted to get rid of Thompson. Five men were selected: Mundell, the marshal; Hodges, the postmaster; McIntosh, called Big Mack; Herb Wright; and Lee Harlan. They went to Garvey's saloon and teed up, then started out for the Thompson tent. On the way they met Thompson coming out of Mrs. King's boarding house — a one-room, half-sod, half-dugout a block west of Main street. Mundell knelt and took a shot with his Winchester, but fell short. Thompson said, "Raise your sights." The next shot came closer. Thompson said, "Try it again." The third shot struck the center of his knee cap.

The five reported back to the committee, which sent Dr. Chase to investigate. The doctor found Thompson at Mrs. King's; he reported that he would be a cripple, but would live. The committee then voted to finish him and put Bennett out of the way, and the same five volunteered. They went first to Bennett's store, and told him, "Bennett, Thompson said you got him in trouble; he wants to see you." Bennett started to get his coat and hat, but one of the men stepped in front of him, saying, "If you don't want to die here, go now." They walked down the middle of the street through the falling snow, Bennett bareheaded, in his shirtsleeves, thumbs in vest armholes, across to the King mansion. When they went in, Hodges said, "Bennett, don't you know you must die for jumping that claim?" and drew his pistol. Bennett grabbed the gun just as it cracked, the bullet going through his right palm and into his forehead. Thompson was lying on a cot. They fired twenty-three shots into him.

When the five reported again, the committee voted to care for Tracy the same way. But Tracy by this time had got leery. When they got there, he had his team hooked to a light rig, and his wife in ready to start. One of the men hollered, "Stop, or we'll shoot," but he left in a high run for Kansas. Big Mack, weight two hundred pounds, crawled a quarter horse weighing about 850 and started after him, but his horse gave out 'fore he got through the sand hills north of the Beaver. Tracy went to Meade Center, and got permission to sleep in the jail overnight.

The committee sold the store and the barn. They paid Norton his back wages, and he left. They paid a preacher, the Reverend Overstreet, seventy-five dollars. Seems he'd held a service just before they started out to plant the boxes, preaching on "The wicked will meet a timely end." The King boy got twenty-five dollars for driving his bulls to Boot Hill; each of the escorts got the same. Mrs. King got fifty dollars for the grave lot; the doctor got a rake-off, but how much I dunno. It all found a place.

This case with several others was reported to the federal court at Paris, Texas. There was one man they did not aim to send or let go – Windy Smith. (He wasn't careful which way his vapor run or how stormy; when it broke out on him it was like a blizzard). Somehow he showed up before the grand jury, and seems he headed the show. Directly afterwards they fixed a big supper with Windy the main man, and he died on the way home. But Attorney-general Garland doubted his jurisdiction, and so the case was never tried. There was no law for No Man's Land except what the people made themselves.

I left Beaver and rode out to my cabin at the bone pile on the Ochiltree flats. I seen a fresh trail leaving – four horses, one wagon. At least I thought it was fresh; the ground was dry, no dew, when one can't well tell a new trail from one six days old. It showed two horses were almost together. Brother Harry always drove with one horse setting on the tongue, so I followed in a trot. I soon found him at a cow camp.

He had married his girl, and turned in at a camp on the new railroad in the Texas Panhandle and freighted for the business men. They called the place Desperado; it was across the river from my old Canadian stage station. It was going to make a city: one long street, two saloons on corner lots diagonally across from each other, several large tents and more little ones, some old wagons, and of course dogs. Red Holly ran one saloon – the Red Wolf – and John Preston, the other – the Wild Horse.

Peelers would come to town, fill up on tiger milk, and come down the main cowpath at nothing to one, taking a pull at all dogs on the move. Holly toted the only star, and the citizens looked on him to keep down fear. One day when business was pickin' up too fast, Preston crossed over to the Holly refreshment stand and said,

"Marshal, you stop this shootin'; someone'll get hurt." But Red did nothing. New men kept coming to town, and the business just went on slidin' uphill. Again Preston called on his rival, and urged him to stop the shooting. Holly said, "Stop it yourself, if you want it stopped." Preston had no coat on, nor no gun; but he said, "Just pin your star on me." Holly took off his badge, reached across the bar, and pinned it on Preston's shirt front.

Preston still unarmed walked out in the middle of the street and waited to meet the bunch coming in a dead run and shooting in every direction. When they were about a rod away, he throwed up his hands and hollered, "Stop!" The horses stopped, and they all rode up to him. He said, "Now boys, you're going to hurt someone. Go lay off your guns." One boy said, "Fellers, he means business; let's talk to 'im." Another said, "You want my gun?" Preston said, "No, go lay it in Holly's saloon." But they said, "We'll give 'em to you, but we won't give 'em to Holly." "Well, lay 'em where you please," he told them. "Have a good time, but don't hurt anyone." So they laid the guns behind the Wild Horse counter, and Preston took the crowd to the Red Wolf and set up the drinks. He did this three times. But the big trade was on the Preston side of the street, which made Holly sore.

The boys kept up their run till dark. At nine o'clock Preston called them again to the Holly parlor. By this time Holly was slobberin' at the mouth. He reached for his pistol, and Preston dove for his. When the guns cracked, both went down. Some time later Preston got up off the floor, found his face all wet, and the room dark and full of smoke. He felt his head – said afterwards he knowed if hit in the head and not killed, he

PEELERS WOULD COME TO TOWN AND FILL UP ON TIGER MILK

Saloon scene, Tascosa, Texas, early 1880's

was all right – and found a patch knocked off over his left eye as big as a fifty-cent piece. He felt his pistol cylinder – only one load left in the chamber. He ran behind the bar to get another gun, fell over some form, and seen it was Holly. He felt him over, and found a hole in his forehead. Then he went outside, and the boys came back in with him. They lit the lamps and drug Holly out from behind the bar. He was hit just over one eye and was out perpetual. Each fellow then hunted up a roost for the night. Next day they laid the ex-marshal away in the sleep that knows no waking.

Brother Harry got to thinking the ruff element was getting too familiar, so on his last freighting trip to Dodge he got a special jug for himself and a little croton oil, which he mixed in. He hid the jug in an out-of-the-way corner of his premises, then in his haste to get away he plumb forgot it; and with a tear in the eye nearest the crowd, he rolled out. The report was that that very evening someone discovered the prize, and all hands took in on the wake. The party soon broke up; they scattered like quails, everyone hitting a high lope for cover.

Harry and I drove up to see how things were getting along at the dugout on the Palo Duro. When we got in sight of the place, we saw several wagons there. We drove up and a tall man about fifty with a gotch eye came out. That was my introduction to a man generally known as "Dad"; we learned later he was the only black sheep of a respectable family in New York state. He had broken open our cabin and generously let a family in, but now he ordered all to leave, including me. He let it be known he was upheld by the committee at Grand Valley. I said, "Go get your committee," and he started off on the nine-mile trip afoot. In the cabin was a woman and child; her husband was away and she was scared. I said, "Lady, I put up this cabin last year. I own it. Remember this is your home till your husband fixes you a good house to go to. All we ask is that if a bad storm comes we may come in for shelter. Don't worry; that committee won't bother you." In a day or so Dad came back. I said, "Here, man, you can take the claim west. I'll help you dig a well and fix a house." So we got real chummy.

That was about the way it went during the next two years in No Man's Land. I helped several to settle near me. The committee, backed by Scranage, was made up of Missouri families that had located around the townsite. They invited us to sign up with them, but we said, "We'll settle differences here; you confine your operations to matters down the creek." Brother Delos and Jim Staton came and took claims on the Chiquita, just north of the Hardesty camp. The committee ordered them to vacate in twenty-four hours, or suffer, etc., etc. The notice was signed by J. C. Shriver, secretary.

A Sunday school had started up at the Fulton post office, a few miles east, and Shriver was superintendent. I went there and introduced myself and said I was innocent of any intent to wrong or hurt anyone; and he said he would withdraw from the deal. Later a fellow who hadn't been at the Sunday school sent word they'd visit us on a certain night if we didn't leave. We had a Sharps .45, a Winchester, a shotgun, and several pistols. We dug pits in three different draws and laid there two nights. Then a couple of us drove down to Grand Valley and asked the committee to call it off. They agreed, and we took dinner with the secretary and forgot it. Several in our settlement tangled with Scranage & co., but we weren't run out.

We did little farming. We just prospected, layed in the shade when it was hot, and watched other people. A family would move in, starve out, go somewhere else. Down the creek they planted a little cane and waited for rain. Finally Delos and Staton left, also a few others. Several said they would pay me to care for their claims, so I held on.

Brother George stayed with me part of the time. We made several trips down to the Canadian canyons to cut posts. In crossing the flat we had to drive several miles out of our way on account of cracks in the soil ten inches wide and several feet deep. There was a cabin that was a sort of landmark. Starting back we would see it ahead of us first thing in the morning; by noon we had turned off to get around the cracks, so it would be off to our right; at sundown it would drop down behind us over the horizon out of sight. It was only a little flat hut, but at times it was blurred with mirages till it looked thirty feet high. In that country a person could see rain coming down, and drive a day and a half before he got to where it fell.

I piled my posts at Staton's place on the Chiquita, where I happened to be staying at the time; and I hauled them to all the towns around. But collecting my pay was something else again. The boys at the Hardesty camp would give me an invite now and then, and that helped. Then I still had the bone business. Also I trapped a few gray wolves for the bounty. But they were hard to catch. They would go in packs of twenty-five or thirty.

Nobody raised anything. All that could skinned travelers; when travel played out, they skinned one another. Young men not working were killing range cattle and supplying beef to the border towns in Kansas.

Others were driving horses west; there was a regular thieves' run up the Beaver with hideouts along the way.

The Chitwood boys, living near Sod Town, east of us, caused several to worry about livestock. In the fall of '88 a good team of mules was taken from near Gate City. Then Jim Chitwood and a partner came to town, and the bunch took them in. Jim said, "Men, I tell you we had nothing to do with your mules. But I know who has 'em. If you'll pick out your best man, give him two six-shooters and my gun, and let him just herd me along, we'll bring in your team. You can hold my pard till your man comes back." So they tied the guarantee to a post, hung two guns on their worst man, and started Jim out. Just think of a hayseed herding an outlaw across fifteen miles of strange country without losing his head!

They came to some red breaks, with just a narrow path crossing; when you started down you could not stop. They crossed several. Then coming to the last one, Jim said, "Now we're close to the bunch. You give me my gun – you can ride right behind and guard me – and we'll get 'em." They went down that way, but when the guard got to the bottom he was looking into the end of Jim's gun. Jim took his pistols, set him afoot, and started him back up the lonesome trail home.

Meanwhile at Gate when the trade began to look fishy, they stood their hostage on a termater box under a hotel sign, a rope around his neck and tied to the signboard. This was at dusk. After supper they took up the slack so he would cough and slobber at the mouth. At about 1 a.m. their bad, bad man hove in with his tale of woe. Then they took more slack out of the rope over the sign, and went to roost. The next morning the man still stood on the box, but his neck was too long; so they put up a new head board in their grave yard.

Once I met Jim Chitwood and three of his partners. He was well dressed, wore a bone-handled gat, had keen gray eyes, nose awfully hooked down, nice manners. One boy had dark eyes, badly gotched; the two others were just ordinary, yet a little shy. They stopped at the Hardesty camp while the boys were all out. Some settlers followed them up the Beaver and surrounded the camp, but let them all get away. Then the settlers went to their hangout, loaded up their goods, tore down their cabins, set fire to everything that would burn, and ordered them to pull for the Kansas line. They found one of the stations down the creek from my place. The man that kept it was a tall, gangling fellow, with long neck, little head, hog eyes, brindle fur, number eleven shoe – good man in his way, if you liked his way. He claimed he was an innocent settler, had never seen the Chitwoods. He had a shed stable with a stack of coarse hay making the north side; on the west end of the stack it seemed the hay was carefully laid. The men moved a post leaning against this end, opened a door that was covered with hay, and there was a stall inside with a nice bay horse tied up. It was a horse that had been missing for some time, and there was a reward on it. The men took it along, but let the station keeper off with a warning.

An outfit named Johnson from over near Duck Pond moved in on the north side of the Beaver, northwest of Grand Valley, and joined the Grand Valley vigilance committee. There were about three families of them. They soon had one good sod house built and several others started. Then in comes a family named Aldrich, and settled about a mile west of them. (I never saw this name spelled. It *might* have been "Eldridge," but judging from the pronunciation I do not think so). They had a bunch of cattle and several large boys, sixteen to twenty years old. First the Aldrich stock got to eating the Johnson grass; then the Aldrich bunch drove over to get surface coal on the Johnson cow chip ground. The lines were all imaginary, but the Johnsons took in after them with shotguns. Several long distance skirmishes followed. There was a sod wall near the creek a half-mile south of the Johnson mud huts; so when an Aldrich started to town, a Johnson would run to head him off, and the one getting to the sod wall first would chase the other back.

At the final show the Aldrich boys beat the Johnsons to the sod wall, and ran them back toward their home. Old Man Aldrich came up just then and hollered, "Keep after 'em! Run 'em to cover!" and they followed them up and chased them into the house. But the oldest Aldrich boy got too close; he peeked over the top of a sand hill about twenty steps from the soddy, and some-one inside touched off a Sharps .50 and busted his head wide open. His father and a brother got him and dragged him home.

The Johnsons reported to the committee, which met to work out a settlement. I did not attend this meeting, but I was present at others and I know the way they generally handled things. The president was a man named Davis – a tall, slim, red-muzzled Puke, green-eyed, and ragged. He always had his mind made up before it started, and he would express himself in a few words, and the others would agree. One or two might get up and talk – just a little spouting – and then they would take a vote, and that was the end of it.

It was decided that each family should pay a fine of fifty dollars, and leave No Man's Land in thirty days. The Johnsons had nothing, but Aldrich had cattle, so the committee sold his cows at five dollars a head and paid the fine. The Aldriches moved south into Texas, but the Johnsons just ignored the order and stayed. One time Aldrich came up to my place and asked me to sign a petition to the committee requesting them to put the Johnsons out. I said, "They had no right to put anyone out. I tell you: you get some of the s Half Circle boys to help, and we'll bring your cattle home, and there won't be a shot fired." But he didn't want to chance it. As I remember it, he finally replevined his stock after the men that bought them moved to a place where there was courts.

Three days before Christmas in '87 I was piling posts at the place on the Chiquita, when Joe Cruse and his wife drove up in an open buckboard. They said, "Tell the s Half Circle boys there'll be a dance at Hardesty Christmas eve; we want 'em all to come." They were on their way to Beaver, forty-five miles northeast. I said, "Joe, it's almost noon. You won't get to Beaver 'fore midnight. You see that storm in the north? Wait till I get you a comfort." But he drove off in a slow trot. Near the Fulton post office he met the s Half Circle foreman, Tom Hungate. Tom told him, "Turn back, Joe, and put up at the camp; then I'll drive in with you tomorrow." But he said, "No." Then Tom said, "Well at least turn back and get some blankets." He said, "No, we'll stop at Fulton and get a blanket for Mrs. Cruse." But he drove by the post office without stopping. That night ten inches of snow fell, with a strong wind and the mercury below zero.

Came Christmas eve, and the s Half Circle boys and I all started for the dance. We stopped at the Hardesty cow camp near Hardesty, kept by Tom Hungate's brother, Cap Hungate. One of their boys had been to town; he reported that the Cruses had not returned from Beaver. This boy was pretty drunk, so when we started for the dance we left him sleeping, tying the door on the outside so he could not wander off. It was still cold.

When we got to Hardesty, Cruse had not showed up yet. Billy Bailey was worried; he said, "I'm not satisfied – I know Joe would be in if he could." The dance was held in a sod house across the street from the saloon. It was well attended, but something seemed wrong; people kept saying, "Joe'll soon be in." Billy tended bar, also played the fiddle in the saloon. He was a good fiddler, but that night he would only saw off sketches of plaintive tunes. At midnight he treated the crowd, saying, "Well boys, this is the last. Joe would be here if he could." As soon as the saloon closed, the dance stopped.

Several of us put our mounts under a shed and spent the night in Cruse's house. It was a good three-room sod with a board floor and very nice furniture. Tom Hungate and I took the best bed. The next morning we started out to hunt Joe and his wife. Some of us took the road past Fulton, which hit the Dodge trail and led into Beaver from the south. We stopped to inquire at Cap Hungate's cow camp, then at the s Half Circle headquarters, getting in to town rather late. And this is what we heard when we got there.

Three boys had taken the trail down the river and reached Beaver before we did. Cruse had not been seen there, but a team had been brought in from thirty miles south on Second creek, that empties into Wolf – neckyoke on, traces and lines dragging. The boys figured Joe's team might have drifted there with the storm, so they started back by the Fulton road. Sixteen miles south they passed around a tract fenced across the trail. At the southwest corner of this fence they seen a mark where a wheel had cut in a drift. A short distance away in a gulch they seen the seat of the buckboard above the snow. It was plain Joe had been trying to get around the fence, and run into the gulch and got stalled. They turned up the gulch, and found some burned matches. A little farther up on a wind-swept bend Joe lay on his back; his wife lay by his side, her head on his breast, both nearly covered with snow. They were taken back to the cemetery to continue their sleep forever.

I Settle Down for Keeps

Early in 1889 Congress passed an act for the opening of Oklahoma. The time was set for high noon of April 22. This Oklahoma was a tract of country right in the center of the Indian Territory; it was south of the Cherokee Strip, and the Chisholm trail ran along the western edge. I knew the country and knew it was good. I made up my mind to take a homestead. My father had given up his Comanche county venture and was back at Caldwell. Charles, George, and Delos were there too, all rarin' to go. I started back to join up with them.

I drove through Beaver City and struck Kansas at Englewood. I stopped at the Day camp; found Day had lost out, and Bob Edgar owned the place. I followed down the Cimarron. I saw some people loading a good mower and stopped to help them; and they loaded a good plow on my wagon. Then I learned they did not own any of the stuff; they had come from the west, and were just helping themselves as they passed through. The settlers had pulled out, leaving machinery of all kinds, even their furniture. I rode through one fourteen-mile stretch where every house was vacant. I was told all the land was mortgaged.

The road was full of movers on their way to Oklahoma. The streams were up, and we helped each other across. When I got to Sumner county it was raining. My folks were ready to go. Father and Delos went in a wagon; Charles, George, and I rode horses. We went down the Chisholm trail, mixing in with the caravan.

The trail was full of covered wagons, two abreast, sometimes three; and horsemen on each side. Once I rode up to overtake Delos and father, who were several miles ahead, but I never seen a break in the line of wagons.

Charles and I decided to run in together at Kingfisher. It was forbidden to enter the country before the opening day, so when we got to Buffalo Springs, just north of the line, we turned off the trail and circled west to ride in from the west side. We got to the line at 11 a.m. the morning of April 22. We saw quite a lot of people strung along south of us waiting for the signal. There were seventeen bunched up where we were; two were men I'd known in No Man's Land. We laughed when we met up again; it was amusing. We lined up ready to start.

Soldiers were supposed to guard the boundary and give the signal, but there were none where we were. At 11:55 the bunch on the hill south of us moved out, and we yelled and started. Charley and I led the crowd by a hundred yards. I drove my stake soon after I crossed the line; it was the southwest quarter of section ten, due north of Kingfisher. Charles rode on, but failed to get a claim. Several others staked the same quarter I did, so we had a long-drawn-out contest at the government landoffice. It was hard to prove who got there first when so much was happening, and since Charley didn't wait to watch I had no witness. Anyhow I lost out. But Jim Staton, who had married my sister Anna, got a good quarter thirty miles northeast. Their family still owns it.

In November I went back to No Man's Land after my stuff. I had left two cows and yearlings with Tom Hungate. One cow had brought a new calf, and was attacked by a pack of "loafers." She tried to fight them off. Two boys seen what was happening from a point four miles away, and rode to the rescue; but when they got there the wolves had eaten up the calf and half of the cow.

I sold the three claims – mine and Staton's and Delos's – for fifteen dollars, loaded up my goods, and came away. I sold my Ochiltree section for ten dollars, and in 1890 I sold my quarter in Comanche county for five hundred. When the Cherokee Strip was added to Oklahoma and opened in the fall of '93 I joined the run again. This time I was successful, took a claim on Turkey creek northwest of a good Oklahoma town named Hennessey, that had grown up on the spot where the freighters had been killed in '74.

My adventuring was over. I put my place under cultivation, stayed there, and prospered. A few years back I sold it and a quarter I had bought adjoining; I was too old to farm it any more. I am the only one left of our family. The last one to go was my sister Anna, who died last year in Oklahoma City. I am past ninety years old, and I am not holding up as I would like; I just ain't first class all around any more. As for this sketch I wrote, I think everyone should leave a mark of some kind along the path they travel.

Index

Index

Index